The Birth of a Political Self

This book provides a psychoanalytic reading of works of literature, enhancing the illuminating effect of both fields.

The second of two volumes, *The Birth of a Political Self: The Jean-Max Gaudillière Seminars 2001–2014* contains seven of the "Madness and the Social Link" seminars given by psychoanalyst Jean-Max Gaudillière at the École des hautes études en sciences sociales (EHESS) in Paris between 2001 and 2014, transcribed by Françoise Davoine from her notes. Each year, the seminar was dedicated to an author who explored madness in their depiction of the catastrophes of history. Surprising the reader at every turn, the seminars speak of the close intertwining of personal lives and catastrophic historical events, and of the possibility of repairing injury to the psyche, the mind and the body in their wake.

These volumes expose the usefulness of literature as a tool for healing, for all those working in therapeutic fields, and will allow lovers of literature to discover a way of reading that gives access to more subtle perspectives and unsuspected interrelations.

Jean-Max Gaudillière studied classical literature at the École normale supérieure (ENS) in Paris before becoming a psychoanalyst. He was a professor at the École des hautes études en sciences sociales (EHESS) and was a member of the Center for the Study of Social Movements (CSSM), founded by Alain Touraine, research director at the EHESS.

In the weekly seminar called "Madness and the Social Link," held for forty years at the EHESS, Gaudillière combined his clinical work with the exploration of literary works dealing with the madness of war. The focus of his clinical work was the impact of historical catastrophes on personal lives.

He is the co-author of two books written with Françoise Davoine: *History Beyond Trauma* (2004) and *A Word to the Wise* (2018, Routledge).

"It is with great trepidation I endorse this book as I fear I cannot do it justice. It is an awesome book made up of seven seminars given by Jean-Max Gaudillière and transcribed by his wife, Françoise Davoine, much as Francesca Bion did for her husband, Wilfred Bion. This book is more than a study or exploration of important authors and moments of history; it is itself an act of creation using materials from antiquity to the present, opening profound experience of war, death, madness, and creative use of our many capacities, ways of sensing, feeling, knowing. A book in which primary–secondary processes interact and add life to life.

The seminars begin with imaginative amplification of Bion's autobiographical writings and end interweaving Kerouac and Vonnegut. In between are writings using myth, poetry, neurobiology, and more as materials to open dimensions of psyche, culture, society. It is a book I will be reading for a long time and I cannot recommend it highly enough as a partner for your – our – journey."

Michael Eigen, PhD, author, *The Psychotic Core, The Sensitive Self, Contact with the Depths, The Challenge of Being Human*

"The privilege of learning from the brilliant teachings of a practicing psychoanalyst who passed away five years ago, made possible thanks to the relentless efforts of his life-and-work partner, Françoise Davoine, is a rare, precious, and uniquely instructive experience. But it is much more. Gaudillière had a keen interest in and a deep understanding of literature, especially novels and plays that staged people wounded so deeply that they had lost their social connectivity. The literary texts, with the help of Gaudillière as their midwife, yield exceptional insights in an aspect of literature rarely, if ever, analyzed: the way it can first show, then cure, the breaking of the social bond, the repairing of which is indispensable for life. Only within sociality is it possible for a political self to emerge, act, and thrive."

Mieke Bal, Amsterdam School for Cultural Analysis

"Jean-Max Gaudillière's seminars are breathtaking in their erudition, the enormous sweep of their understanding, and the core, deeply clinical truths they regularly rediscover: that family trauma leads to generational madness; that, in the place of madness, time has stopped and the social order has been perverted; that the silenced 'political self' comes to life at the unconscious intersection of the patient's and therapist's history. Years ago, toward the end of an anxious bit of travel for my family, Jean-Max said: 'It's OK. I'm here.' How grateful we are to Françoise Davoine that we hear that voice still, and that, through his seminars – which, as an occasional guest, seemed to me more intellectually alive than any I had ever experienced – Jean-Max, his patients, and all those whose trauma he brings to us continue their teaching."

M. Gerard Fromm, PhD, Distinguished Faculty, Erikson Institute, Austen Riggs Center

"Jean-Max Gaudillière and Françoise Davoine have widened our understanding of 'madness.' And they have done so in a way that lead us to recognize: 'Yes, but of course.'

The words of my deceased colleague Gaetano Benedetti come to mind when thinking of my dear colleague and friend Jean-Max:

> 'It is a comfort, in such troubled times in society, to have the memory of colleagues who have dedicated their professional lives to a discipline like psychotherapy which [......] effectively represents one of the most noble efforts to relieve the [......] suffering [of the mad person]. This suffering was once – and sometimes still is – considered to lie outside the realm of therapy, whereas it lies in fact at the very heart of it.'"

Brian Koehler, PhD, MS, New York University

The Birth of a Political Self

The Jean-Max Gaudillière Seminars
2001–2014

Jean-Max Gaudillière

Transcribed by Françoise Davoine
Translated by Agnès Jacob

Routledge
Taylor & Francis Group

LONDON AND NEW YORK

First published in English 2021
by Routledge
2 Park Square, Milton Park, Abingdon, Oxon OX14 4RN

and by Routledge
52 Vanderbilt Avenue, New York, NY 10017

Routledge is an imprint of the Taylor & Francis Group, an informa business

Published in French by Hermann 2020

British Library Cataloguing-in-Publication Data
A catalogue record for this book is available from the British Library

Library of Congress Cataloging-in-Publication Data
Names: Gaudillière, Jean-Max, author. | Davoine, Françoise, transcriber.
Title: The birth of a political self : the Jean-Max Gaudillière seminars 2001-2014 /
Jean-Max Gaudillière ; transcribed by Françoise Davoine ; translated
by Agnès Jacob.
Other titles: Lectures. Selections. English
Identifiers: LCCN 2020015612 (print) | LCCN 2020015613 (ebook) |
ISBN 9780367523336 (hardback) | ISBN 9780367523343 (paperback) |
ISBN 9781003057475 (ebook)
Subjects: LCSH: Psychoanalysis and literature. | Psychoanalysis.
Classification: LCC PN56.P92 G37913 2021 (print) | LCC PN56.P92 (ebook) |
DDC 809.001/9–dc23
LC record available at https://lccn.loc.gov/2020015612
LC ebook record available at https://lccn.loc.gov/2020015613

ISBN: 978-0-367-52333-6 (hbk)
ISBN: 978-0-367-52334-3 (pbk)
ISBN: 978-1-003-05747-5 (ebk)

Typeset in Times
by Swales & Willis, Exeter, Devon, UK

To Jeanne, Batiste, Emile, Kalea, his grandchildren

Contents

Prologue

The title of this book is borrowed, with the author's permission, from *The Political Self* by Rod Tweedy, the much-appreciated editor of my *Fighting Melancholia: Don Quixote's Teaching*, published by Karnac Books, before the latter was acquired by Routledge.

This book presents seven more seminars given by Jean-Max Gaudillière, which I transcribed after the previous seven – published under the title *Madness and the Social Link* – during the summer of 2017, at the invitation of Jane Tillman, Director of the Erikson Institute of Education and Research at the Austen Riggs Center.

Writing these transcriptions, which I described in the prologue of *Madness and the Social Link,* allowed me to make new discoveries when I referred back to the pertinent literary works, to find exact references. I had always wondered about Jean-Max's passion for Bion and Kerouac. I knew only Bion's theoretical works, and had not read Kerouac at all. I had been content to listen and transcribe, until I started to look for the passages Jean-Max had quoted, and found, as a result, the guiding theme of this second volume of seminars.

After the seminar "with" Hannah Arendt, the works Jean-Max chose were written under the influence of events where death was imminent, during the major catastrophes of the centuries that witnessed them. That is where we found the resources needed to confront the transferences "wavering between living and non-living" that Winnicott places at the heart of "cultural experiences." I will review in brief the experience of the encounter between the practice of the psychoanalysis of madness and trauma and the successive books examined in the second part of Jean-Max's series of seminars at the EHESS, entitled "Madness and the Social Link."

Bion's contribution to this psychoanalysis is to be found in his autobiographical books where he recounts his experience of World War I, at the age of 70, in exile in Los Angeles. Several times, the phrase "I died at Cambrai, at Amiens, at Ypres" acknowledges his connection with his own ghost left on the battlefield with his companions, a ghost to whom the psychoanalyst in *A Memoir of the Future* confesses: "I was so afraid to meet you." This makes Bion conclude that one only becomes an analyst in the interferences of transference, whence a political subject resistant to the erasure of traces can emerge.

The events in Bion's *Memoir*, written in the present, take place on the battlefields of the Somme, but also those of Austerlitz and Stalingrad, depicted by Tolstoy in *War and Peace*, by Vasily Grossman in *Life and Fate* and by W. G. Sebald in *Austerlitz*. Seminar 9 discusses the role of chance in our practice, when causality cannot function because everything that upholds the social link has broken down.

When this happens, there emerges an agency that negates all alterity, against which madness fights, bringing about critical situations that the analyst should not try to evade. These situations are discussed in Seminar 10, through Jean Cassou's *La mémoire courte,* Marc Bloch's *L'étrange défaite*, Molière's *Tartuffe* and Goethe's *Faust, Part Two*, which makes an emphatic distinction between the madness of *Narr*, who reveals political abuses, and the perverse madness of *Tor*, embodied by Mephistopheles.

Martin Cooperman, analyst at the Austen Riggs Center and survivor of Guadalcanal, used to say that an analysis of madness takes only a week, but it takes years to get to it, it takes years for the protagonists to come out of hiding: the patient hiding behind his symptoms and the analyst behind his theories. They can then encounter each other, after the loss of all their qualities. Robert Musil's novel, written in the 1930s during the Nazis' rise to power, explores the imminence of the war that no one sees coming in 1913, through Ulrich, *The Man without Qualities*. His fight against stupidity is the subject of Seminar 11.

I was familiar with Rabelais' literary works – he is the subject of Seminar 12. What I didn't know was that in addition to being a healer of the body and the psyche – "better to write about laughter than tears" – he was also closely involved in political action aimed at preventing the imminent outbreak of the European wars of religion. *The Fourth Book*, written at the end of his life, takes us for a ride, as Jean-Max says, through the dangers of the century, refusing, however, to draw alongside the Isle of perversion. Rabelais' expression "How to raise time thanks to higher sense?" would later be taken up again by Yvette Guilbert. An end-of-century *diseuse*, she portrayed the women forced into the street in her first repertoire, and created a second medieval repertoire, after returning from the brink of death. She described her art with precision, opposing the interpretations Freud, her admirer, made in their enduring correspondence.

"Music before all else." Jean-Max, who was a musician, read *On the Road* to the syncopated rhythm of jazz, the sound Kerouac caused to resonate, in an effort to infuse life in the zones of death that never stopped haunting him. My reservations about him quickly melted away when I saw how insistently his writing described the explosion of the American dream during wars and economic crises, and how it revealed his love for his older brother, who died when Jack was 4. Seminar 13 insists on the syncopated rhythm of an analysis whose highs and lows set in motion time that had stopped in the lethal zones of trauma.

The final seminar discusses *Timequake*, a trembling of time, Kurt Vonnegut's last book, which, he says, brings to an end the narration of his captivity in the cellar of a Dresden slaughterhouse when the city was destroyed by the incendiary bombs of the British and American air forces. I had read *Slaughterhouse-Five* without noticing the repetition of the expression "memoir of the future" that Bion used as the title of his last fictional work, while he was exiled in Los Angeles, at the time when Vonnegut's bestseller was published.

The major constituent of the psychoanalysis of madness and trauma is arrested time, whose tremors reverberate through the silence of generations. I hope the reader may discover, as he reads these seminars, that it is possible for time to be set in motion again.

Françoise Davoine
Paris, December 2019

1 Seminar 8: 2001–2002
Wilfred Bion (1897–1979)
Questions of memory

A Memoir of the Future

Bion was taken for a lunatic. The three parts of *A Memoir of the Future* were written in the United States, where he took refuge in 1968 in Los Angeles, to escape "the cosy domesticity of England." The three books are entitled *The Dream* (1975), *The Past Presented* (1977) and *The Dawn of Oblivion*, published in 1979, the year of Bion's death. This book of dialogues, with its typographical inventions, was inspired by *Tristram Shandy*,[1] which, in turn, was inspired by *Don Quixote*. The character of Captain Bion brings to mind Tristram's uncle Captain Toby Shandy, who is endlessly telling his war stories, after he fought in Marlborough's army against Louis XIV.

Bion was born in India. His language bears the traces of the English spoken in his native country by his nanny, who told him the stories of the Mahabharata. When he was 8, he was sent to England alone, to be schooled, and always felt like a misfit.

Reading Bion is not always easy, since he does not present a unified theory, and does not aim for systematisation. If you have no particular question to ask when you read him, he will not teach you anything. His famous grid is a tool he invented to help himself think. Therefore, we will submit our questions to Bion in the last period of his life, focusing on his work of fiction *A Memoir of the Future*, and his two autobiographical books *The Long Week-End, 1897–1919* and *All My Sins Remembered*,[2] in which he says he died during World War I.

From *War Memoirs* to *A Memoir of the Future*

Bion was the analyst of Frances Tustin and Samuel Beckett, but he did not found a Bionian school. His work spanned the century, and when he took his leave we inherited it all. His first book *War Memoirs 1917–1919*[3] is the story of a young man who volunteered for the war and became a tank commander at the age of 19, when his entire crew was killed. In 1915, Bion had been rejected by the army's recruitment office, until his father used his influence. At the front, he kept a diary instead of writing the daily letters he had promised his parents. When the diary was lost in the confusion of the post-war period, he wrote it again with the precision granted by traumatic memory in search of a witness. I stepped into this role easily, since I spent my youth in Picardy and recognised in his descriptions the villages, the poplar trees, the canals, the fog, the rain, the mud, the roads and the rivers, and could picture his battles on that land. Through this common bond, a friendship was born between us.

As I did for Hannah Arendt, I am not going to work *on* Bion, but rather *with* him. I will converse with him about the loss of his second diary, which he found again and reread in Los Angeles in order to write his other books. He was not the first author to lose the manuscript in which he recorded his war experiences. The same misfortune befell the narrator of *Don Quixote* at the start of the first novel.[4] In Chapter 8, Cervantes left the knight suspended in a freeze-frame:

> On, then [...] came Don Quixote against the wary Biscayan, with uplifted sword [...] while on his side the Biscayan waited for him sword in hand [...]. But it spoils it all, that at this point and crisis the author of the history leaves this battle impending, giving as excuse that he could find nothing more written about these achievements of Don Quixote than what has been already set forth.
>
> (p. 49)

The narrator finds the lost pages among the old papers a young boy intends to sell in Toledo to an old-clothes dealer, but they are written in Arabic, the language of his years of slavery in Algiers.

The loss of the original text is at the root of the inscription of trauma. Stored in cut-out memory, it returns intact, in a language one has "no desire to call to mind," according to the first sentence of *Don Quixote*, but which will emerge in the transference. Cervantes was 45 when he was jailed again in the Seville prison – after a dishonest banker accused him of theft – where Don Quixote appeared to him in his cell. In the author's preface, Cervantes calls him his son and entrusts him with enacting the delirium of his war and his slavery.

Bion would be able to write about his war experiences fifty years later. When he was in exile in Los Angeles, in 1968, at the age of 71, he heard again, all around him, the American accent of the soldiers who had fought by his side – a time he did not want to call to mind either. In *The Long Week-End*,[5] an American officer, Captain Robinson, arrives as reinforcement:

> we did not think of him as a man of different nationality so much as of the same nationality with peculiarities which, when we did notice them, were very peculiar peculiarities [...]. For example, he did not seem to understand our jokes.
>
> (p. 214)

Robinson was later killed in combat. Bion no doubt came upon him again in Kurt Vonnegut's bestseller *Slaughterhouse-Five*,[6] published in 1969, in which the author describes his captivity in an underground slaughterhouse in Dresden, until, on the morning of February 15, 1945, he and his companions came out to find the city completely destroyed. The expression "memory of the future" is used several times in the novel.

Who is speaking? A voice from beyond the grave

It is the voice that says: "I died in Cambrai in 1917," when the entire crew of his tank was killed. Bion is connected to them, and to the soldiers who replaced them, in a plural body of survival. It is to them that he owes the microhistory made up of pencil-drawn maps of the front line, as they advanced metre by metre, with no detail forgotten, noting the atmosphere of the day, the weather, the hour when the fog lifted, and he could see the poplars that told him where he was when he was lost.

These maps are vitally important. The map of the Citadel of Namur, where Captain Toby, Tristram Shandy's uncle, was wounded in the groin, plays a crucial role in his healing. As long as he tries to explain to polite visitors what happened to him in battle, his wound worsens from the effect of traumatic revivals, until a large map of the citadel pasted on the wall allows him to name the landmarks, in time and space, of the circumstances in which he was left for dead.

The memory of the subject of trauma, who died, as Bion died at Cambrai, on the battlefield, is a living agent looking for an other, not merely a recording device. When mortal danger is unspeakable, it is expelled and remains suspended above our heads, like the huge rock in Magritte's painting *A Sense of Reality*. This expulsion is accomplished by means of fragmentation whose leftovers return from the outside through visual, tactile, olfactory or auditory hallucinations. All the senses are used to investigate the catastrophe that remains imminent. But there is still a problem: how to conceive of an "outside" when the threat obliterates the limits between inside and outside. Expulsion and fragmentation are an attempt to create an outside in a world without alterity. But each fragment carries the same terror, like Mickey Mouse's bucket and broom endlessly multiplied in Walt Disney's *Fantasia* and Paul Dukas' symphonic poem *The Sorcerer's Apprentice*.[7] Traumatic memory of details eliminates gaps. There is no void. The details hold together through contiguity, unforgettable.

In *The Long Week-End*,[8] Bion is in a ditch with Sweeting, who asks: "Why can't I cough sir?" Bion looks at his chest and sees that the whole left side has been torn away. He makes Sweeting sit down and tries to bandage him, but the soldier collapses, as if relieved, and calls his mother: "Mother, mother, mother." The unforgettable scene keeps repeating for a whole page: "I could not stand it. [...] Sweeting, *please* Sweeting ...

please, please *shut up.*" They are in a shell-hole. Exhausted, Bion tries to reassure his comrade: "There will be some bearers shortly." But he knows that it's almost over:

> His eyes were glazed over. Enough life flickered in them at my words for him to say, "You will write to my mother? Won't you?" – "Yes, of course." [...] And then I think he died. Or perhaps it was only me. [...] Sweeting. Gunner. Tank Corps.

(p. 249)

Fragments return as flashbacks, in traumatic revivals. Forty years later, in 1956, Bion travelled by train across the battlefields of France. Through the window, he saw all the details emerge out of the land – T. S. Eliot's "The Waste Land"[9] – and the past was present:

> As I write these words I know that I have not forgotten what happened that night at English Farm, what was going to happen [...] at Cambrai, at Amiens, in the "train bleu" after years in the black areas of a second world war.

(p. 128)

War Memoirs is the raw material for *A Memoir of the Future*, which tries to create a memory that forgets, in Book Three, *The Dawn of Oblivion*. When he published *A Memoir of the Future*, Bion's colleagues thought he was crazy. They preferred to limit his work to his theoretical texts written up to 1966. Yet his fiction follows directly in the traces of William Rivers' article – published in *The Lancet* in 1918,[10] and written in London during the bombardment – stressing the difference between repression and suppression. Wearing a fool's cap – in a theatre of fools about the folly of war – Bion succeeds in starting a conversation, which he calls "psychotic transference," with something that defies any possibility of dialogue.

Dialogues in *A Memoir of the Future*

In 1970, nine years before his sudden death from leukaemia, when he was planning to go back to India for the first time, Bion takes us, whether we like it or not, into an England that has just been taken over by a totalitarian power. The man who died at Cambrai and at Amiens addresses the denials of his century. In the house where the character named Alice lives with her husband Roland, two men with impersonal gazes open cupboards and draw up methodical lists of their contents. Roland finally says: "'But we are not deceased – yet.' The men consult an official-looking paper: 'Our list says you are deceased. [...] It's nothing to do with us, but contact the liquidation people'" (pp. 16–17). The liquidation people impose the "banality of evil," an expression coined by Hannah

Arendt at the end of *Eichmann in Jerusalem*.[11] By destroying otherness, the totalitarian agency destroys access to speech.

When there is no other, the subject of trauma wanders through a memoir of the future, where the expulsed fragments stop time from passing. Bion scoffs at analysts who lecture about psychosis without entering into its transference: "Psychotics are a feather in the cap of analysts," who do not ask: "How is it possible to speak of a thing in its absence, knowing as we do that it cannot be absent?" In other words, how can we elicit the symbolic order which makes it possible to name a thing in its absence, when that thing is a haunting presence? This was also Wittgenstein's dilemma. Like Bion, he was haunted by the war on the opposite front line, and was "at a loss," as he wrote in the *Investigations*, "when the tool with the name 'N' was broken."[12] His response was to invent a language-game, with an other who is able to play.

The language-game invented by Bion is a dialogue seeking a "thou" between various characters, including versions of himself at crucial stages in his life. Starting with germ cells called "somites," he gives the floor to himself at age 20 months, 8 years, 17 years and 22 years, as well as to Captain Bion, "Myself," P. A. (the psychoanalyst) and others such as "Bion," who admits to Dr Watson: "I could never flame with life again after James, Ernest, Charles and I were extinguished at Cambrai" (p. 150). The psychoanalyst, P. A., is dreading going back to Amiens, for fear that he should meet his own ghost, left behind when he died there on August 18, 1918, as he says, in the last battle fought by his tank section (p. 257).

In California, he rereads for the first time his *War Memoirs*[13] and writes a "commentary" on them, in the form of a dialogue between "Myself" and "Bion" aged 21, who admits to the older man: "I never recovered from the survival of the Battle of Amiens" (p. 218). His traumatic dreams are political, since they fight against the erasure of traces. The young Bion tells "Myself" about a recurrent nightmare in which he desperately holds on to the muddy bank of the River Steenbeck, but keeps slipping towards the "raging torrent." "Myself" replies: "Your 'dream', as you call it, sounds a better description of the 'facts' than the facts. The crossing of the Steenbeck swallowed up many an English soldier" (p. 118).

To gain access to this type of dream without associations, in which the dreamer is holding on to the clear-cut limits of the dream frame, Bion says that the analyst should be "without memory or desire." He too must be able to step out of time and acknowledge his presence in such an experience without past or future, through some coincidence. Then a first mirror is created for the ghosts who walk through mirrors and through time.

In *A Memoir of the Future*, I come upon a sentence (p. 135) that strikes me as such a coincidence. "The voice" making the following statement comes from the future/past: "Where's my fire? Bring me my fire will you! There are some topless towers here that require burning." And I see myself with Françoise, at the top of the Twin Towers, during the week before

September 11, 2001, carrying in my backpack Bion's books that I had just bought at the Karnac bookshop in Manhattan, for this seminar.

Attention to detail is not the same thing as the free-floating attention that conveys signifiers thanks to what Lacan calls the "crystal effect of language," since the symbolic order has collapsed. It registers suppressed uncanny impressions, which Bion picks up in his clinical vignettes. Often the patient picks them up first. An example is given in Pat Barker's *Regeneration Trilogy*, during a session between William Rivers and his patient Prior, who notices that his analyst stutters at times. This observation will allow a big step forward in the analysis of them both. Later, Prior will tell Rivers: "You write like you stammer."[14]

Bion also writes like he stammers. He uses adverbs like "absolutely," "very" and "completely," which French translators often omit to smooth out the text. But the folds formed by adverbs must not be ironed out, since their laterality provides a side glance at the big picture. Bion writes: "The date and certain facts may not always be exact," but they are "very clearly stamped upon one's memory," when everything is in "such terrible confusion." The worst thing, in act of the translation, is to abolish transference: "I am going to convey the feelings," says the French, whereas Bion allies himself with the reader and says: "our feeling."

This kind of memory is that of a subject who constantly shows that he is dead and that he can write. We hear his breath, his commas, his inability to tell: "we could not tell." "We" are also the ones who cannot tell, his group of *buddies*, a plural body of survival, among whom there is an "absolutely straight" Irishman. The translation eliminates the adverb, as if to attenuate the Irish guy's straightness. In fact, he will die soon afterwards. Why take away his "absolutely"?

Pub conversations

I will give you the example of a patient who was confined to a psychiatric hospital, and was the sole survivor of a group of buddies who killed themselves during their hospitalisation. Long afterwards, he brought to the session the story of the madness machine. As with war machines, it is better to keep them in working order than to pretend there will be no more war. He is a pétanque player (a French game of lawn bowling), and until recently has been getting a perfect score every time. He says: "I am the killer," but is afraid that madness will return. Everyone is looking at him, like before, when everyone talked about him while he made his way to the sessions. His sidelong glance spots a man to his right, in the square – a man he has never met, wearing dark glasses. Although everyone takes him for a world champion, a god of pétanque, this man makes him tremble with anguish. The stranger works for the great totalitarian system from which his family escaped by coming to France, and has come to spy on him. In *A Memoir of the Future*, the character of the killer is called "Man."

Without thinking, I propel myself into the town square and say: "The man is me," asking myself what I mean by that, *ce que je veux dire.*

Wittgenstein insists that the French expression *vouloir dire* ("to want to tell") adds another dimension to the verb "to mean," an act of volition: *I want to tell.* "I want to tell him something about *myself,* which goes beyond what happened at that time. [...] Not [...] on grounds of self-observation, but by way of a response (it might also be called an intuition)."[15] This paragraph of the *Investigations* comes just at the right time because, in effect, I told him something about myself.

The repetition of madness, like military manoeuvres, seeks, on the sidelines, an unspecified other, who in this case is the total stranger I am willing to embody when I say: "It's me," since no one else can be reached. The following week, he misses every time he throws. What happened? By taking the place of the threatening man – "Get out of my way!" – I transformed the totalitarian agency into a relational situation that I had once experienced and had disclosed to him at the start of his analysis.

My present response was a repetition of my first reaction to his delusion, when everyone was talking about him and I myself was losing my bearings to the point that after a session, I almost had an accident. Then I had an intuition: "These are pub conversations," I said. That's what I had "wanted to tell" him to put an end to our confusion, and it was about *myself.*

As it happens, I spent my childhood and adolescence in a café run by my mother in Picardy, where my father found a job and transplanted the family from our native Burgundy. I had just wanted to tell my patient about my dread when I would cross the café, stiff as a puppet, with the eyes of the habitués on me, and their jokes ringing in my ears. His delusions stopped at once, since he was no longer alone when he faced the persecutory agency his family had never spoken about, although their mute terror had been passed on to him, leaving him in utter solitude. I had stood by his side, in a present "when time ceased to flow," as Bion says in *The Long Week-End* (p. 263).

Returning to normal life doesn't solve the problem. Speaking of veterans' homecoming, or soldiers on leave like himself, Bion observes that they were not relieved. They were disgusted with the home front, with the "blah, blah, blah" of newspaper headlines, with people who have no idea what it's like, who don't want to know, who think that rehabilitation will do the trick:

> The Turkish bath was very refreshing; I felt so clean. It's not *real*, you know; just a kind of trick. Really, of course, one stinks. They have a way of making people look so life-like, but really we are dead. I? Oh yes, I died – on August 8, 1918. [They] wanted me to enjoy my leave, not to be dwelling too much on [...] the horrors of war.
>
> (p. 265)

ARF: a folded word

The pétanque player's delusion invoked a masked stranger to give me the place of the impossible other, so I took it. This was Freud's problem in the beginning, when he wrote, in pencil, on the train coming back from Berlin where he had visited Fliess, his *Project*,[16] which raises the question: How can a subject emerge from the impact of the huge energy of the Real, which he calls Omega? He invents a number of filters to break down this energy, which he calls successively Phi, the primary process composed of images of words and of things (*Repräsentaz*), and Psy, the secondary process composed of representants of representations (*Vortellung Repräsentaz*), called signifiers by Lacan.[17]

This last filter makes the Real forgettable by passing it through the sieve of the repressed unconscious, "the discourse of the Other," made up of signifiers. But when there is no other, big or small, and therefore no repression, Freud points out on several occasions – in the *Gradiva*, the *Uncanny* and *Moses* – that another unconscious is at work. We call it a cut-out unconscious, composed of surviving images belonging to the primary process. In such circumstances, time stands still, since its flow is measured by symbols, and nothing is forgotten since nothing is inscribed in the past.

Bion gives a concrete illustration of this experience. After he shouted "Get out" to his crew, and after Sergeant O'Toole pushed him away from the open door of the tank:

> [a] bullet had spattered, missing my head [...]. The near miss they said [...] made a loud crack – or killed you. As I looked at my map and hands in the tank I felt I was floating about four feet above myself [...]. This dis-association, de-personalization, was a way of achieving security – spontaneous, automatic, but potentially costly as it involved *not knowing* of the imminence of death.
>
> (p. 132)

The experience of having faced death without being aware of it is recorded by the "seismograph" of our soul, as Aby Warburg calls it.[18] But a human being is not a photographic plate. In order to be able to live, we compress this recorded experience by expelling words and images that are no longer connected to each other by the symbolic chain and pertain to the primary process. Socrates, a veteran of the Peloponnesian War, calls them "primary elements without reason" (*próta stoicheia aloga*) in the *Theaetetus*[19]. Bion calls them "beta-elements." These "surrealist" elements – a word invented by Guillaume Apollinaire while he fought on the same front line as Bion – were identified by Marcel Duchamp as "prime words divisible only by themselves and by unity."[20] They tend to be intertwined, according to Socrates, who goes on to say: "it is their interweaving which makes the *logos* both speech and reason." Bion calls this process the "alpha-function."

When these prime elements enter through the eyes, they are expelled and come back as visions; when they enter through the ears, they are heard as real voices. According to the voice-hearers of the Hearing Voices Movement, hearing voices is a particularity demanding to be shared, instead of being labelled a pathology. Sometimes these elements overwhelm you to the point where you no longer know who you are. The mathematician René Thom calls "catastrophe" a zone in which "form and substance merge," except for some shapes surviving on the border of this area. He experienced such a "catastrophe" after he was awarded the Fields Medal in 1958. His competitor was John Nash, "a beautiful mind"[21] whose voices and visions did not prevent him from winning the Nobel Prize in Economics in 1996. René Thom recounts:

> Afterwards came a period of depression. Whatever progress has been made on the mathematical side since then has been done by others. [...] And so, I handed the reins over to them. But I had to do something! The result was catastrophe theory.[22]

(pp. 18–19)

Thom defines catastrophe as a break in continuity, and identifies forms on the border of this zone for which he has mathematical formulas. One of them is the pleat:

> When a space is projected onto something smaller than its own dimensions, it accepts the constraint, except at a certain number of points where it concentrates its primary individuality. It is this singularity which gives rise to resistance. The concept of singularity is a means of gathering the entire structure in a single point.

Bion provides an example.

In the first part of *The Long Week-End*, dedicated to his childhood, the trace of this fold is heard in the ARF phoneme, an utterance resulting from the compression of "Our Father," the beginning of the Lord's Prayer (p. 12). At critical times, language is creased. These creases are not affected by time. This thought makes me slip into a reverie: if ideologies erase and turn to dust the traces of previous generations, in order to create new men and women, then those people become generations of vacuum cleaners. Still, children keep track of such stupidity.

For young Wilfred, the symbolic chain was broken when his father accused him of lying when he was telling the truth. The boy proclaimed his good faith, becoming afraid that *Arf Arfer* would appear:

> Arf Arfer was very frightening. Sometimes when I heard grown-ups talking they would indulge in bursts of meaningless laughter. "Arf! Arf! Arf!" they would go. This would happen especially when my sister or

I spoke. Then we would go into another room and practice. "Arf, arf, arf!" [...] and in the end it would make us laugh because it sounded so silly. Sometimes it would be puzzling to know why the grown-ups were so big and why they spoke as if we were "silly." [...] Arf Arfer was related, though distantly, to Jesus who was also mixed up with our evening hymns.

This word, folded up into compacted phonemes in a crease of traumatic memory, is chanted by the 4- or 5-year-old child to resist the stupid betrayal of his relatives.[23] This talisman would turn out to be troublesome for Bion's first inept analyst, nicknamed FIP ("Feel It in the Past"), since it is neither an effect of repression nor a neologism – sign of psychosis in the eyes of obtuse psychiatrists. It indicates a fold in time, which will be unfolded by Bion to become the "thou" of Captain Bion, "Myself."

In Book One of *A Memoir of the Future*, while Captain Bion is staring at a speck of mud trembling on a straw, he sees trees walking:

How they walked – walk! Walk! They went like arfs arfing. Arf arf together. [...] What 'appened then? 'E fell on 'is arse. And 'is Arse wuz angry and said, Get off my arse! You've done nothing but throw shit at me all yore life and now you expects England to be my booty! Boo-ootiful soup; in a shell-hole in Flanders Fields. Legs and guts ... must-'ave bin twenty men in there – Germ'um and frogslegs and all starts! We didn't 'alf arf I can tell you.

(pp. 53–54)

The chapter ends with surrealist words worthy of *Finnegan's Wake*.[24]

"Arse 'ole" is another folded word Bion creates from the Protestant hymn "Our Souls" – written in 1415 about the Battle of Agincourt, in which the English thoroughly defeated the French. He sang it at Oxford University, where he found himself right after being discharged. His arse gets angry when the hymn reminds him of the shell-holes full of Germans, French and English soldiers with their guts ripped open. The manipulation of these words is not an intellectual exercise, since physical strength is needed to disassemble the syllables until they cause bursts of laughter.

Talismans

As we have seen, Wittgenstein insists on the verb "to want" in the French expression *vouloir dire*, "to mean."[25] This will to say, at work in pleated words, requires that the same will be present in the listener. Bion and Wittgenstein put their readers to work, asking them to follow the same procedure with their own little pleated words. I will give you an example.

The expression "asshole at the police station" was the folded word of a patient, a college teacher who came to see me in a delusional state. As a child, he had condensed in this expression his father's departure, when he was arrested at dawn by the police, during the post-war purge, for suspected collaboration with the Germans. As he was taken away, his wife said: "Give them everything." The boy interpreted this to be her request that he prostitute himself to the police, and later in life he extended this interpretation to his students and his colleagues. He was being spied on by the police, who used transmitters hidden in his watch, and even in his teeth. One day, he brought me proof of a student's prostitution in the form of a note explaining her late arrival to class. And I lost the precious note. Very embarrassed, I admitted at our next session that I could not find it. From that day on, he stopped having delusions. The ever-present traumatic event was now inscribed in my memory and could therefore be forgotten.

According to the late Martin Cooperman, an analyst working with psychosis at the Austen Riggs Center, who was a flight surgeon at Guadalcanal:

> an analysis of madness takes a week, but it takes years to get to it. At first, the analyst hides behind his theories and the patient hides behind his symptoms, until they both come out of hiding and can finally meet.

Bion's "arse 'ole" and this patient's "asshole" stored the memory of catastrophic events, when the pact of language was broken. It was a talisman.

The word "talisman," like the word "dragoman" – the spokesman of the Great Mamamouchi in Molière's *The Would-Be Gentleman*[26] – came to us in the seventeenth century from the Arabic language which provided translations of Plato. The word is borrowed from the Greek *telesma*, meaning "rite." In *Phaedrus* (244e), the one who wants to recover from madness must take part in cathartic rites, *katharmôn te kai teletôn*.[27] When the unspeakable and the unimaginable return like phantoms, mere trifles make it possible to create, *telein*, a pleat in which a minimal identity of the subject can take refuge. Confronted with the betrayal of his own people, he can resist thanks to this word unlike any other, which he keeps in his mouth until he no longer needs it. Joe Eagle Elk, the Sioux medicine man, would tell patients assailed by the dead who demanded their due: "Take a stone and clasp it tightly in your hand."

This talisman bears witness to the moment when danger erupted on the scene. Like in the story of Tom Thumb, it marks the passage making possible the return to the world of the living, a fragment of one's history providing a minimal guarantee. A crisis in the analysis attempts to call up the secret little thing against all odds. It is the ultimate expression of a pleat: without even knowing what is folded inside it, it counts on a fortuitous encounter to combine its resistance with that of a second in combat, a therapist, worthy of the name *therapon* – in Homer's *Iliad* – capable of being more than an observer.

Vertex

According to Bion, the vertex is the angle from which the analyst considers a word or an image. *Arf* can be viewed from several perspectives. "We find something bizarre about seeing because we do not find the whole business about seeing puzzling enough," Wittgenstein writes. The one who cannot recognise "the imponderable evidence" revealed by the subtleties of a gaze, a gesture or a tone of voice is "aspect blind."[28] The short clinical vignettes in Bion's theoretical works illustrate his awareness of subtle signs shown by his patients, beyond what they are saying. He gives two personal examples in the first part of *The Long Week-End* – entitled *India* – and Book One – *The Dream* – of *A Memoir of the Future*.

The nanny looking after Wilfred and his sister – "our Ayah" – was older than their parents and gave them affection: "Our mother, on the other hand, was peculiar: [...] warm and safe and comfortable. Then suddenly cold and frightening."[29] The two children quarrelled constantly, exasperating their parents. To calm them down, their father decided to read them bedtime stories, one more dreadful than the other, in their opinion. Even more awful than *Alice in Wonderland* was the story of Little Meg, Andersen's *Little Match Girl*.

"At the start her mummy and daddy died. Then she had to look after her little brothers and sisters. Of all the stupid things – she tried to sell a box of matches 'at a street corner'." But the streets of a large European city are something completely foreign to the Bion children, who live in the Indian countryside and only know the jungle. The worst thing in the story is that the girl couldn't sell any matches. "The next night was worse still. The rich man, or a policeman whom he summoned, wanted to take Little Meg and her children to gaol!" A terrible "Arf Arfish" feeling took hold of Wilfred and his sister. From then on, they began to scream as soon as they saw their father coming into the room with the storybook (pp. 26–27).

The failure of Bion's father's belief in the soothing virtues of fairy tales echoes that of mainstream psychoanalysts in the healing virtues of dream interpretation, as shown in Chapter 8 of *The Dream*, Book One of *A Memoir of the Future*:

> The dreamless sleep ended. The day was as empty of events – facts proper to daytime – as the night had been empty of dreams. [...] The world of reality, facts, was no longer distinguishable from dreams, unconsciousness, night [...]. The thinker had no thoughts, the thoughts were without thinkers. Freudian dreams had no Freudian free associations; Freudian free associations had no dreams. Without intuition they were empty; without concept they were blind.
>
> (p. 33)

When a dream does not spring from repression, it needs a different vertex to create a first mirror through which metaphors come to light. Let me give you an example. At the Prémontré psychiatric hospital in the North of France where we became analysts, a man condemned to life internment for a crime he said he did not commit introduced us to the patients in the locked ward where we had just arrived. He gave us an order: "Write! Write that schizophrenics – like the silent young man who took me by the hand to show me around – follow a scent back to its origin, and if you can't smell it, they punch you in the face." They act like Cassandra, "the foreigner, whose nose is that of a bitch, smelling the scent of blood," says the Chorus in Aeschylus' *Agamemnon*.[30]

When he smells it, in Chapter 36 of *The Dream*, Bion speaks of "feeling sane enough to be afraid, and to respect [this] fear." In this case, Arf Arfer intervenes when speech collapses: "Sometimes in my dreams I thought I heard Arf Arfer arfing. It was a terrible frightening noise. [. . .] Arf Arfer was not to be trifled with." Indeed, no longer being frightened of one's fear is worse than anything.

In *The Long Week-End*, Bion has just escaped death once again. Beforehand, while acting as tank commander, he had felt his fear, until a shell exploded and his crew pulled him out of the tank. That's when he became aware of a new sensation:

> The tank was shaking continuously like a wobbling jelly [. . .]. I was not aware of being afraid, which, from the point of view of comfort, is as good as not being afraid. [. . .] When I realized that both violent slam and wobble occurred at intervals which were rhythmically connected, I knew we were very near the bursting point of a heavy shell. I felt we should move; there was nowhere to go.
>
> (p. 130)

When we are shaken up in critical moments of analysis, the same question arises: What to say? Where to go? "Bloody noise! Bloody silence!" Bion writes. The French translation of the adjective "bloody," *sacré*, indicates that the sacred sounds of silence are splattered with blood. When you are paralysed with fear, Wittgenstein's advice is: "Play out your fear."[31] Two texts dictated into a recorder by Bion in 1977 – two years before his death – make it possible to tame wild thoughts thanks to a rhythm.

Taming Wild Thoughts[32] through rhythm

Aeschylus' play *The Persians* – staged in 472 BC – is about the return of defeated Persian King Xerxes from the Battle of Salamis where Aeschylus fought. Xerxes orders his men to whip the sea as punishment for her refusal to help him. But the sea laughs at him, as we can read in a superb verse, spoken in another tragedy, *Prometheus Bound*: "*Pantôn te kumatôn*

anèrithmon gelasma" ("The countless smile of the many-sounding sea").[33]
Rythmos starts in the womb. It is measured time, scansion, the number
counted out, but also perceived through the skin, the nose, the eyes, the
gestures, the words – everything that can create a symbol provided an other
is touched by it.

Bion speaks of rhythm as a primordial stage in the genesis of the
unconscious:

> I am suggesting that besides the conscious and unconscious states of
> mind, there can be another one. The nearest I can get to giving it
> a provisional title is the inaccessible state of mind. It may become
> inaccessible because the foetus gets rid of it as soon as it can. [The
> foetus] has feelings or primordial ideas [like] an awareness of its heart-
> beat or an awareness of feelings of terror, of sound, or of sight – the
> kind of sight experienced through the pressure on the optic pits [...] –
> all that may never have been what we would call either conscious or
> unconscious.
>
> (p. 50)

I wonder if he was not thinking of the first chapter of *Tristram Shandy*,[34] in
which the embryo tells the reader about his parents' carelessness when he
was conceived. He complains in the following terms:

> Now, dear sir, what if any accident had befallen him in his way alone? –
> [...] and that in this sad disorder'd state of nerves he had laid down
> a pray to sudden starts, or a series of melancholy dreams and fancies
> for nine long, long months together? – I tremble to think what
> a foundation had been laid for a thousand weaknesses both of body
> and mind, which no skill of the physician or the philosopher [or the
> psychoanalyst] could ever afterwards have set thoroughly to rights.
>
> (p. 6)

Like Captain Shandy – the only one to take care of his nephew Tristram
from the beginning of his life – Captain Bion can easily identify with the
embryo:

> And I, in this peculiar world in which I now find myself, am both in
> need of nourishment and of somebody with whom to communicate, not
> because I have an awful lot to say, but because I find myself in the state
> of mind with which I am distressingly familiar – the state of mind in
> which I can only say I am abysmally, literally and metaphorically,
> ignorant.

That is, the state of the foetus abysmally unaware of what awaits him:
"That is one reason why it is a matter of some urgency to me to be able to

find some sort of network in which I can catch any thoughts that are available" (p. 31).

The Persian poet Omar Khayyam, quoted by Bion in *Taming Wild Thoughts*, said in the eleventh century that his only solace in war was the rhythm of "the brave music of a distant drum." As Captain Toby did, Captain Bion remembers: "I was incredibly moved when I heard the distant music of the bagpipes of a Highland division that was to accompany us in battle." He speaks of this music again in *The Long Week-End*:

> It is bagpipes [...]. Listen! We watched the rhythmical sway of the kilts [...].
> In that war the 51st Division, Highland territorials, had won a reputation
> second only to the Guards ... We had already learned [...] that our lives
> depended on the stout hearts of the infantry who were in action with us.
>
> (p. 141)

Lacan, who never saw action at the front, proposed a negative definition of the Real: the Impossible, that which "never ceases not to be inscribed." Hence his refusal to theorise psychotic transference at the end of his *Écrits*: "On a Question Prior to Any Possible Treatment of Psychosis."[35] Bion is not content with a preliminary question. He strives to transmit in a positive light this specific transference, which is considered impossible by analysts fascinated with negativity.

In Chapter 33 of *The Dream*, he shows us how to overcome the impossible:

> Leonardo da Vinci drew those writhing coils of hair, those swirling
> masses of water, to remind you of the form that lay concealed within
> the formless infinite. He could see them and drew them for you. What
> he could not see or help was that you would not be made to look [...].

He could not foresee that "you [...] were a 'consequential idiot'. [...] Still at it, still playing [at] cause and effect!" (p. 156). The forms hidden "in the formless infinite," outside of temporality, are not subjected to causality, even "psychic causality."

When the experiences brought to us have neither words nor images, we must be attentive to surviving forms hidden in formless infinity: an invisible blush, a sound as inaudible as that of one hand clapping – as Zen puts it – or the petrification Wittgenstein evokes: "I turn to stone and my pains continue."[36]

At the end of the text he dictated into a recorder in 1977, Bion cleared the way for the psychoanalysis of madness:

> When someone who is wide awake has one of those experiences, we
> say that he is hallucinated or deluded; that state of mind has not
> been investigated because it is so much simpler to put that patient
> into a mental hospital or into an entirely different state of mind by

the administration of drugs. And anyway it has to be investigated by someone who is wide awake, fully conscious, and in possession of all his senses. When I say "all his senses" I do not mean all of what my contemporaries and what rational and reasonable people call "sense"; I include senses of which I myself may not be fully or particularly aware – the uncertainty principle, the incompleteness principle. So even the mathematicians cannot help me very much, because I think they themselves have reached a similar impasse in this problem of trying to elaborate what they call rigorous thought or rigorous thinking.

(p. 50)

And he added:

we do need some sort of discipline, rigour of thought. I haven't said what kind of rigour. [...] There is not much room for dogmatism or bigotry; that has gone too far; that seems to me to cross the point of no recall.

Like Hannah Arendt, Bion appeals to our judgement (p. 51). He himself is merciless in his judgement of an analytic practice that discredits the patient's inventiveness, attributing it to his psychotic structure. Still, he remains optimistic, encouraging "embryonic" analysts in supervision to use their imagination (p. 43) and to concentrate on elements of the past that occur in the present. Otherwise, how could we play our part in the theatre of fools? "I am a messenger sent by God," a madman told the psychiatrist. "Don't listen to him," shouted another, "I never sent anyone."

Thoughts without a thinker

Bion is interested above all in thoughts without a thinker:

it may be what is a "stray thought," or it could be a thought with [or without] the owner's name and address upon it, or it could be a "wild thought." The problem [...] is what to do with it. Of course, if it is wild, you might try to domesticate it [...]. If its owner's name and address is attached, it could be restored to its owner, or the owner could be told that you had it and he could collect it any time he felt inclined. Or, of course, you could purloin it and hope either that the owner would forget it, or that he would not notice the theft and you could keep the idea all to yourself.

(p. 27)

He focuses mostly on thoughts without "any kind of ownership or even any sort of [...] genealogy" – those that turn up in our dreams and seem ordinary to psychoanalysts, although they are not, since they bring back "events which are notorious and which are historically known to us, both in our private histories and in the history of the race." In that case, the analyst must change his vertex, for these are not simply what is "said to be dreams." He would be well advised to take these events into account and ask the patient "where he went and what he saw [...] when [...] he was asleep," although the latter insists that "it was only a dream ... Freud was one of those peculiar people who seemed to think that dreams are worthy of further consideration" (p. 28).

Since analytic discourse does not provide a suitable vocabulary for speaking of the "stray thoughts" encountered in the course of these voyages and visions, Bion proposes to place them in "a box." He says the box will contain:

> something that is physical [...] a "beta-element." I don't know what it means [...]. But anyway, there it is, in case a strange creature should exist [...]. There is something a bit more sophisticated: that is to say a similarly physical creature, but one that arouses in me primordial thoughts or feelings, something that is a sort of prototype of a mental reaction. These I shall call "alpha-elements."

Bion doesn't know much more about them, except that when he has experienced them, he was told that he had been extremely restless in his sleep.

The box he describes is a ghost trap. At the end of Book Two of *A Memoir of the Future, The Past Presented*, ghosts are speaking to ghosts. That of the psychoanalyst, Ghost of P. A., says that he died in battle at English Farm, at Berles-au-Bois. When one of his men appears, the ghost of Auser, Ghost of P. A. tells him: "I loved you, but I couldn't save you." The ghost of Auser doesn't blame him: "Never mind, old boy. [...] Sorry I lost my tank, but there were a lot of them ..." Auser's ghost is happy to see P. A., the psychoanalyst: "It's jolly nice to see you again – I hope you are glad to see me too." And the psychoanalyst replies: "I am indeed – but truth to tell I've always been afraid of meeting you" (p. 423). This phrase should be taught to all "embryo-psychoanalysts," to prepare them for the occasional sessions in which they are going to meet ghosts, perhaps even their own ghost. The phrase applies to critical moments when the ghosts of the analyst and of his patient force both of them out of hiding, so they can finally speak to each other.

Bion's box brings to mind the black boxes of two discoverers. It resembles the box Saussure placed in the safe deposit of a Swiss bank. He had placed in it the *Anagrams*[37] – his quasi-delirious theory made up of fragments of Ennius' Saturnian verses, forerunners of Latin poetry. They would be published in 1979 by Jean Starobinski. Later, in Geneva, he taught his famous *Course in General Linguistics*, published after his death, in 1913, from notes taken by two disciples. There is also "Newton's trunk," discovered by antique dealers in 1936, in which the scientist had stored delirious measurements of the Temple of Jerusalem.[38] In order to name this strange transference, Bion relies on Shakespeare's lines in *Macbeth* (Act V, Scene 5), later used by Faulkner: "A tale told by an idiot, full of sound and fury, signifying nothing."

Macbeth and Palinurus[39]

Where am I taking you now? On a boat, sailing off on Bion's broad culture, which he quotes to converse with his experiences in the present. At the Battle of Amiens, where he dies for the second time, the fog is so dense that he can't see his hand. He feels he has lost his capacity to act as a soldier. Although he was awarded the Victoria Cross, he is filled with dread, begins to cry and quickly makes measurements on his map to regain his composure. He doesn't feel adequate to the task, and in any case the fog is so thick that his mapping is false, "but better to have wrong measurements than no measurements at all." He thinks he sees trees walking, like Macbeth's woods walking (Act V, Scenes 4 and 5), which are really soldiers. His speech becomes phonetic and gives a beat to "a formless infinite." Bion's broad culture provides him with tools to speak to insanity; this is what makes me seek his company and want to converse with him.

In the next chapter, "Myself" takes up François Villon's refrain *"Où sont les neiges d'antan?"* ("Where are the snows of yesteryear?"),[40] followed by a lamentation:

> Poor Newton! Poor Shakespeare! Poor Galileo, Descartes, Freud, Milton [...]. The "famous ones" [...] the mute, inglorious ones, where are they? They saw the Promised Land, the mirage, the fame which is man's last and first infirmity of noble minds, the weakest of which was that of the steersman Palinurus, thrown into the sea by a god.
>
> (p. 55)

This brings us to Book V of the *Aeneid*.

Aeneas has survived the catastrophic defeat of Troy thanks to Venus' protection. Following in Homer's footsteps, his mission is to establish the Julio-Claudian dynasty, with Augustus as its first emperor. After he leaves Carthage and abandoned Dido, he comes ashore on the coast of Sicily. The religious vertex of the tale depicts the rivalry between two groups of gods; Juno's intention is to prevent the hero from reaching his destination. His fleet catches fire; Jupiter plays the firefighter, but Juno stirs up a storm that sinks four ships. Children, women and old men are left behind in Sicily where Aeneas founds the city of Segesta, before sailing away on the flagship whose helmsman is Palinurus; Cape Palinuro, between Naples and Pozzoli, is named after him. Venus, Aeneas' mother, negotiates with Neptune.

Finally, the god promises that her son will have a safe trip in exchange for a sacrifice: "Only one shall there be whom, lost in the flood, you will seek in vain; one life shall be given for many" (*Unus pro multis debitur caput*) (Book V, verse 815).

For Bion, the influence of the animist culture of the Greeks and the Romans is augmented by the Hindu religion of his nanny – "our Ayah" – whose influence his parents feared:

> I suspect that my father and mother were afraid I would "get ideas" if I were allowed to have contact with any kind of "pagan superstition" at variance with the pure, unsullied belief of our puritan and their missionary forbearers.
>
> (p. 15)

Passing through the two gates of sleep – the gates of horn and ivory – Bion accompanies Aeneas on his journey among the dead, to meet Palinurus.

Aeneas' father, Anchises, whom Aeneas saw in a dream, advised him to visit the Cumaean Sibyl and, after finding the Golden Bough, to go to Lake Avernus and descend to meet him in the Elysian Fields (Book V, verse 735). The visit to the underworld, called *Nekuia* in Greek, takes place in Book VI, when Aeneas puts Cerberus to sleep with drugged cakes, and unsheathes his sword to defend himself against the shadows pressing in at the gates. These are the souls of the dead who did not receive proper burial, *inops inhumata turba*, and cannot cross the Styx (Book VI, verse 325). Charon, the ferryman, pushes them back mercilessly with his oars. This is when Aeneas recognises the downcast shadow of "the helmsman Palinurus," who entreats him to take him across the river (Book VI, verse 341). His ghost also speaks for the young officer who died at Amiens, with so many of his brothers in arms, who had no burial.

Aeneas believed Palinurus had drowned during the sea voyage from Libya, "while he marked the stars, [and] had fallen from the stern, flung forth in the midst of the waves [...] tearing away the helm" (Book VI, verse 337). These events are recounted at the end of the previous book. Palinurus was leading the fleet, *Palinurus agebat agmen* (Book V, verse 833), when the god Sleep, sitting atop the stern, invited him to lay down his head, offering to replace him at the helm. The wary steersman objects:

> Me do you bid shut my eyes to the sea's calm face [...] I whom a clear sky has so often deceived? (Book V, verse 849) Such words he said and, clinging fast to the tiller, never let loose his hold, and kept his eyes upturned to the stars.

But Sleep shook a humid bough dipped in the Styx over him, and when he fell into a sudden slumber, flung him head first into the sea. In the following book, Palinurus corrects Aeneas' version of events and tells him what happened next: he swam to a shore where some cruel men killed him (Book VI, verse 359).

Palinurus is quoted in Chapter 13 of *A Memoir of the Future*, when "Myself" objects to the traumatic revivals that tormented Captain Bion in the previous chapter: "He says the consistency of his mind never recovered" (p. 55). "Myself" rails against the mirage of promised glory after the war, to men:

> waiting Palinurus-like to be hurled from the throne of the stern, the leader [...] by whose position all are ordered to steer. Even Aeneas is hurled from his trust in his steersman by a god whose true face is a disguise, which conceals yet another god behind the mask of a benevolent, calm, inviting, alluring, seducing sea.

Palinurus is the hero of all those who were "betrayed by Memory" (p. 55).

When a patient has delusions, we might ask what gods are speaking through his mouth, and which of them might be betraying him. In his dream, Bion visits the places of traumatic memories filled with powerful emotions. To his patients haunted by ghosts, he brings his cultural references, in a continuous dialogue with the soul of his dead comrades, to whom his works are dedicated, in a never-ending attempt to give them a resting place.

Poetry

Paradoxically, the impossible to inscribe never ceases to look for inscription through a "transitional subject" – Benedetti's expression – emerging from thoughts without a thinker, which the analyst tries to catch as best he can. How to catch the impossible, to say and to imagine? At the Boston Planetarium, which we visited years ago, some young astrophysicists showed us how, in order to think about unimaginable waves detected from light years away, they had coloured in the zones that had been recorded. The same applies to "the gross darkness" which Bion calls a "vacuum" in *Taming Wild Thoughts*, borrowing the French term *néant* ("nothingness") from Victor Hugo's *Legend of the Centuries*. Speaking of beta-elements, he says that he could call them by the names of colours, to make them visible: "the blue of the sky, the red of blood, the yellow of ochre, the colour that is made out of earth" (p. 30). And in *A Memoir of the Future*, he uses – to capture the shades that give this vacuum consistency – a method borrowed from Freud, who needed "artificially to blind himself" to explore the dark places of the mind (p. 42). The same is true of Kenzaburō Ōe, whose heroes are often one-eyed.

From a certain perspective, Bion says, a tennis net is a collection of holes assembled together, just as words are made of empty spaces between syllables. In *The Long Week-End*, he recounts that as a child, he recited his prayer to "Geesus," asking him to "pity my simple city," all the while wondering where this poor city of his might be found (p. 13). The suffix "-ity," coming from the Latin *-itas* – as in *simplicitas*, "simplicity" – had been created by Cicero to name abstractions – the quality specific to a thing, *oiotès* in Greek. The city emerges in the empty space between the syllables, and its quality is as imaginable as that of the pitiful destroyed cities he would come across during the war. The unimaginable city of his childhood will become as incredible as the "poor destroyed cities" of his youth.

In *Taming Wild Thoughts*, Bion catches another wild thought in the net of his idleness, which used to make his parents nervous: "Why don't you two play together?" He catches it with two verses from Shakespeare's *Cymbeline* (Act IV, Scene 2), spoken at the funeral of a young girl: "Golden lads and girls all must, as chimney-sweepers, come to dust." Bion knows the author's name, his address (Stratford-upon-Avon), and since he is long deceased Bion takes possession of his words. "I know, I know," he tells himself. But what is it he knows? Probably that we are sick to death of the Shakespearian texts we were forced to learn in school. One scholar even claimed that "chimney-sweepers" could be a reference to dandelion leaves. For Bion, the wild thought creates the image of a graveyard for the "golden lads" who have come to dust – those of his regiment who carried the promise of dandelion flowers whose seeds are blown far and wide by the wind. The simple funeral lament in *Cymbeline* revives an emotion sown four centuries earlier (p. 33).

To catch the strange things of the madness of war, Bion introduces a poetic time-space, bathed in the mournful atmosphere of Palinurus and *Cymbeline*. The third part of *The Long Week-End*, called "War," starts: "The world was all before. The iron gates of my Paradise clanged to behind me as I walked, alone, solitary in my anonymous glory to face the dawn of the freedom for which I had waited so long." His paradise in boarding school had been a hell: "Oh no, not again! Exactly: not again. No more; no never more." Another time opens that can only be glimpsed from a poetic vertex. The passage from childhood to war takes place through a tunnel at Bishopsgate, on:

> dark, sodden, sulphurous Liverpool Street – and this was *it*. Surely it *must* be a pool whose stench-borne waters close over one for ever. So like the shell-hole – no, no; not yet. That was later, or long ago; take your pick.
>
> (p. 104)

The reader is not given such a choice. An autobiography implies an autobiographical pact with the reader, who is immediately drawn into a time that does not pass. Bion admits:

> The only place I can live is the present. [...] I cannot forget what I cannot remember. Fear of the future greatly resembles a past I cannot remember, because it is buried in a past that did not take place.

At the same period, 1979, Winnicott's last paper, "Fear of Breakdown,"[41] speaks of Bion's experience:

> The patient needs to "remember" this but it is not possible to remember something that has not yet happened, and this thing of the past has not happened yet because he was not there for it to happen to. The only way is to experience this past thing for the first time in the present, that is to say in the transference.

Each experience of war, like war itself, is unprecedented. Speaking of the Battle of Lepanto, Cervantes was already saying it was an event the likes of which had never been seen before. Afterwards, everyone says: "Never again" and the next one produces a brand-new hell. Language is stripped of its rational and poetic functions, since metaphor is impossible where no Other is present. But as soon as, by chance, "a passionate witness to events without a witness" is encountered, as Dori Laub says,[42] the phantom of the metaphors starts to stir.

François de Malherbe's poem "*Consolation à Monsieur du Périer sur la mort de sa fille*" ("Consolation to Monsieur Du Périer on the Death of His Daughter")[43] is a good illustration. It begins and ends with two famous lines: "*Ta douleur, du Périer, sera donc éternelle?*" ("Your sorrow, du Périer, is it to be eternal?") and "*Et, rose, elle a vécu ce que vivent les roses, l'espace d'un matin*" ("And, rose, she lived the life of roses, the space of a morning"). Malherbe corrected his original version – "*Et Rosette a vécu ce que vivent les roses*" – by removing three letters – "tte" – in the daughter's first name. From Rosette, she was transformed into the rose, and the poem triumphed!

What is a beautiful verse? In this case, it performs a ritual for a father whose pain is boundless. A single word, not a metaphor, transforms the young girl from being like a rose to being the rose. The theme of the passing of time is banal, but poetic licence provides access to a world where thoughts are buried in the future: Bion's future when he enters war, where he had never been, but where his comrades have already died with him. *The Ghost of the Rose*, a one-act ballet by Carl Maria von Weber, based on Théophile Gauthier's poem, and performed by Diaghilev's Russian Ballet, is not the *carpe diem* of Ronsard's famous poem "*Mignonne allons voir si la rose ...*" ("Sweetheart, Let Us See if the Rose ..."). It is a literary and musical genre called "epitaph."

Bion's interactions with patients struggling with madness were of this type. Though in his 1974 *Brazilian Lectures*[44] he confessed that he no longer had the strength to transform projections of solid objects, he had the strength to transform them into literature and warned Brazilian analysts against ready-made theories. *A Memoir of the Future* has prophetic accents like those of Artaud when he claimed, in 1933, that it was imperative to know "whether now, in Paris [...] sufficient means [...] could be found to permit [a theatre of cruelty], or [else] red blood will be needed right away, in order to manifest this cruelty."[45] At some critical moments, when a ruthless agency enters the sessions, psychotic transference comes face to face with cruelty.

A Memoir of the Future enacts the three stages of this transference, whose aim is to escape from a waking nightmare, *The Dream*, to confront the traumatic present of the past, and *The Past Presented*, so that *The Dawn of Oblivion* may rise and usher in the future. Otherwise, the dead deprived of burial come back to protest, as Jean Cassou does on their behalf in *La mémoire courte* (*Short Memory*), written after World War II: "And the dead? What did they die for? To cut out their memory is a second death."[46] Bion voices the same protest, given his experience of the previous war.

Learning from war experience

In his book *Learning from Experience*,[47] Bion discusses not only his experience as an analyst, but what he learned from his war experience and never talked about until his exile in Los Angeles. It is a complex experience, in the sense of *plecto* – "to weave" in Latin – through "psychotic transference," which creates a connection in order to explore the dynamics of disconnection. This requires a change of vertex, making it possible to detect interferences.

The war also forced Bion to change his perspective – as he recalls in *The Long Week-End*[48] – from the one he had when he volunteered: "Patriotic, I had realized it, was all I could be" (p. 117), in situations where he understands nothing at all:

> We stood there and waited for something to happen. We had not even begun to realize that nothing happens in war, or [...] nobody knows what happens. I would have thought I was being made a fool of if I had been told that, even years after that war and yet another like it, I still would not know something so simple and obvious as who had won.
>
> (p. 120)

In Chapter 6, he is at Ypres, "Wipers," the English "Verdun," resonating with "wiped out." The dead metaphor pushes its ghost towards the extermination to come:

> The Salient [...] had to be held. [...] These words have little meaning to anyone today, but as an ancient this is the only way of making my voyage through time; from now on it can be only to islands in the mists of memory, described in words which likewise have no meaning to anyone today.
>
> (p. 124)

Like the "Nightmare Canal," which was a rallying point for his tank section. It "was not the place for chat." And that which cannot be said appears during the night, many years later: "Even now [over 70 years later] the menacing streets of Ypres and this Nightmare Canal can return to me and leave a stain of foreboding on the brightest day" (p. 124). Cervantes must have had a similar thought when he baptised Don Quixote *de la Mancha* – "the stain" in Spanish. When the veteran has recollections, what is recollected? Something, says Bion, "where the present used to be," wiped out and at the same time unforgettable.

Earlier, in Chapter 5, he had arrived in Le Havre, then boarded a train for Belgium. Officers had separate compartments from those of the men:

> making unmistakable the gulf that separates US from THEM. Our men, my men, or *The* Men? The name of the inhabitants of the Earth. Or perhaps "Men!" as one would address them before battle. It seemed queer that [they] should suddenly have become estranged and separated as we now approached the Line for which we had prepared so long.

But even this word loses its meaning:

> Much later I had a similar crisis of etiquette when cheerful, jolly Smith suddenly became "It" when a shell splinter entered his brain and we could not get his limbs to pack properly into the grave. "Him," "Corporal," "Matey," "Smith" – time was getting short and it made things awkward if we had to make a grave to fit him.

(or It)

What does a man become at this limit where he is no longer recognised as a subject? Bion asks himself this question, experiencing it almost physically (p. 119).

At the front, finally, he is a rookie who hurries jerkily – with the "staccato" seen in films of the trenches: "Later I realized that any figure, every figure walked in the same way. Even our faces had become standard, strained, covered with a slimy sweat" (p. 126). Now he is entering deeper and deeper into war; the ochre mud becomes reddish, gunfire is more intense:

> Things seemed to be livening up; many more guns were firing. Machine-guns, five-nines – "What did you do in the Great War Daddy?" ... "What are five-nines Daddy?" ... "What ..." "Oh, eat your bun, your damned bun ..." I still feel I am in too much of a hurry to explain all that. And anyhow it is out of date; they do things better now.

(p. 127)

The veteran has nothing to say to the next generation. Sometimes a story remains unheard by his children but reaches the third generation and the ones that follow. Often he has left notebooks, like those that patients bring me, because I ask for them. Sometimes someone has delusions that enact, in the present, past events without a witness.

Bion wonders about his own indifference. Near the famous Canal, he meets his old classmate Bonsey in an infantry regiment. They are both surprised to run into each other: "'Good God! It's you Bion isn't it?' 'Bonsey! E. K. Bonsey!' I remembered him at school, a couple of years older than I, studious, wearing spectacles; I neither liked nor disliked him." As his crew is marching back from battle, Bion looks for Bonsey, to exchange a few more words:

> but he had been killed. *Requiescat in Pace* – "See you in Peace-time old man." I was shocked; I was shocked to find I did not care. I was to become more familiar with the intense comradeship of war, every scrap of gesture, intonation, etched apparently indelibly. A week later it was over and yet not so.
>
> (p. 143)

Later, in Chapter 16, after the Battle of Passchendaele, Bion was summoned by their alcoholic major, who was nevertheless completely reliable at critical times. The major announced that Bion would be recommended for the Victoria Cross, at the age of 19. Bion had been afraid that the major wanted to see him because Highland troops had been fired at by friendly fire. In London, when the general tried to portray him as having "the right stuff" to be a hero, "[h]e seemed to doubt it. So did I." The general asked about the battle for which Bion was commended: "It had all the elements of a first class drama but obviously a hopeless cast" (p. 173).

Rather than exclaiming: "My God! What terrible suffering!" as people also do when they encounter psychosis, we should realise that we are dealing with a sophisticated dynamic which strives to shatter all the links of ordinary language and invent new ones. In Chapter 6 of *Learning from Experience*, he tells us what war has taught him: to be attentive to gestures, to changes in facial expression, to clothing, to a smile or a tone of voice – expressing beta-elements that seek some resonance on the part of the analyst (p. 13). Unfortunately, his first impulse might be to get rid of "personal" impressions, as he has been taught, and if things go wrong, to recommend medications or ECT, now very much in fashion. However, Claude Barrois, former medical director of the psychiatric department at the Val de Grâce military hospital in Paris, and author of *La psychanalyse du guerrier*,[49] warns that chemical treatment of trauma prevents the functioning of the thinking apparatus. Bion is convinced that such an attitude also shuts down the thinking apparatus of the therapist: someone who cannot analyse his own reactions in his relationship with the patient, he says, should not hold the position of analyst.

An analyst at the psychiatric hospital: Prémontré, 1970

At the start of the 1970s, we arrived as sociologists at the Prémontré psychiatric hospital in the North of France – on the battlefields of wars waged for centuries – and we became analysts there. We were members of the Center for the Study of Social Movements (CSSM) headed by Alain Touraine at the École des hautes études en sciences sociales (EHESS) in Paris. With his agreement, we were to carry out research on "Madness and the Social Link," which became the topic of the weekly seminar we gave for forty years. At the hospital, the medical director Edmond Sanquer was a Breton of few words, the son of a sea captain. He introduced us to the staff. We were given white coats and we accompanied the nurses on their rounds to distribute medication, getting to know the patients at the same time. "They don't take them anyways; they throw them in the toilet," the nurses said, not fooled. Many "residents," as they were called then, mentioned previous wars. After some time, we realised that to get to the hospital by car each day, the road cut through graveyards with a sea of white crosses on each side, across the battlefields where our grandfathers, as well as Bion, had fought. We had not noticed them at first, as if this was a normal landscape.

When we arrived, were greeted by a tall, ageless man, blonde and thin, fitting the typical description of a schizophrenic in those years, and were impressed by the civility with which he granted us the honour of showing us his madhouse. The nurses filled us in about him. He had lived in a small village with his parents until their death, and had been cared for by the neighbours afterwards. Then psychiatry came into his life. One day, in the common room where we used to spend time, another patient asked us:

– What is a sociologist?
– Someone who is interested in social movements.
– Oh, you are a bachelor!

Indeed, either we were engaged in objective observation or we entered into a relationship with him. Our host, who overheard the exchange, came closer, very interested. He said he was conducting research himself, on "ideopathology," with a supervisor in Paris named Paolo Herzog. I asked him if he had met him. Not at all. He had gone to Paris twice, had circled the Gare du Nord where his train arrived, and had returned home. We told him that our Paolo Herzog was known as Alain Touraine, a fact he was very happy to hear.

One day the medical director saw patients with the whole team, so that they could be introduced to a new intern. Just as he was starting his interview with the ideopathalogy researcher, he was called away on an urgent matter and asked me to continue in his place. This put me in a state of confusion, of which the patient was aware, so that he went ahead and introduced himself.

He touched my arm as if to say: "Don't worry, I don't mind. Anyway, it won't take very long." The following night I fell into a dreamless sleep and awoke feeling very anxious, with my arm paralysed – the arm the patient had touched. Charcot may have interpreted this as a hysterical symptom, but I prefer Bion's explanation. This man had been willing to take my anxiety upon himself: "I've been through worse, it won't kill me." In the confusion that took hold of me, I felt the betrayal of our conversations. In the night, beta-elements had been transferred to me through an interference.

In Chapter 10 of *Learning from Experience*, Bion speaks of the patients' ability to trigger strong emotions in the analyst, who can transform them by acknowledging them. At that time I had not yet started to explore "the past presented" by war on this territory, where the ploughs still dug up an amazing number of weapons and ammunitions. But, without knowing it, I was registering day after day, through a new social link with the patients confined there, sometimes for ages, the madness of wars, which led me to Bion.

English Farm, Nightmare Canal

In Chapter 7 of *The Long Week-End*, Bion takes part in his first battle at the front, in November 1917, near Cambrai:

> In the dark we could just distinguish some remains [...] English Farm they called it. This is where our tanks were to rendezvous for battle. [...] Some German bombers unloaded. [...] Then a star shell fell on our route. We stopped instantly. [...] The entire line of tanks [...] what an age they took to open fire. [...] The dread of the immediate future weighed heavily on our attempts at being carefree. No weight so leaden as the weight of freedom from care. Perhaps [...] I should have run away. Too late, too late.
>
> (p. 128)

It was there that Bion experienced dissociation, a dread that he could later recognise in his patients. He needed over fifty years to describe precisely the origin of this intuition as a psychoanalyst:

> As I write these words I know that I have not forgotten what happened that night at English Farm, what was going to happen on the St Jean-Wieltje Road at Cambrai, at Amiens, in the "train bleu" after years in the black areas of a second world war.

Here, he refers to the train he took in 1956 to revisit battlefields that appeared to him in the present of 1917: "I see them still in the watch fires of a thousand sleepless nights, for the soul goes marching on" (p. 128). Like Fabrice del Dongo at the Battle of Waterloo,[50] he had no idea what was happening and learned from newspaper reports that it was a great battle.

While he searches on the map for Hill 40, he and his crew are wallowing in mud, in primitive tanks rolling on timber beams to avoid falling into holes. To the right, he sees tree stumps, and a wood is in fact marked on the map just to the right of Hill 40. Shells are exploding:

> The enemy could see us and his artillery were aiming concentrated fire at us. He could not miss. Yet miss he did, and this contributed to the delusion of safety. And then I realized, in one of my repeated glances in the direction of the trees, that they were not trees but our infantry advancing in line with their rifles slung on their shoulders. I had imagined that infantry used their rifles for shooting; not so – not in Ypres Salient. Imaginary security; imaginary aggression? Yet men died.
>
> (p. 131)

He speaks through the voice of Dante and Macbeth, and this is not a metaphor since he is at the gates of Hell: "Battle orders I wanted [...]. Would nobody tell me what to do?" (p. 134).

In the next chapter, he reports to the major – who tells him: "Sit down my dear chap" and offers him a glass of port – to confess that he had lost his tank, which got stuck in the mud. The intelligence officer asks him to point out the place on the map. But he can't answer, because he keeps thinking of the desiccated corpse with which he had shared his shell-hole: "It – or was it 'he' [...] was lying andrews-cross-wise. [He] didn't stink, for which I was thankful" (p. 138).

In Chapter 10, Bion comes back to the nightmarish experience of a canal he described in Chapter 6 as "Nightmare Canal" (p. 124). "Nightmare" is composed of "night" and "mare." "Mare" is present in the French *cauchemar*, whose first part, *cauche*, means "to press down on," in the Picard dialect, and comes from the Latin verb *calcare*, meaning "to trample." What oppresses us in a nightmare is a ghost, the incubus or succubus that comes to lie over us or under us. In Greek, the word for nightmare is *ephialtès*, "that which jumps on you." Ephialtes was an Athenian who supported democracy. In 458 BC, he was assassinated by an aristocrat. Did his ghost haunt Athenians? Nightmares often haunt veterans until their death, as we heard from our fathers, who didn't understand how they could still be trampled every night so many years later.

Descartes was assailed by three nightmares, on November 10, 1619, in his stove-heated room in Ulm, when he was a soldier in winter quarters in Ulm during the Thirty Years' War (1618–1649). We know about them thanks to his first biographer, Adrien Baillet.[51] Afterwards he left the army and travelled through Europe until he settled in the Netherlands, where he changed his address several times. In his case, too, it took a long time to tame the dread they inspired.

It was not until 1637 that he wrote his *Discourse on Method*,[52] in order, he says, to "conduct my own method of reasoning." The passage "like a man who walks alone in the darkness, I resolved to go so slowly and circumspectly that if I did not get ahead very rapidly I was at least safe from falling" (p. 137) refers to the terrifying winds from the beyond in his first nightmare, which threatened to make him fall at every step and carry him away. Three years later, in 1641, his Sixth Meditation "rejects [...] as ridiculous, the general uncertainty respecting sleep, which I could not distinguish from the waking state." Waking from his third nightmare, he had been scared by the vision of many lights in his room, like will-o'-the-wisp, evoking the souls of the dead.

Descartes also describes traumatic memory, which:

> can never connect our dreams with each other [...]. And, in truth, if someone, when I am awake, appeared to me all of a sudden and as suddenly disappeared, as do the images I see in sleep, so that I could not observe either whence he came or whither he went, I should not without reason esteem it either a specter or phantom [...] rather than a real man.
>
> (p. 134)

In his correspondence with the princess Elizabeth of Bohemia, who suffered from melancholia and asked for his help, he analysed her traumas through his own experience, thanks to transference, like a genuine psychotherapist.[53] The psychotherapy of trauma is as old as wars. We are far from the dualism promoted by Cartesians, which, as Descartes wrote to Elizabeth, he had posited first in order to go beyond it. In other words, "dissociation" was his first tool of survival, which he analysed using his own method, and could abandon afterwards.

What is at stake is not knowledge, but the very existence of events that require an interference to testify to their existence. This interference can take the form of laughter, for instance in the Theatre of Fools, which drags onto the stage mirthless grandees who take themselves seriously. The same seriousness prevails among psychotherapists who diagnose psychosis in the unmotivated laughter of patients who mock them. A fable was dedicated to the subject long ago. The Abderitans summoned Hippocrates one day, worried about Democritus' fits of laughter. In his fable "Democritus and the People of Abdera," La Fontaine writes: "How I have always hated the opinions of the mob!"[54] Hastening to restore the reason of this laughing fool speaking to himself about atoms, "children of a hollow brain, invisible phantoms," Hippocrates finds him "sitting in leafy shade, beside a brook. [...] Having put aside mere trifles of conversation, they reasoned upon man and his mind."

Going beyond the *Witz* connected with repression, the fit of laughter opens onto the territory of the sacred. Aristophanes' comedies are inseparable from tragedies, like *kyôgen* between performances of Noh theatre. Bion displays a degree of humour when he says, in *Attention and Interpretation*: "I have no idea what someone's psycho-analysis involves. This is not false modesty, but a condition of work."

Subverting mainstream psychoanalysis

Bion's experience with patients suffering from "disturbances in thinking" drove him to bring into question orthodox transference, in situations where "thoughts are things and things are thoughts, and they have personality."[55] He proposed a new reading of the myth of Oedipus, drawing attention to the disparity of elements composing the Sphinx, which are not linked by a "chain of causation." Her riddle – "What walks on four legs in the morning, two legs at noon and three legs in the evening?" – reminds Bion of something other than Oedipus' answer.

In *The Long Week-End*, he remembers the time when a friend told him:

> When you go on leave don't go see Cohen. I went – it was dreadful. He has lost both eyes, his right arm and both legs. [...] He [...] just has a silly grin. The nurse told me afterwards that every now and then he becomes terrified, cowers down in a corner of the room and sucks his thumb. Once he told his doctor that at these times he could see [...] his mother rise out of her grave and walk slowly toward him. [...] "For though the body dies the soul shall live for ever." I hope not, with all my heart I hope not.
>
> (p. 186)

Clearly, the Oedipus complex is not the only answer.

What lives forever are the names Bion recites like a prayer: "Their name liveth for evermore."

> In the hearts and minds of the survivors it did, til they also died. [...] the 5th Battalion [...] who sang [...] we were swallowed up amongst so many new boys that we hardly existed. Despard: killed in action. Bayliss: died of wounds. Cohen: wounded. [...] Ball: [...] he was such a nice fellow [...] til that day he got under the tank. [...] Hauser, Quainton [...] and myself.[56]

In the same way – through the voice of the captive who escaped from slavery in Algiers – Cervantes recites the names of the comrades who died in Tunisia, at the siege of La Goletta in which he took part. He bequeaths them an epitaph in the form of a sonnet.[57]

The psychoanalysis of madness and trauma is familiar to Bion since his war experience. In Chapter 27 of *The Long Week-End*, just before the Armistice, he is shocked by his men's disappearance: "No one had heard of my men; my section had simply disappeared." He tried to talk about it with two of his comrades, who listened and seemed to understand, but had nothing to say: "I learned that when no one has anything to say the time has come to be silent" (p. 219).

Bion's assertion resonates with Wittgenstein's last sentence in the *Tractatus Logico-Philosophicus*, written on the front line at the same time: "Whereof one cannot speak, thereof one must be silent."[58] But, like him, Bion did not stop at that point: "The debate with myself did not cease. *That* was not so easily dealt with then or since." When Wittgenstein returned to Cambridge after ten years spent in Vienna in a post-traumatic state, he resumed practising philosophy (as a therapy), and claimed, in the *Philosophical Investigations*, that we can break the wall of silence since we cannot help showing what we cannot say, by using what he calls "ostensive definitions." But showing to whom? This is where psychotic transference comes into play.

To answer this question, Bion advances certain elements that mainstream psychoanalysis "has not sufficiently examined," but which do not go unnoticed by patients who consider their analysts' interpretations "unjustified." In 1959, he writes: "Psychoanalysis must free itself of restrictions of the classical method, as unsuitable in these cases as classical mechanics are from the perspective of quantum mechanics." In both cases, the research deals with interferences.[59]

Later in the text, he gives the example of a stammerer who shows the interruption of the symbolic chain "by muscular movements of the tongue, the lips and the vocal chords" (pp. 158–159). The speaker cannot say "I am angry," but there is anger, producing high and low tones. If the analyst can perceive this resonance through "his own personality," Bion says, and through his history, instead of warding off this interference, a transitional subject emerges from the interaction. Still, it is not an easy task.

Dream of terror

In *The Long Week-End*, Bion recounts his failure, in the summer of 1918, to enter into such an interaction, and the terrifying dream he had afterwards. An officer who died in action had to be replaced. A man named Cannon was assigned to take his place, although Bion would have preferred Sergeant O'Toole. Very hurt by the rejection, O'Toole asked to speak to Bion in private:

> "Sir, I don't want anything more. I don't mean I want to be invalided out – no shell-shock for me. But this time sir, I feel I want six feet of earth and nothing else. I know it's got to happen; I feel it in my bones sir. Will you write to my people sir?" I told him that of course I would but I did not think there was any need to think of that. I am amazed now that even allowing for my not yet being twenty-one I could say

anything so silly. Both of us had had far more than our ration of escapes; both knew it.

O'Toole is grateful: "'Thank you very much for letting me talk to you sir.' He saluted and went off." O'Toole never missed a chance to say "I'm an orphan." After failing to make contact with him, Bion felt as if he was orphaned of himself (p. 237).

That night he dreamt a terrible dream, from which he awoke just as he was about to go into action during the great English offensive near Amiens:

> The dream was grey, shapeless; horror and dread gripped me. I could not cry out, just as now, many years later, I can find no words. Then I had no words to find; I was awake to the relatively benign terror of real war. Yet for a moment I wished it was only a dream. In the dream I must have wished it was only a war.
>
> (p. 238)

The "protopathic" dimension of extreme pain – observed by William Rivers during the first stage of the experiment conducted with Henry Head on the regeneration of nerves – is similar, he says, to that of an injury to otherness suffered by the traumatised officers who were his patients at Craiglockhart.[60] Such is the absolute terror of Bion's dream without content, stemming from the total loneliness that Sergeant O'Toole tried to share with him. An organic wound becomes more tolerable at the "epicritic" stage, where thresholds appear little by little, like psychic pain filtered gradually through the transference. This nameless dread still haunts Bion years later, although he tries to break it up into small fragments that are as terrible as the ousted "thing," if the filter of another, his alpha-function, is absent.

These are the heterogeneous elements composing the Sphinx in the Oedipus tragedy. They appear in dreams "which are not Freudian dreams," since they originate outside the symbolic chain, from an agency called *Nemesis*, which intervenes when the law, *Nomos*, is broken. *Nemo* means "to share" in Greek. When *hubris*, "excess," breaks the law of sharing called *Moira*, injuries to otherness are inflicted and are passed down through generations, activating dreams that show ongoing chaos.

Bion's war is indelible. At the very end of *The Long Week-End*, he speaks of Asser's death, as it was described to him by a prisoner of war. Ordered by the enemy to surrender when his tank was surrounded, he replied, revolver in hand: "I'm damned if I will." This story, which "added nothing" to what he had already guessed, was extremely disturbing to him. His first impression was "one of utter waste." His second reaction was incomprehension:

> After Cambrai it was obvious to me [...] that I could have been killed
> a number of times over [...] then a feeling that I would never in such
> circumstances do my duty. [...] I do not understand courage such as
> Asser's [although] I can easily understand all the *explanations.*

His third impression is the attachment he felt to this young man, "always
cheerful, modest, unassuming. [...] the very language of love, like the word
'love' itself, can hardly be used in the presence of the thing itself. [...] 'And
I, only, am left alone to tell thee'" (p. 271). At the ceremony in the palace
where he is awarded the Victoria Cross, he is unable to reply to the king's
congratulatory words, and can only think: "For God's sake get me out of
this hole" (p. 189).

On August 8, 1978, a year before his death, he was still talking to his dead
comrades by dictating into a recorder the thoughts that would constitute
Cogitations. In *The Passing of Arthur,* a tale Purcell had set to music a century
and a half earlier,[61] Tennyson says: "The faces of old ghosts look in upon the
battle" – the Battle of Camlann fought by the king before he went off to the
Isle of Avalon – the way to which, the Celts say, can only be found by chance.
Asser's ghost looks upon the Battle of Amiens – where Bion died a second
time on August 8, 1918, when his whole crew was burnt to death:

> The bodies [...] poured out of the door of the tank as if they were the
> entrails of some mysterious beast of a primitive kind which has simply
> perished then and there in the conflagration [...]. This experience is
> similar to others I have had in the past, but the similarity refers only to
> the known facts, not to the unknown. In this respect there are new
> experiences [requiring] methods of recording [...] the unknown [...]
> that cannot be described in ordinary terms.
>
> (pp. 368–369)

A fable of our time

As Freud wrote in 1912 at the beginning of his *Gradiva,*[62] Bion found
"valuable allies" among writers and poets, who have their own methods of
recording thoughts without a thinker, coming from the unknown. After his
exile to Los Angeles, Bion became one of them. Beforehand, in 1968,[63] he
had written some notes, published in *Cogitations,* about the marketing of
thoughtlessness; he attacks "poisons for the mind," such as "the miracle of
pharmacology. Drugs are substitutes employed by those who cannot wait
[...] which destroy the ability to discriminate the real from the false"
(p. 300). Bion compares their addiction to messianic ideas, twisted around
a void like a knot that attracts curiosity, greed, envy, hatred and destructive
paranoia, although such turbulences may also engender growth and
maturation (p. 299).

Then, in July 1971, he introduces a revolutionary discovery taking place in the year 30070: "psycho-analysis" (p. 329). The term is made up of *psyche* – "mind" or "personality" – and *anal*, derived from an anatomical structure concerned with the evacuation of waste products from eating. In short, psychoanalysts develop purifying rituals intended to placate the remains of what they have devoured. But since this is not effective on a large scale, a religion develops around using rare metals in the form of representations of excretions called Money; these innovations are supported by psychoanalysis. But greed led some elements to substitute inferior substances like paper to the precious metals, which then led some dissident psychoanalysts to subvert the religion of Money in favour of the religion of "Science."

Brainwashing and statistics reached a very considerable degree of efficiency. Eager to remain at the forefront of progress, psychoanalysis established "scientific criteria" to recruit its own candidates and to separate psychotic personalities from those that are not, putting the former in loony bins. Some candidates were placed in the "not yet" category. In those times, the hierarchy hunted down and destroyed all signs of potential growth.

At this point, a troublemaker named Smith, alias Bion, makes his appearance. He becomes an analyst, after his war experience. His peculiarity is refusal of the established dogma instilled by "prolonged and deep analysis" – and his interest in psychotics – like his patient who takes herself alternately for the Virgin and the Duke of Wellington. Regarded with suspicion due to his analytic relationship with a person who, "in the quaint terminology of the time, was a menace to herself and others," he makes things worse for himself by advocating the scrutiny of the present and *the unknown* rather than the investigation of the past, and by speaking of thoughts without a thinker and other such nonsense. Consequently, in those barbaric times, he and his patient are both in danger of "having their brains scientifically and humanely destroyed" by various drugs and other mechanical procedures. Worse still, his patient turns hostile and wants to get rid of him.

Bion's relationship with his American colleagues is also unsuccessful: "They are puzzled by, and cannot understand me." Above all, they don't understand psychotic transference, which requires the analyst to work with his own failings. His patient, who wants to get rid of him, is in fact seeking to destroy the ruthless agency that abused her and took his place, so that she can face it and rebel. By admitting his own faults as an important element of the transference, a reliable otherness is created (p. 332). Bion learned to be an analyst during the war, which taught him that the "minimum necessary" is sincerity (p. 367): "I do not think [...] a patient will ever accept an interpretation, however correct, unless he feels that the analyst has passed through [an] emotional crisis as a part of the act of giving the interpretation" (p. 291).

Ceasefire: November 11, 1918, 11 a.m.

On that date, in a train carriage in Rethondes, the Allied generals were meeting with the German High Command: "all the usual military precautions would be maintained. This I supposed was a way of saying the war was over." The men were exhausted: "We could certainly understand that if our army stopped fighting it might well be impossible to start it again." A grenade explodes under the caterpillar tracks of a tank; one of Bion's men is killed on the spot. It takes him time to realise what the small red spot on his gunner's chest means, a red mark like that over the heart of Arthur Rimbaud's "Le dormeur du val" ("Asleep in the Valley").[64] "Dear Madam, I regret to inform you that your son ... was killed by accident when the war was over..." "What about his wife and children? [...] he was too young and can't have had any. Oh yes he had though; and she was expecting a baby. 'Dear Madam, I regret to inform you that your husband...'"[65]

In the morning, his sergeant, Cannon, appears, clicking his heels. Bion is startled, like he is each time a bullet makes them all duck, sweat, curse. He is not a fanatical warrior, but gives an order for parade. The men refuse to come out of the barracks. Cannon clicks his heels again. Their captain admits: "Those clickings were getting on my nerves." The men finally come out: "I could have wept with relief. Alone in the hut, I wiped the sweat off my face and tried to stop my trembling."

What happens when all this is over? Bion says: "I was 21 and had not yet experienced what it was to be a relic." These are terrible words, for they speak of the passage from a carefree past to a present in which all the survivors have become a living memory: "Though we did not realize it, we were men who had grown from insignificance to irrelevance in the passage of a few short years." The only way out is to write, as Bion did fifty years later. *The Long Week-End* ends with these words:

> No one could explain that if the British Empire did not share the same fate it was because of a few poets. But what can poets do against nuclear fission or, even more potent, some germs being carefully tended and nurtured by biologists of marvelous skill and foresight – as is the way with the clever toolmaking animal, man?
>
> (p. 287)

Christmas comes. It's important to "Keep the men occupied" to keep away dark thoughts. "Everyone suddenly burst out singing," wrote the poet Siegfried Sassoon, but Bion says: "our songs had alcoholic overtones. Too many faces were missing." He can't bring himself to sing, even after the war: "Never, never again. I was not unhappy – indeed I often felt that I was much happier than most. But no more singing: never" (p. 191).

In his article "Scientific Method," dated January 1959, Bion compared what takes place in the analysis of psychosis with the scientific method described by Henri Poincaré in *Science and Method*.[66] In Chapter 1, entitled "Selected Facts," Poincaré protests against greedy and stubborn plutocracy, but also against virtuous and mediocre democracy ready to turn the other cheek, and in whose bosom wise men without curiosity would not die of illness, but certainly of boredom. Yet nothing new would have been created without some selfless fools who died in poverty, and discarding utility, took pleasure in investigating nature, since it is beautiful.

Bion attempts to draw psychoanalysts out of their boredom by stating that psychotic transference, though useless for corporate interests, generates a new social link, bringing pleasure and beauty on both sides. It stems from "selected facts" that tie the patients' symptoms to the analyst's life experience through deep resonances. In *Cogitations*, he adds: "In this respect [the analyst's] position is not unlike that of the soldier in war who is aware of his own troubles but not of his enemy's." When the enemy is present in a session and attacks the transference, the analyst must keep in mind that he is struggling with his patient to bring into existence a social link, where such a link has ceased to exist. The "selected fact" is the interference, producing turbulences in the analyst, which creates a space for freedom between them.[67]

"The answer is the misfortune of the question" (Blanchot)

The seminars given by Bion in Brasilia in 1975 and in São Paulo in 1978[68] are published as discussions with Brazilian analysts who submit clinical cases to him, without any psychobabble. These discussions are followed by "four papers." The first, entitled "Emotional Turbulence" – published in 1976 – brings into question Freud's concept of the "caesura" of birth.[69] Bion suggests that "the foetus might have a proto-mind and personality, or could develop its proto-mind into a mind after birth." Therefore, it would be useful to have a way of knowing what the foetus thinks (p. 309). Later the individual can do his best to cut the umbilical cord, but will never succeed in silencing what was recorded by his foetal cells, coming from his environment.

What has been cut out of the foetal experience returns in emotional disturbances, at critical times in childhood, adolescence and old age: "When the analysand is too young or too senile, too retarded or too premature" to express these disturbances verbally, the analyst must find "the limits of wavelength that bind the polyspectral 'area'." The next element in choice depends on chance, that is, on "some force other than the conscious human being who chooses" (p. 297). In the psychotic turmoil of communications during the session, "tones of voice, smiles, gestures, silences" offer the analyst a chance to connect them to his own impressions and thereby gain access to another universe. Failing this, as Maurice Blanchot says, "The answer is the misfortune of the question."

Bion gives an example of the insatiable curiosity of children. As a child, he was constantly pestering his parents: "What's that, Daddy? – A cow. – Why is it a cow, Daddy? – Because his Mummy and Daddy were cows. – Why were they cows, Daddy?" And so on ... Every good answer stimulates "further questions and further problems" (p. 300). This is the process of growing up: we open our eyes, take a step, and a new world opens every time. The same is true in analysis: every bit of progress opens a new universe, instead of solving the problem, but it can also lead to a clash between the analyst and the patient, threatening to interrupt their common research.

This is where Sanskritist Charles Malamoud's parable is relevant. It is the story of two carts that collide while taking two wise men to a place of sacrifice. Instead of despairing, they rebuild a new cart out of the fragments of their two broken ones. When a sudden collision occurs in the transference, it is important to recognise it and adjust – *arariskô*, "patch up" – the scattered pieces in order to build a new vehicle.

According to Bion, "ignorance is filled with knowledge" (p. 301). How does he know this? "Thanks to his *phrenes* – the Greeks' physical thinking apparatus, the Japanese *hara*" – which rises and falls like a powerful breath when agitated. Fortunately, the answer obtained stimulates another question. But unfortunately, since man abhors a vacuum and hates ignorance, he fills the space created by his unanswerable questions with psychoanalytic theories resembling authoritative statements (p. 302). Bion gives another example.

"It is curious that this term, 'caesura', was misprinted in the original paper by Freud as 'censure'" (p. 304). This slip has political consequences. By confusing the discontinuity of the cut-out unconscious – which manifests itself through word-things and surviving images – with censored signifiers of the repressed unconscious, our mental turbulences, and those of our societies, end up bursting into violence. Of course, we can always tell ourselves, relying on the media: "We all know this." But what "we all know," Bion insists, "prevents us from realising that something – we know not what – has not yet emerged from the turbulence. Are we then to inhibit the turbulence? Or are we to investigate it?" (p. 303). He continues, taking a political stand:

> The general tendency is to bury newborn ideas by inviting the one who proposes them to enter an institution, calling him a genius, or calling him crazy and locking him up, so he will not disturb the "sanity" of other.

In any case, "escape from self-knowledge" leads to "self-murder" or to "killing another group or society or culture" (p. 305). Fortunately, as he writes at the end of *The Long Week-End*, there are always poets – Homer and Shakespeare – who ignore the caesura and "listen to the inarticulate and formulate states of mind that did not exist in their time: ours." If we break away from the inhibiting influence of psychoanalysis, we can listen to interferences – at the origin of radio astronomy – which lead us into sacred territory (p. 306). Bion takes the example of the word "bloody": "'Bloody' does not have much to do with the white cells, red cells, or whatever. It is, in fact, an abbreviated way of saying, 'By Our Lady'. So it is really part and parcel of [the] sacred" (p. 307).

This territory is part of the social field that, Bion argues, Freud too often considered a given. But he warns us that "the revolutionary becomes respectable – a barrier against revolution. [...] That war has not ceased yet" (p. 331).

Making the best of a bad job

"Making the Best of a Bad Job" is the title of Bion's last paper, written in 1979.[70] It deals with the turbulence occurring in transference, whether the analyst speaks or not. Of course, he could try to conform to what is expected of him, but he would be insincere.

"All is fair in love and war!" Bion reminds us: "The enemy's object is so to terrify you that you cannot think clearly, while your objective is to continue to think clearly no matter how adverse or frightening the situation." And he adds: "[This] calls for courage" (p. 322). Then he goes over all the forms of thought of which "the body keeps the score,"[71] starting from the foetal stage:

> I suggest that there is no reason why [the foetus] shouldn't *feel* [...] some stages of fear, of intense fear [...] as the shadow of a future we don't know any more than we know the past, [kept] as memory traces. [...] It seems to me that [...] certain [...] developments are too *premature* and too precocious to be tolerable. Therefore, the foetus [...] does its best to sever that connection. At a later stage, the individual can shut himself up.
>
> (p. 309)

Bion gives the example of a 30-year-old man who lives as a recluse in his room, with the curtains drawn. He brings a Smith & Wesson revolver to the sessions, which he lays ostentatiously by his side, in order to have the means of putting an end to the analyst's interpretations:

> Luckily [...] having been an instructor in small arms, I paid a great deal of attention to that Smith and Wesson. It did rather distract me from paying attention to what the patient was saying, and I think the patient was similarly saved from having to pay too much attention to what I was saying.

After giving other examples, Bion concludes that there is no reason to think that the foetus has not felt "intolerable pressure in the amniotic fluid, and even after he changes to a gaseous medium." The revolver illustrates a prototype of visceral fear that Bion has experienced in war. In other cases, this fear is expressed through incontrollable tears flowing even before birth. This fear without a subject is passed on to the foetus by what Socrates calls "a wrath [...] transmitted through some lineage,"[72] like a projectile seeking a target. The fear could be expressed through a revolver, with which the analyst happened to be familiar, and speaks to both of them of unspeakable feelings.

In the third paper, entitled "Evidence," published in 1976, Bion illustrates this inversion of vertex by referring to Clouzot's film *The Mystery of Picasso*,[73] in which Picasso is painting on a sheet of glass so that the picture can be seen from either side:

> Using my hand, I suggest something of this sort: look at it from one side; there is a psycho-somatic complaint; turn it round: now it is soma-psychotic. It is the same hand, but what you see depends on which way you look at it, from what position, from what vertex ...

A little further on, Bion asks: "Is it possible to talk to the soma in such a way that the psychosis is able to understand, or vice versa?" (pp. 318–319).

Bion's conclusions are the same as those drawn by analysts who speak to babies abandoned in nurseries:

> It is important to recognize that there is a world in which it is impossible to see what a psychoanalyst can see [...]. We are investigating the unknown [...]. We may be dealing with things which are so slight as to be virtually imperceptible, but which are so real that they could destroy us almost without our being aware of it. *That* is the kind of area into which we have to penetrate.
>
> (pp. 319–320)

This area is the sphere of wandering ghosts coming back through "achiral" images, without a reflection in the mirror.

Lacan experienced such an absence of reflection when, after the war, in 1947, he visited Bion and John Rickman – Bion's second analyst.

Lacan's visit to Bion[74]

Lacan had noticed that as early as 1939, British psychoanalysts were helping to create a national army in which "the mental instruction of recruits" was held to be "an essential factor of morale." He discovered that

"British psychiatrists made use of their newly emerging science in what could be called the synthetic creation of an army."

As far as the selection of officers was concerned, Lacan observed that "it was made on the basis of horizontal identification, which Freud neglected in his work in favour of the identification [...] to the leader." He was surprised to find a large number of British psychoanalysts in the war, in contrast with their total absence in France during World War I[75] and World War II, when he himself stopped practising. Indeed, the psychoanalysis of psychoses had developed with traumatised soldiers elsewhere in Europe and among Anglo-Saxons. Perhaps Lacan's disdain for Anglo-Saxon psychoanalysis stemmed from the reserved reception he received from Bion.

Lacan expected him "to share the flame of his creation," but their encounter was rather guarded. He had to content himself with observing Bion's "large physique and [...] swimmer's chest, his face [...] frozen in an immobile and moonlike mask, accentuated by the fine commas of a black moustache." After diagnosing him as a solitary being, he turns instead to Rickman, who is much more jovial, speaks warmly and passionately, and has a less forbidding tawny moustache.

At the end of his five-week stay in England, Lacan concluded that the British victory was "of a moral order" contrasting with the "panicked dissolution of [the French population's] moral status," a population "victim of the systematic misrecognition of the world by each individual." A book testifies on this dissolution: *L'Étrange Défaite*,[76] written by Marc Bloch, historian and cofounder, with Lucien Febvre, of the Annales School of History, and of the School where our seminars are held. Born in 1885 and recruited as an intelligence officer in World War I, he volunteered for service again during World War II, when he was 54 and the father of six children. After the fall of France in 1940, he joined the French Resistance and was killed in a ditch by the Nazis.

Still, as Don Quixote says: "all comparisons are odious." At the age of 17, Lacan had been terrified to find his father unrecognisable when he returned from the front. For solace, the young Lacan joined the surrealist movement. A similar story was told by World War I historian Stéphane Audoin Rouzeau about his own family, in a book written for the centennial of World War I, under the title *Quelle histoire*.[77] What a story, indeed. His own father cut off all relations with the author's grandfather, a traumatised veteran, treating him like an outcast; he joined the surrealist movement and became a friend of André Breton. Like Hannah Arendt, the historian defends his right to judge such a rejection. Captain Bion's return to civilian life, despite his two decorations, was far from glorious either, as his second autobiographical book testifies.

The body politic

All My Sins Remembered[78] was published in 1985 by Francesca Bion after the death of her husband, as the planned sequel to *The Long Week-End*. It starts when Bion is at Oxford, enrolled as a history student, completely lost, still a virgin, and knowing nothing about psychoanalysis. The comrades who survived went off in different directions. His nights are haunted by nightmares:

> I did not see, I did not see that peacetime was no time for me. I didn't know, however many pretty ribbons I put on my wartime uniform, that wartime also was no time for me. I was twenty-four – in 1921 – no good for war, no good for peace, and too old to change. Sometimes, it burst out in sleep. Terrified. What about? Nothing, nothing. Oh well, yes! I had a dream. I dug my nails into the steep and slippery walls of mud that fell sheer into the waters of a raging, foaming Steenbeck. Ridiculous! That dirty little trickle? If blood is thicker than water, what price the thickness of my dreams? [...] I woke up. Was I going crazy? Perhaps I *was* crazy.
>
> (p. 16)

In his last paper, "Making the Best of a Bad Job," Bion analyses his dreams, which, according to Francesca Bion, haunted his nights:

> Suppose we regard being asleep as being in a particular state of mind in which we see sights, visit places, and carry out activities [...] not usually carried out by us when we are awake [...]. (p. 327) A man has much muscular activity. When awake, he says he has had a restless night. Where did he go? What did he see? Who was he? [...] What is certain is that [the] physical activity which the patient has experienced is unmistakable [...]; he often admits, unwillingly, that he is tired (pp. 329–330). [...] After all, what is wrong with the factual event when the person is asleep? (p. 328).
>
> (p. 327)

Bion considers that the problem is not that of the individual, but of the physical body seen from a political perspective, that of the body politic.

Charlotte Beradt testifies to such political dreams in her book *The Third Reich of Dreams.*[79] A Jewish doctor is called in to treat the Führer. He is the only one who can cure him and he treats him in accordance with the Hippocratic oath. When the doctor wakes up, he is devastated. Bion would say that his dream is "a battleground" where Nazi propaganda, under the guise of recognition, condemns him to death.

As Hannah Arendt noted in her analysis of Rahel Varnhagen's traumatic dreams,[80] a memory takes shape during the night that is cut out in the daytime. *All My Sins Remembered* starts with the statement that when the young war veterans are back home, they are unable to speak to each other, despite having been extremely close at the front: "We could not reminisce about the war; and we had nothing else to talk about." Hence, hallucinatory dreams without an address. The analyst must be able to locate their source, and try to tune in to some wavelength despite the white noise. The patient "is like a fossil, unaware of what he testifies to. Things have been recorded, of which he has not the least idea" (p. 25). In such a case, an overdose of theories kills the self by eliminating the elements that tie him to History (p. 27). Apparently, animistic societies are better able to deal with this problem.

In a text on animism published in *Cogitations* and dated February 17, 1960, Bion describes the mechanism of destruction used by the mental apparatus to get rid of intolerable things that are recorded by sense impressions. In contrast, animistic rituals – using objects dear to collectors – transform unprocessed beta-elements into alpha-elements that can be shared and symbolised. Bion calls the things we eliminate to fend off distress, ever since our birth, "proto-real." What use is distress, if not to make a *tresse* – meaning a "braid" in French – intertwining proto-real elements with a song, for instance, such as my favourite Mexican song *"Gritten las piedras del campo"* ("The Stones Shout in the Countryside"). To say that stones have knowledge is not a metaphor, for they can speak to some people when no other mouth speaks to them. The Sioux ritual formula during ceremonies, "all my relatives" places rocks at the top of the hierarchy of beings, since they need neither plants nor animals to be. Humans, who need all of these, are at the foot of the ladder, despite their "humanistic" claims, as Artaud said when he was visiting the Tarahumaras in Mexico.

"The child and the spells"

When animism does not work, things take their revenge, until a rhythm emerges in the midst of helplessness, *Hilflosigkeit*. This is what happens in Ravel's *L'enfant et les sortilèges*,[81] with a libretto by Colette, in which the things and beings destroyed by the child speak up to attack him, until the final appeasement. The child feels their ferocity even when he has his eyes closed.

Colette wrote this text at the request of the director of the opera in 1915, and sent it to Ravel, whom she had met briefly in 1900. He was fighting near Verdun in 1916 and stopped composing, except for *Le Tombeau de Couperin*, composed on the occasion of his mother's death in 1917; Ravel produced no other work until 1919. This lyric fantasy, *The Child and the Spells*, performed for the first time in Monte Carlo in 1925, "brings to life the fury of war and the revenge of things on human omnipotence."

Alone in his room, the Child, who is 7, refuses to do his homework: "I want to punish Mama," someone we don't see, except for a hand and a finger. She has left the room, saying: "Think of how you've hurt mummy." In a fit of anger, he throws the china cup and teapot, stirs up the fire in the fireplace, torments the squirrel in its cage, pulls the cat's tail, destroys the old clock, tears up his book, pulls off the wallpaper and shouts: "I am free, free, naughty and free!" falling into the armchair, which pulls back.

Struck dumb, he hears the things speak among themselves. "We don't want the child anymore," they say, without addressing him. And he witnesses the revolt of those he tormented: the clock and the torn-up book, the old Wedgwood teapot and the broken china cup, the fire that crackles: "I burn the naughty ones;" the shepherd and the shepherdess, the amaranthine goat and the blue dog on the Jouy print linen – all of them hostile, ignoring him when he cries: "I am afraid!" Fallen from the heights of his omnipotence, the Child thinks for the first time of taking care of the squirrel: "He bound up the wound of the squirrel!" the objects sing in unison. At the end of the play, the "enchanted beings" come back to become his allies.

Confronted with the destruction of the subject, the analyst may dismiss "the conception to be formed of the handling of the transference in such treatment,"[82] like Lacan, and define the problem as psychotic structure. But in fact, he falls off his armchair, which pulls back like that of the Child, and discovers in himself flaws he never suspected. If he takes up this challenge, he sets up joint research with his patient, which Bion unhesitatingly calls "scientific," since its objective is "to establish – be it imperfectly – the truth."

This is the task Rickman and Bion undertook at the Northfield military hospital in 1942–1943, in the course of the six-week duration of "the first Northfield Experiment."[83]

John Rickman, Bion's second analyst, was a Quaker and a disciple of William Rivers. Like him, he treated war neuroses when he came back from the front. He also went to Vienna, where he and Ernest Jones established the foundations of British psychoanalysis. His analyst was Melanie Klein. He recommended her to Bion, when he himself started to work too closely with him. Before World War II, military psychiatry and the British army were in a critical state, described by Bion in his article "The War of Nerves," published in 1940 – a title Ben Shephard borrowed in 2001 for his wonderful book *A War of Nerves*.[84]

In 1941, John Rickman published an account of the short psychotherapy of a soldier wounded in the North of France. He was paralysed in one arm, which he nursed with great care, trying to warm it, while speaking of his best friend killed in the same battle, who "would have given his right arm for him." Rickman understood that the arm did not represent the body of his comrade, but their severed bond. Although the soldier was indifferent to this interpretation, Rickman encouraged him to talk about his friend. In this process of mourning, the patient started shaking and was overcome with grief, while his arm gradually recovered normal function. Within a few weeks, he was able to return to training.[85]

The Northfield Experiments were influenced by Tavistock psychoanalysts like John Bowlby, Tom Main and Michael Foulkes. Rickman and Bion were recruited in a military hospital in Northfield, near Birmingham, to treat traumatised soldiers. The first experiment lasted six weeks, during the winter of 1942–1943, after which Bion and Rickman were dismissed – an end reminiscent of Laurel and Hardy's final tour.

When Bion and Rickman arrived at Hollymoor Hospital, the psychiatric service was dirty and chaotic. Their goal was to incite the soldiers to assume responsibility, not to have them live in a libertarian democracy, as they would be accused of doing. Bion was known for his research on small groups, to which he is often primarily associated.[86] He became interested in this while he was involved in the selection of officers in 1942. When he observed soldiers performing tasks, he did not select those with the greatest expertise, but those who became the centre of relationships in what he called "leaderless groups."

Drawing on their experience, Bion and Rickman confronted the chaos that greeted them when they arrived, and asked the men to organise groups around activities they were free to choose. The only requirement was to meet at 12.30, for half an hour – a meeting designated by the military term "parade," where the analysts would let the men speak, only contributing their impressions on what was not being said. The assumption was that "if one couldn't be loyal to his friends, he couldn't be the enemy of his enemies."

To test them, one group asked to be taught to dance. Bion, who remembered his shyness after his return from World War I, encouraged them. As the weeks went by, the disorder came to an end; the experiment had clearly succeeded. But during an unannounced visit, Bion and Rickman's superiors found the dancing lessons on the ward shocking. The hierarchy quickly ended the experiment. A second experiment was conducted by Foulkes, who applied the same principles but was more skilled at dealing with his superiors.

In 1947, in a paper delivered to the British Psychoanalytical Society and published in *Cogitations*, Bion addresses the historian, who must be "more prominent in the investigation of guilt of the parties to the last war [without] being manipulated by the emotions of the group" (pp. 341–342).

Gregory Nagy: *Sunt lacrimae rerum* ("the tears of things")[87]

We invited Hellenistic historian Gregory Nagy, professor at Harvard, to speak in our seminar on May 23, 2002, at the suggestion of our friend, Hellenistic historian Nicole Loraux.[88] Nagy is a specialist of Homer,[89] whom he hears from the vantage point of his Hungarian culture. Like Bela Bartok, his father travelled through Hungary looking for the remaining bards . According to Nagy, the *Iliad* emerged from the stories veterans of the Trojan War told each other, between *philoi*, and which were passed down to their grandchildren with very little change, since these stories stem from a memory that doesn't forget.

Gregory Nagy commented on the scene, in Book I of the *Aeneid*, where Aeneas lands in Carthage, after he fled the destruction of Troy. He is waiting for Queen Dido in front of the temple built in honour of Juno, and contemplates the bas-reliefs described by Virgil in a vision on the Acropolis, taking his inspiration from the metopes on the north side of the Parthenon. Nagy emphasised the art of the relief, engaging the sense of touch, absent from two-dimensional "filmy" pictures. Three-dimensionality adds to the visual and auditory image the power to model it. The passage from *pingo* – "to paint" – to *fingo* – "to sculpt" – creates a "fiction" in the positive sense of the word, which allows touching. This possibility is given by the use of the genitive – unknown in English and French – which in Greek means "in connection with." Nagy proposes giving this passage a reading that augments the classical tradition by reference to the Cycladic and Orphic versions.

The bas-reliefs on the Temple of Juno represent the suffering of the men and women of Troy who, for the Athenians of the fifth century, were the enemy. Aeneas, who would later found Rome, becomes aware that even the Carthaginians – Rome's future enemies – recognise the torments of the Trojans. Looking more closely, Aeneas recognises himself: "It's me!" This is the scene where Aeneas tells his friend Achates: "*Sunt lacrimae rerum et mentem mortalia tangent*" ("There are tears 'in connection' with the universe, and mortal things touch the mind") (verse 462). Victor Hugo borrowed *Sunt lacrimae rerum* for the title of one of his poems.[90]

Res means "the universe," as in Lucretius's title *De rerum natura*.[91] There are tears connected to the whole universe, and what do they touch? Not the heart, but the mind, *menten*. It is a cognitive process – in Greek, *manthanein* – "to know"; it is where "mathematics" comes from. Tears touch the part of the person that is able to learn.

Aeneas speaks about knowledge when he feels pity, and he cries. Here, the driving force of terror and pity is different from its use by Aristotle.

He also tells Achates: "*Salve metus*" ("Dispel your fears") (verse 463). We are all right, we are in a civilised place where people understand us. Ironically, this scene takes place in Carthage, which will be destroyed by the Romans a century before Virgil's birth. In fact, legend has it that Scipio the African, author of the famous phrase "*delenda est Carthago*," wept as he ordered Carthage to be destroyed, and quoted the passage in the *Iliad* where Andromachus mourns the death of Hector. In tears, Aeneas recognises the massacre of Troy: *agnoscit lacrimans* (verse 470). Here, the poetics of terror and pity concerns people who may not have not our admiration, but who prove they are civilised.

Before weeping, Aeneas saw, laid out in order, *ex ordine* (verse 456), the Trojan War battles. Without looking at them in sequence, he would not have recognised himself. This scene is a screen memory, reminiscent of Book VIII of the *Odyssey*, where Ulysses, landing on an unknown shore, was greeted by Nausicaa and taken to the banquet of the Phaeacians, as an anonymous castaway. There, he hears the bard Demodocus, the local Homer, singing about the destruction of the Trojans. The fact that he recites the horrors of the war, in detail, is essential. Suddenly, the narration stops while Ulysses weeps. The camera zooms in on him; he cries like a woman whose husband was killed, with her whole family, and who will be taken into slavery. Anyone who reads this passage recognises Andromache, whose husband and son were killed. Ulysses recognises himself in Astyanax's murderer and sheds Andromache's tears.

In *Ion*,[92] Plato describes the emotions of the Athenian spectators when the *Iliad* is recited by the rhapsode before 20,000 citizens during the Panathenaic festival that takes place every four years. Civic grief made 20,000 pairs of eyes cry when the bard describes the suffering of the Trojans, not of the Achaeans. For instance, Andromache, "smiling through her tears" as she sees her baby Astyanax cry, terrified by the crest of Hector's helmet while he kisses him. After their farewell, she turns around several times to catch a last glimpse of him, to keep in her memory. The verse is elegiac; her sorrow mixes pleasure, *terpsis*, with pain. Terror and pity are eroticised. When language is frozen, says Nagy, the hymn (from *hymen*, the virginal tissue) – connecting pleasure and pain through rhythm – transmits to the next generations "total recall," immemorial, inscribed in the name of truth, *aletheia*, meaning "without oblivion."

Even when there are no words, transmission cannot be stopped. Transference teaches us that as soon as the analyst's mind is touched by something which strikes a chord, a relief springs up. This passage from a filmy narrative to relief – in both meanings of the word – is always impressive.

Frozen tears

At the end of his unfinished autobiography *All My Sins Remembered*, in Chapter 14, Bion gives a moving account of an experience where he remained frozen, "numb" and insensitive. In 1945, his first wife, actress Betty Jardine, whom he had married in 1939, died in childbirth while he was away on a mission. He had begged Betty to have a baby, and "her agreement to do so had cost her her life." The account starts with an asyndeton – with no connection to the previous chapter dealing with his resistance to Melanie Klein's interpretations, and his disinterest in money. The scene takes place on a weekend, when he is unable to touch his baby, little Parthenope, who lost her mother – nor can he bear to be touched by her. The scene ends with the conclusion of Hamlet's "To be or not to be" monologue: "Nymph, in thy orisons be all my sins remembered,"[93] whence the title of Bion's book.

Bion had hired a couple to look after his baby, but he realised "as never before [that] something was wrong, must be wrong." That weekend, he was sitting on the lawn while the baby crawled to a flower bed and called to him to come to her. "I remained sitting." She started to crawl towards him, hoping he would pick her up. "I remained sitting." She continued to crawl and her calls became distressful. "I remained sitting." He watched her try to cross "the vast expanse" that separated her from her daddy. "I remained sitting but felt bitter, angry, resentful. Why did she do this to me? Not quite audible was the question, 'Why do you do this to her?'" Unable to stand it any longer, the nanny got up to fetch the baby. Bion stopped her: "No, let her crawl. It won't do her any harm." They watched the child crawl painfully: "She was weeping bitterly now but sticking stoutly to her attempt to cover the distance."

Bion is passing on to her what he has lived through in the war, and he knows it: "I felt as if I were gripped in a vice." The compulsion was stronger than him: "No. I would *not* go." Fortunately, the astounded nanny got up and picked up the child without his consent. The presence of this other, and her dumbfounded expression, pulled him out of the filmy, two-dimensional picture: "The spell snapped. I was released." He was released from the fate that took him back to the present of the trenches where his buddies were crawling while he could do nothing to save them. Fortunately, the baby stopped crying when she was comforted by maternal arms: "But I, I had lost my child. [...] It was a shock [...] to find such a depth of cruelty in myself" (p. 70).

What gives the scene its sharp outline is the presence of what Hannah Arendt calls "a horrified other."[94] Bion understood that his child was trying to take care of him.

In this confusion of times, at the end of Chapter 12, Bion foresaw the transgenerational transmission of trauma. He presents an internal dialogue between himself and his "thou," where the latter demands that he pay the bill for the two previous wars: "Excuse me, it's the Bill." He protests, since in August 1914 no one told him that there would be a bill to pay. But he finally agrees: "Oh well, all right. Just put it on the bill. Two great wars and victories. I'll pay later." His interlocutor insists: "Yes, certainly sir. In whose name shall I make it out? Your baby's? Or her children's children?" Unable to think of an answer, he protests that he can't use his brain when he keeps being interrupted. But the thou is relentless and decides for him: "Sorry sir. I'll just put it down to your daughter and her offspring. She's too young to mind anyway" (pp. 64–65).

Bion was no longer there in 1998 when Parthenope was killed, at 53, in a car accident, along with her daughter. But he knew, ever since the war, that there is no causality in tragedies, only Ate, fatality – from the verb *aô*, "to drive mad" – and that Aeschylus, Homer and Shakespeare make it possible for him to record the memory of all his sins, as he made it possible for his patients to do.

Asking questions

Francesca Bion published Bion's last texts in a book entitled *Bion in New York and Sao Paulo*.[95] Speaking of his famous grid, Bion says he considers it a tool to transform the vague impressions we are left with at the end of a session into a three-dimensional tool: "it has, as far as I am concerned, served a useful purpose which has made me think that others might find it profitable to invent and apply a grid system of their own." These were his last thoughts a few weeks before his death in 1979, when he was preparing to return to India for the first time.

The author's note introducing the talks in this book could serve as a postface to this seminar:

> I thank all who participated in these discussions with their objections and agreements. Many who read this book will feel that my replies are inadequate and incomplete. That they are inadequate I must admit; that they are incomplete I regard as a virtue especially if it stimulates the reader to complete the answers. I wish the reader as much enjoyment as I had in speaking; if it sends him to sleep may I wish him "Sweet Dreams" and a profitable awakening.
>
> (p. 6)

On the previous page, Francesca Bion emphasises the scope of this statement:

> He believed that "the answer is the misfortune of the question." It was the problems that stimulated his thinking, both in his private and professional life, never the answers. His contributions were always an extension of the questions. He would say: "I try to give you a chance to fill the gap left by me."

In his preface to the *Philosophical Investigations*, dated "Cambridge, 1945," Wittgenstein had expressed the same view fifty years earlier: "I should not like my writing to spare other people the trouble of thinking. But, if possible, to stimulate someone to thoughts of his own." The *Investigations* are composed of short paragraphs that give the reader a chance to fill in the blanks, in a transference between writer and reader.

Both Bion and Wittgenstein were war veterans whose purpose was to engage speech by showing what cannot be said and by asking new questions, perpendicular to the steady hum of clinical sessions and theoretical references. To help us understand, Bion tells a story that introduces this third dimension. He had been a hyperactive child who would be prescribed Ritalin today, since he drove his parents crazy with his questions. To make fun of him, he was asked regularly to recite the poem at the end of "The Elephant's Child" in Kipling's *Just So Stories*,[96] written for Best Beloved – the author's adored eldest daughter Josephine, who died of pneumonia in 1899 at the age of 6. This is how the story goes.

The little elephant was like the young Bion, filled with insatiable curiosity that irritated his dear family and the other animals in the jungle, so that they kept spanking him. But he remained very polite, while continuing to ask the questions that preoccupied him. The major one, although he had never seen a crocodile, was to know what they ate. All the animals were outraged until the bird Koloko told him where he could find the crocodile, far away, in the great Limpopo River.

Having reached that shore after a long trip, he finally met the crocodile and asked him the question he had been pondering. When the latter asked him to come closer, he did not suspect that it was him that the crocodile intended to eat, suddenly seizing his nose and pulling on it. The little elephant arched his back as he pulled away, so that his nose began to stretch. It would have been the end of him if the great serpent Python had not grabbed hold of a tree and twisted himself around the back legs of the elephant. Tired of fighting this resistance, the crocodile gave up and let go of his prey.

Then the little elephant went home, discovering along the way the benefits of his traumatic experience: he could now "[pull] fruit down from a tree, without waiting for it to fall," cover his head with "a new, cool slushy-squishy mad-cap whenever the sun was too hot," and "sing to himself, down his trunk [...] louder than several brass bands." Once he was back home, it was his turn to spank all his dear family, until his parents learned the lesson and went to the great river to have their noses stretched into trunks.

The story ends with the poem that Bion now recites to his New York audience:

> I keep six honest serving-men:
> They taught me all I knew;
> Their names are What and Why and When
> And How and Where and Who.
> I send them over land and sea,
> I send them east and west;
> But after they have worked for me,
> I give them all a rest.

When he used to recite this poem as a child, the adults would double up with laughter, Arf, Arf, Arf, but he never understood what the joke was. They compared him to that stupid Elephant's Child, but he didn't find that amusing. "We are not amused," said Queen Victoria (1819–1901), Empress of India when Kipling (1865–1936) wrote his *Just So Stories*, published in 1902. Later Bion set out for the Great War in France, where the crocodiles did not get him, as they did Kipling's only son, who went missing in 1915. When Bion came back, he asked no more questions until he met John Rickman, who rescued him from the spanking of orthodox analysts, enabling him to become an analyst after his own fashion, using his knowledge of war trauma to work as he pleased, and asking his patients questions that his analytic family considered intrusive (p. 10).

Hearing voices

But, as the poem says, "serving-men" have to be given a rest. In his May 28, 1977 article on wild thoughts,[97] Bion speaks of "thoughts without a thinker which wander about without a destination or an owner," and which "the analyst doesn't know what to do with" (p. 31). These "unclaimed" thoughts may be registered by a child or an adult who hears voices in search of a home. The worst thing that can happen to such people, Bion says in his next article, written on May 29, is to be labelled schizophrenic and sent to a psychiatric hospital where they will be given drugs and electroshock to silence their voices, and even worse to convince them that they are mad or stupid (p. 50).

Haunted by his nightmares, Bion refuses to play the role of the barracks corporal who sends his patients to the hole; he considers that analysts who prescribe these treatments do not deserve that name; he sees his patients as "effective collaborators" and trusts the impressions that these wild thoughts trigger in him, when they resonate with zones of which he is unaware. These stray thoughts require that the analyst be rigorous in the identification of these interferences, using a method "as scientific as Heisenberg's Uncertainty Principle, Gödel's incompleteness theorem and revolutionary quantum mechanics" (p. 49).

The most precise image he can give of the psychotic conference is undulatory: "I am set in motion by rhythmic communications" (p. 31). He advises the "embryonic" analyst in supervision to use his imagination and to dare to say what he experiences during the session (p. 45). Thus, fossil voices can find a home by touching the analyst, instead of being engulfed in the giant statistical ear that will classify them. The purpose of oscillatory transference is repression, since one "cannot remember what [one] cannot forget."

In Chapter 4 of *All My Sins Remembered*, Bion reflects on his autobiographical writing and compares memory without forgetting to "molten rock [that] solidifies into lava [...] – white hot energy, revolt, rebellion – [that] cools and solidifies into further layers of crystallized debris," identified in the transference particle by particle:

> A gross example is this writing which is inseparable from making marks on paper: some of them are marks which conform to accepted rules of grammar, articulate speech; others do not. I cannot know what it is my intention to record until I have recorded it; and then I shall not know [like a fossil] what I have recorded nor what it is of which I am a record. So I have, snail-like, left my trace on this piece of paper.
>
> (p. 25)

His life resembles the Finnish epic Kalevala,[98] whose heroes are in search of the Sampo. No one knows what that is, like in *The Hunting of the Snark*,[99] which turns out to be "a Boojum, you see," or like the analyst unknown to himself, whom each patient has him discover:

> We may long to say "I am [...] Freudian or Kleinian [or Lacanian]" – any label which is "respectable." But every psychoanalyst has to have the temerity, and the fortitude that goes with it, to insist on the right to be himself and to have his own opinion about this strange experience which he has when he is aware that there is another person in the room [...]. I have suggested this: discard your memory; discard the future tense of your desire; forget them both, both what you knew and what you want, to leave space for a new idea. A thought, an idea unclaimed, may be floating around the room searching for a home. Among these may be one of your own which seems to turn up from your insides, or one from outside yourself, namely from the patient.[100]

When Bion recommends discarding memory and desire, he is not advocating neutrality or laziness, but the conditions making it possible to gain access to the patient's time-space, limitless and timeless:

> Unfortunately, it doesn't happen as often as we would like; the two personalities do not often meet. But they may meet closely enough to be aware that there is something more in the room than material a computer can process.

(p. 12)

And he adds:

> If you are an officer in a battle you are supposed to be sane enough to be scared, but you are supposed also to be capable of thinking. It sounds ridiculous to say that people sitting in a comfortable room in full peacetime have to be capable of anything – but they do. The analyst is supposed to remain articulate and capable of translating what he is aware of into a comprehensible communication. That means he has to have a vocabulary which the patient may be able to understand [...]. It sounds absurdly simple—so simple that it is difficult to believe how difficult it is.

(p. 14)

In *A Memoir of the Future*, the character of Alice quotes a passage from Tolstoy's *War and Peace*:[101] "Do you remember what Prince Andrei says on hearing a remark: 'That is sooth, accept it'" (Book III, Chapter 7). In his New York lectures, Bion points out: "What does matter is what we, the analyst and the patient, have *not* seen before," which makes both say: "Yes, that is true. That interpretation is right; that observation is correct." We will examine Tolstoy's remark more closely in the next seminar.

Notes

1 Sterne, L., *The Life and Opinions of Tristram Shandy, Gentleman*, Alma Classics, 2017.
2 Bion, W., *A Memoir of the Future*, Routledge, 2018; *The Long Week-End, 1897–1919*, Karnac Books, 1982; *All My Sins Remembered*, Karnac Books, 1985.
3 Bion, W., *War Memoirs 1917–1919*, Karnac Books, 1997.
4 De Cervantes, M., *Don Quixote I*, Ormsby, J. (Trans.), Baker & Taylor, 2013.
5 Bion, W., *The Long Week-End*, op. cit.
6 Vonnegut, K., *Slaughterhouse-Five*, Research & Education Association, 1996.
7 Disney, W. (Dir.), *Fantasia*, 1940.
8 Bion, W., *The Long Week-End*, op. cit.
9 Eliot, T. S., "The Waste Land," in *The Complete Poems and Plays*, Faber & Faber Poetry, 2004.
10 Rivers, W. H. R., "The Repression of War Experience," *The Lancet*, February 2, 1918; delivered before the Section of Psychiatry, Royal Society of Medicine on December 4, 1917 by W. Rivers late medical officer, Craiglockhart War Hospital.
11 Arendt, H., *Eichmann in Jerusalem*, Viking Press, 1964.
12 Wittgenstein, L., *Philosophical Investigations*, Ascombe, G. E. M. (Trans.), Basil Blackwell, 1986, section 41.
13 Bion, W., *War Memoirs*, op. cit.
14 Barker, P., *The Regeneration Trilogy*, Hamish Hamilton, 2014. See *infra* Seminar 6 on William Rivers.
15 Wittgenstein, L., *Philosophical Investigations*, op. cit., section 639, p. 1676.
16 Freud, S., *A Project for a Scientific Psychology*, S.E.1, Hogarth Press, 1895.
17 Lacan, J., *The Seminar of Jacques Lacan: The Ethics of Psychoanalysis*, Book VII, W. W. Norton & Company, 1977.
18 Warburg, A., "A Lecture on Serpent Ritual," *Journal of the Warburg Institute*, 2(1923): 1938–1939.
19 Plato, *Theaetetus*, Liberal Arts Press, 1955, 202a.
20 Duchamp, M., *Du champ du signe*, Flammarion, 1975.
21 Nasar, S., *A Beautiful Mind*, Touchstone, Simon & Schuster, 1998.
22 Thom, R., *To Predict IS NOT to Explain*, Tsatsanis, S. P. (Ed.), Thombooks Press, 2016.
23 Bion, W., *The Long Week-End*, op. cit.
24 Joyce, J., *Finnegan's Wake*, Wordsworth Editions, 2012.
25 Wittgenstein, L., *Philosophical Investigations*, op. cit.
26 Molière, *The Would-Be Gentleman*, Kessinger Publishing, 2010.
27 Plato, *Phaedrus*, Focus Publishing/R. Pullins Co., 2003, 244e.
28 Wittgenstein, L., *Philosophical Investigations*, op. cit., pp. 212, 215, 228.
29 Bion, W., *The Long Week-End*, op. cit., p. 9.
30 Aeschylus, *Agamemnon*, Cambridge University Press, 2004, verse 1095.
31 Wittgenstein, L., *Philosophical Investigations*, op. cit., p. 188.
32 Bion, W., *Taming Wild Thoughts*, Karnac Books, 1997.
33 Aeschylus, *The Persians*, Kessinger Publishing, 2010; *Prometheus Bound*, Dover Thrift Editions, 1995, verses 89–90.
34 Sterne, L., *The Life and Opinions of Tristram Shandy, Gentleman*, op. cit., p. 6.
35 Lacan, J., "On a Question Prior to Any Treatment of Psychosis," in *Écrits: A Selection*, Sheridan, A. (Trans.), Tavistock/Routledge, 1977, Seminar III.
36 Wittgenstein, L., *Philosophical Investigations*, op. cit., section 288.
37 Starobinski, J., *Words upon Words: The Anagrams of Ferdinand de Saussure*, Yale University Press, 1979.

38 Verlet, L., *La malle de Newton*, Gallimard, 1993.
39 Virgil, *Aeneid*, Fairclough, H. R. (Trans.), independently published, 2017.
40 Villon, F., "Ballad of Dead Ladies," in *Ballads Done into English from the French of François Villon*, Thomas B. Mosher, 1904.
41 Winnicott, D. W., "Fear of Breakdown," *International Review of Psycho-Analysis*, 1(1974): 61–351.
42 Felman, S. and Laub, D., *Testimony: Crises of Witnessing in Literature, Psychoanalysis and History*, Routledge, 1992.
43 De Malherbe, F., *Oeuvres Complètes de François de Malherbe*, CreateSpace, 2015.
44 Bion, W., *Brazilian Lectures*, Routledge, 1990.
45 Artaud, A., *The Theatre and Its Double*, Grove Press, 1944, Chapter 7.
46 Cassou, J., *La mémoire courte*, Mille et une nuits, 2001. See *infra* Seminar 10 on J. W. von Goethe.
47 Bion, W., *Learning from Experience*, Karnac Books, 1991.
48 Bion, W., *The Long Week-End*, op. cit.
49 Barrois, C., *La psychanalyse du guerrier*, Hachette, 1993.
50 Stendhal, *The Charterhouse of Parma*, Howard, R. (Trans.), Modern Library, 2000.
51 Baillet, A., "Olympica," in *Vie de Monsieur Descartes*, La Table ronde, 1992.
52 Descartes, *Discourse on Method and Meditations*, Dover Philosophical Classics, 2003.
53 Princess of Bohemia and Descartes, *The Correspondence between Princess Elisabeth of Bohemia and René Descartes*, University of Chicago Press, 2017.
54 De La Fontaine, J., *The Original Fables of La Fontaine*, Hard Press Publishing, 2010.
55 Bion, W., *Elements of Psychoanalysis*, Karnac Books, 1983, Chapter 6, p. 22.
56 Bion, W., *The Long Week-End*, op. cit., p. 182.
57 De Cervantes, M., *Don Quixote I*, op. cit., Chapters 39–40, pp. 292–294.
58 Wittgenstein, L., *Tractatus Logico-Philosophicus*, Psychology Press & Routledge Classic Editions, 2001.
59 Bion, W., *Cogitations*, Routledge, 1992.
60 Barker, P., *The Regeneration Trilogy*, op. cit.
61 Lord Tennyson, "The Passing of Arthur," in *Idylls of the King*, Penguin Books, 1983.
62 Freud, S., *Delusions and Dreams in Jensen's Gradiva*, S.E. 9, Hogarth Press, 1907.
63 Bion, W., *Cogitations*, op. cit.
64 Rimbaud, A., *Complete Works*, Harper Perennial Modern Classics, 2008.
65 Bion, W., *The Long Week-End*, op. cit., p. 283.
66 Poincaré, H., *Science and Method*, Dover Publications, 2011.
67 See *infra* Seminar 7 on Hannah Arendt.
68 Bion, W., *Clinical Seminars and Other Works*, Karnac Books, 1987.
69 Freud, S., *Inhibitions, Symptoms and Anxiety*, S.E. 20, Hogarth Press, 1926, pp. 77–175.
70 Bion, W., *Clinical Seminars and Other Works*, op. cit.
71 Van der Kolk, B., *The Body Keeps the Score*, Penguin Books, 2014.
72 Plato, *Phaedrus*, Focus Philosophical Library, 2003.
73 Clouzot, H. G. (Dir.), *The Mystery of Picasso*, 1955.
74 Lacan, J., "British Psychiatry and the War," *Psychoanalytical Notebooks of the London Circle*, 4 (Spring 2000): 9–34.
75 Tison, S. and Guillemain, H., *Du front à l'asile, 1914–1918*, Alma Éditeur, 2013.

76 Bloch, M., *L'Étrange Défaite*, Gallimard, 1990. See *infra* Seminar 10 on J. W. von Goethe.
77 Audoin Rouzeau, S., *Quelle histoire, un récit de filiation, 1914–2014*, Gallimard, 2013.
78 Bion, W., *All My Sins Remembered*, Karnac Books, 1991.
79 Beradt, C., *The Third Reich of Dreams*, Aquarian Press, 1985.
80 See *infra* Seminar 7 on Hannah Arendt.
81 Colette (libretto); Ravel, M., *The Child and the Spells: A Lyric Fantasy in Two Parts*, opera, 1925.
82 Lacan, J., "On a Question Preliminary to Any Possible Treatment of Psychosis," in *The Seminar of Jacques Lacan*, op. cit.
83 Harrison, T., *Bion, Rickman, Foulkes and the Northfield Experiments: Advancing on a Different Front*, Jessica Kingsley Publishers, 2000.
84 Shephard, B., *A War of Nerves: Soldiers and Psychiatrists in the 20th Century*, Harvard University Press, 2001.
85 Rickman, J., "A Case of Hysteria," in *Selected Contributions to Psycho-Analysis*, Routledge, 2003, p. 185.
86 Bion, W., *Experiences in Groups,* Tavistock, 1961.
87 Virigil, *The Aeneid of Virgil*, Charles Scribner's Sons, 1952.
88 Loraux, N., *The Invention of Athens*, Harvard University Press, 1986.
89 Nagy, G., *Poetry as Performance*, Cambridge University Press, 1996; *The Best of the Acheans*, Johns Hopkins University Press, 1999.
90 Hugo, V., "Sunt lacrimae rerum," in *Les Voix Intérieures et les Rayons et les Ombres*, Hachette, 2012.
91 Lucretius, *De rerum natura*, Oxford University Press, 1922.
92 Plato, *Ion*, Jowett, B. (Trans.), CreateSpace, 2016.
93 Shakespeare, W., *Hamlet*, Dover Publications, 1992.
94 See *infra* Seminar 7 on Hannah Arendt.
95 Bion, W. (Ed.), *Bion in New York and Sao Paulo*, Karnac Books, 1980.
96 Kipling, R., *Just So Stories*, CreateSpace, 1902.
97 Bion, W., *Taming Wild Thoughts*, Karnac Books, 1997.
98 Lonnrot, E., *The Kalevala*, Oxford University Press, 2009.
99 Carroll, L., *The Hunting of the Snark*, Book Jungle, 2009.
100 Bion, F., (Ed.), *Bion in New York and Sao Paulo*, op. cit., p. 11.
101 Tolstoy, L., *War and Peace*, Penguin Classics, 2009.

2   Seminar 9: 2003–2004

Leo Tolstoy (1828–1910), Vasily Grossman (1905–1964), W. G. Sebald (1944–2001) and Eric Kandel (1929–)

The history of wars in *War and Peace, Life and Fate, Austerlitz* and *In Search of Memory*

Queen of the seas that are to bear you.

(*Mithridate*, Act I, Scene 3)

Under this Racinian banner, this year's seminar will examine the scientific, social and ethical stakes of the relation between the mind and the brain, as we encounter it in our analytic practice. This discussion follows the "questions of memory" examined in the last seminar with the help of W. R. Bion, one of the major analysts of the past century, whose work was rooted in his experiences at the front during World War I. Bion teaches us that at the limits of *Mind and Matter[1]* – the title of a book by Erwin Schrödinger, inventor of the equations of quantum mechanics – a memory that doesn't forget is striving to be transmitted through transference in our work with madness and in the work of certain writers. Bion himself wrote a work of fiction at the end of his life, *A Memoir of the Future,[2]* a work of fiction we will examine later. Then we will turn to Leo Tolstoy, W. G. Sebald and Vasily Grossman to examine this memory without a text that escapes usual transmission.

Turning to neurobiology, we will mention Eric Kandel, winner of the Nobel Prize in Medicine in 2000, whose books *Principles of Neural Sciences[3]* and *In Search of Memory[4]* offer a careful examination of the mood and personality disorders classified in the DSM-IV. Kandel encourages us to look at our clinical experience and ask ourselves why the causal approach to the brain should exclude research on psychotic transference in a context of madness, even if it is worth nothing to pharmaceutical companies. The literary works discussed in this seminar are a reliable investigation of that context.

The question of causality in history is one of Tolstoy's major concerns in *War and Peace*, quoted by Bion. When we follow the literary heroes of the European wars of the early nineteenth century, we can assert that fiction is able to provide a rigorous framework for the inscription of that which usually escapes transmission. The novel depicts the emergence of an epic subject from countless military and political actions that the historian of the *longue durée*, "long-term history," tends to dismiss: Fernand Braudel calls these actions the "dust of events."[5]

The third author who will support our research is the German novelist W. G. Sebald, and particularly his last book *Austerlitz*, published the year he died in a car accident in 2001.[6] It is a book of stories waiting to be told – given the hero's complete amnesia regarding the first four years of his life, before he was sent by train from Prague to England, to avoid the Nazi round-ups in which his mother disappeared soon afterwards. The book describes the transference between the narrator and the hero, who has become an art historian endlessly investigating the architecture of European train stations and the plans of fortresses, until he finds the traces of his origins.

All along his journeys, he thinks with the help of things, as Bion says: "Things are thoughts and thoughts are things." His memory is full of holes, not from forgetting, but created by a totalitarian system. He compensates the failure of words with photographs having no apparent meaning. The narrator recounts his exchanges with the hero in a style modelled on the discontinuities of their encounters – an absence of paragraphs, very long sentences interrupted by photographs – throughout Europe, with stopovers in Paris, Germany and Czechoslovakia. They met first in Antwerp in 1967 and pursued their random meetings until their separation in 1997.

The fourth writer is Vasily Grossman, author of *Life and Fate*,[7] written with a freedom wrested from Soviet and Nazi ideologies. His prodigious work, saved from suppression and oblivion after his death, is a triumph of inscription of the catastrophes of the last century, an inscription similar to what our patients seek when they combat the erasure of traces by a lawless agency.

A Memoir of the Future or brain lesions

The focus on falsified or silenced historical events, which was that of "forward psychiatry" during World War I, is often neglected by psychoanalysts when treating madness and trauma. In her book *September 11*,[8] Susan Coates differentiates this type of clinical work from classical psychoanalysis, since the former deals with an absence of symbolisation. When these patients confront their analysts with events that failed to be inscribed, they stretch the limits of language. The difficulty lies in a subversion of temporal categories, illustrated by the title of Bion's *A Memoir of the Future*, and by that of German historian Reinhart Koselleck's *Futures Past*.[9]

Bion's book, published at his own expense, takes the form of a dialogue between many characters and different stages of his life. In order to speak of things that defy communication, he gives the floor to his germinal cells called "somites" – cousins of Tristram Shandy's embryo. Indeed, Bion's motto follows Laurence Sterne's, who claimed that his only rule was to follow no rules. In the same spirit, Tolstoy wrote at the end of *War and Peace*: "If we admit that human life can be ruled by reason, then all possibility of life is destroyed." We must take into account arrested time when history stammers. Things are recorded in a memory without a subject, as there is no witness to attest to them.

In his book *In Search of Memory*, Eric Kandel describes different types of memory: explicit and declarative memory, which can be put into words, and neuronal memory, which disappears in the event of brain lesions. But he does not mention symptoms without lesions, as if the new science of the mind tends to eliminate the psyche. In this context, Sir John Eccles,[10] another winner of the Nobel Prize in Medicine in 1963, speaks of "time delay materialism," focusing on lesions that are always yet to be discovered. His point of view, on the contrary, emphasises "the effect of the mind on the brain," as in states of terror when the psyche produces changes in the brain, recently revealed by cerebral imagery.[11]

Tolstoy also foresees the disaster brought about by determinism. In his epilogue, he writes: "But let us assume that what is called science can harmonize all contradictions. [...] Watching the movement of history, we see that every year [...] opinion as to what is good for mankind changes." In 1921, Robert Musil raised the same objection through Stader, a character in his play *The Enthusiasts*:[12]

> Listen, my Institute uses the most modern scientific methods: graphology, pathography, heredity, calculus of probabilities, statistics, psychoanalysis, abyssal psychology, etc. ... For all events in the universes are ruled by eternal laws ... Do you see? Modern science and Detectivism are continually narrowing the realm of chance, of events without order, of the supposedly personal. There is nothing that is a matter of chance. There are no individual facts. Indeed! There are only ... scientific relations.

Such statements eradicate liberty. In transference, autobiography becomes heterobiography. There is something in the psychoanalyst's life, or that of his ancestors, which resonates by chance, and thanks to a gift of words, with the patient's history, making it possible to constitute a plural body of survival with a second in combat, a *therapon*, against the erasure of trances.

We have borrowed the notion of a plural body from Anna Freud's observation of the children from Terezin whom she took in and cared for after the war in a Sussex cottage.[13] They formed a leaderless group that refused to be separated since each child strengthened the others' capacity for survival. At the same time, their "plural body" was amputated of those who had died.

The Dawn of Oblivion

In Book Three of *A Memoir of the Future*, entitled *The Dawn of Oblivion*, Bion describes the genesis of speech:

> This book is a psycho-embryonic attempt to write an embryo-scientific account of a journey from birth to death overwhelmed by pre-mature knowledge. [...] I admit responsibility for what I have experienced, but not for the distortions of scientific sense. [...] I shall not repeat my apology for having to borrow the language of experience and reason despite its inadequacy.
>
> (p. 429)

This is also Sir John Eccles' dilemma when he tries to determine *How the Self Controls the Brain*. A disciple of Charles Scott Sherrington, winner of the Nobel Prize in Medicine in 1932, Eccles wrote his book at the age of 80, after he met Heinz Götze, a German physicist in quantum mechanics. Eccles expresses his gratitude to him and to his wife, thanks to whom he was still alive after a recent accident. Just as hypothetical gravitons are invoked to name something that has never been observed, Eccles calls "psychons" mental events that act on the brain. His colleagues think him crazy, because he oversteps the bounds of biology, which considers that the brain acts on the mind, and not the other way round.

And why not conceive of lesions to alterity, regarding certain events affecting the brain? Eccles considers the mind to be "like a field in the physical sense of the word, but nonmaterial, which can account for known phenomena where the mind interacts with the brain" (p. 43). And why not suppose that "the other" is part of this field?

Shakespeare has spoken of this through the voice of *Richard II* (Act V, Scene 5), in a passage Eccles quotes as an epigraph in his book. Dethroned by Bolingbroke, who would become Henry IV, the king awaits execution and meditates on the subject of this seminar:

> My brain I'll prove the female to my soul, My soul the father, and the two beget a generation of still-breeding thoughts. And these same thoughts people this world In humours, like the people of this world, For no thought is contented.

There is no thought without an other; no thought is isolated.

But when thoughts are deprived of otherness, they can change into things, and ghosts can appear. Bion describes this risk: "A foetal idea can kill itself or be killed [...]. Metaphors can be the ghosts of ideas waiting to be born," says P. A., the Psychoanalyst, in Book Two, *The Past Presented* (pp. 417–418). His interlocutor, Bandmaster, rings a bell at once, addressing time and ghosts: "Time, ghosts! Time to be departed. All change. [...]

Quick ... march! Dead ... fall in! By your coffins ..." (p. 418). They look to another who can inscribe an epitaph that puts them to rest.

At the start of *The Dawn of Oblivion*, Eighteen Years speaks in the midst of the hubbub of the different prenatal and postnatal ages: "I look like being educated by one of those solidified nightmares on the Ypres Canal" (p. 432), which Bion calls "Nightmare Canal" in *The Long Week-End* – as well as by those who died at Cambrai and at Amiens, still present, "for the soul goes marching on" (p. 128). He has become a guide of souls, under the protection of Hermes, the god at the crossroads. With a little luck, an analyst like Rickman, met at the crossroads of World War I, will help Eighteen Years place a coin in the mouth of the dead and lead them to Charon, the ferryman, so that they can cross the Styx, the River of Oblivion. Some children are also guides of unsettled souls: "I have seen this in another life," a young girl who heard voices told me.

When the past is swept away, the soul being guided is reduced to a brain, and the guide is diagnosed as being psychotic. Yet even children know that it's impossible to do without a soul, that it's far worse than having to live with it. Bion is familiar with this risk, which is why he makes his psycho-embryonic attempt to inscribe past events that occurred at different ages: a 3-hour-old embryo, a 15-day-old embryo, and then a young man of 19 who, after the war, has become as old as a fossil. They all live with a "premature knowledge," as Bion puts it.

By opening a dialogue between "the psychosomatic and the somapsychotic," Bion sounds the alarm against stupidity that says: "Well, everyone knows that." He acknowledges the intelligence of children who hear voices, and who wholeheartedly consent to guide the souls that have entrusted themselves to them. They have to recover the habeas corpus, not with its literal Latin meaning: "This body belongs to you," but meaning: "May you have a body." Here, addressing the second person is a requirement for thinking when all others have vanished, as Bessel van der Kolk says in his book *The Body Keeps the Score*.[14]

Freedom of thought

Freedom of thought is the aim of transference with our patients who are exploring the frontiers of language, where the subject has set up camp. From war to war, Socrates, Cervantes, Descartes, Sterne, Wittgenstein and our other interlocutors in this seminar have expanded language in order to inscribe trauma in a memory that can forget. The same is true of scientific research that expands into new domains through scientific revolutions, as Thomas Kuhn[15] calls them, but also through moments of madness experienced by Nash, Gödel, Cantor, or people related to them, such as Schrödinger's wife Anny and Einstein's son Eduard.[16]

The scientific revolution heralded by Eccles in Chapter 9 of his book applies quantum physics to the microstructure of the neocortex, showing that mental action could augment neural response, without contradicting the physical laws of conservation of energy. This theory caused his work to be dismissed. Although he was considered highly qualified by the scientific community, academic publishers rejected his 1969 Berkley lecture on the brain and the "soul," in which he uses this term for the first time, instead of "conscience." "The materialists got the better of me," Eccles said, changing the title of his text to *Facing Reality*.

He then quoted Karl Popper's theory of three worlds: world 1 – the entire material universe, the organic and inorganic world, including the human brain and man-made machines; world 2 – the world of conscious experience, perception, memory, imagination and thought; and world 3: the world of creativity, scientific, artistic and literary.

In terms of psychoanalytic creativity, Freud observed, at the dawn of psychoanalysis, that one would have to be mad to believe that traumas leave no trace. He and Breuer were interested in affects such as fright and hyperexcitability, triggered by a splitting, a state cut off from consciousness. But in September 1897, Freud abandoned this theory of trauma, which he called his "Neurotica."[17]

Literature

The title of this seminar, "Queen of the seas that are to bear you," expresses this aporia. It is a verse taken from *Mithridate*, a play set in the Kingdom of Pontus, where sparks are still flying today. Mithridate, famous for having great resistance to poisons, wanted to consolidate his power against Roman colonisation. He allied himself with smaller kingdoms and orchestrated the massacre of 8,000 Latin settlers living on the Ionian Islands. Racine's play starts when the Romans have decided to get rid of this troublesome fellow. The monarchs of the small kingdoms break their alliance with him, and he is rumoured dead, although no one can say if he is alive or not. For the purposes of tragedy, Mithridate has become betrothed to Monima, the princess of a little kingdom, to whom he has given the royal diadem before their marriage, as a promise that she would be queen.

The tragic knot of the play becomes apparent when Mithridate reappears and learns that during his absence, his two sons, who have different mothers, have taken opposite sides: one is allied with the Romans and the other fights against them. The latter, Pharnaces, intends to become king and marry his father's betrothed. He tells her that she will make him king and he will make her queen, and that she shall be "sovereign of the seas which are to bear [her]." Now you have only to read the play, knowing that Louis XIV and Charles XII of Sweden considered it their favourite tragedy.

The verse I quote expresses a tension that eliminates causality. How can Monima become sovereign of a space that has to carry her? This is like sawing off the branch on which one is sitting, unless Neptune stirs up a whirlwind that sweeps them away. These things used to happen when the gods laughed at mortals: she asked for it; she should have waited for her husband's return. When we look closer, the verses spoken by Pharnaces are more interesting than my summary of them:

> Our marriage and departure must be hastened;
> Our common interests and my heart demand it.
> My ships are ready, waiting to receive you.
> And from the altar you may go aboard,
> Queen of the seas that are to bear you.

Pharnaces doesn't ask her what she thinks. Her sovereignty will be abolished in midline if the sea decides otherwise. By using the vocative case, Pharnaces avoids addressing her as a "thou." In our work, the goal is to reconstitute this "thou" for those who have been annihilated as subjects. But relying on psychoanalytic technique is not sufficient to create alterity. The analyst must use other resources, coming from his life experience. In *The Dawn of Oblivion*, P. A., the Psychoanalyst is asked if he helps his patients, and gives an answer that widens the scope of the question:

> I think there is something to be said for differentiating *knowledge* and *wisdom* [...]. I would say that whatever *knowledge* each of us has must be augmented by *wisdom*. However intelligent, the chance of survival is decreased if the character cannot rely on being wise.

That is when Alice quotes Tolstoy, out of the blue: "Do you remember Prince Andrei in *War and Peace* feeling in the course of a discussion as if an inner voice said, 'That is sooth; accept it.'" Robin replies: "Yes, it impressed me when I read it" (p. 497).

This bit of wisdom is spoken by a traumatised war veteran, Prince Andrei, in a conversation with Pierre Bezukhov, who is just as disturbed for other reasons. For Bion, this phrase summarises the goal of psychoanalysis with those who are caught in the stranglehold of depersonalisation: the emergence of a "thou," considered by Dori Laub – founder of the Fortunoff Video Archive for Holocaust Testimonies – to be the goal of psychoanalysis in cases of extreme trauma.[18] We will trace the constitution of this "thou" from Bion to Tolstoy.

Knock, knock

In Chapter 3 of *The Dawn of Oblivion*, "Somite Thirty" comes on the scene to tell "Boy": "Get back into the Amniotic Fluid," and to warn him not to be seduced by the voice that says: "Glory! [...] Don't lie snoozing in bed."

"Somite Thirty" insists: "Keep warm in bed. Your King and Country want you – you stay in bed." But the Boy imagines himself winning the Victoria Cross, which was in fact awarded to Bion, as well as the Legion of Honour. "Seventy Years" cuts in to deplore the ruckus the somites are making in the dormitory: "Sometimes they all speak at once and it is a perfect Bedlam" (p. 443).

All these voices speaking at the same time are those of young veterans who lost their unlived lives too early, as well as those of embryos tittering on the edge of non-existence, like Tristram Shandy's embryo. These voices are fighting negation personified by the character Man. Bion introduced him to the reader at the beginning of *A Memoir of the Future* as a representative of the totalitarian power that invaded England. He has no concern for individuals, and does not care whether they are dead or alive. When he joins in the discussion, he offers to kill everyone, ghosts included, to silence them once and for all. The problem is solved, except that ghosts, who are experts at coming back, continue to do so.

P. A. comments that children are familiar with this type of memory. The nursery rhymes they sang for centuries have much to say on the subject. "These nursery rhymes say a lot," Bion confirms. In England, the ditty "Ring Around the Rosie" – a rosy rash around the mouth was a symptom of the plague – brings forth the ghosts of the Black Death that ravaged Europe in the sixteenth century. "A pocket full of posies" refers to the herbs carried to ward off the smell of disease. "A-tishoo! A-tishoo!" – the sneeze announcing the illness – is followed by "We all fall down."

P. A. says that in nursery rhymes:

> the archaic chord is struck and vitality is released. If we could strike the chord, the vibrations [...] could penetrate the barriers which at present act as obscuring screens – the need is for screens sufficiently resistant to catch and display the meaning without destroying it by denial ...
>
> (p. 498)

This rhyme goes "knock, knock" on the door of the analyst.

One day a young man was referred to me, suffering from tics that were judged to justify cryotherapy treatment. Between the ages of 5 and 9, he had been abused by a member of his family, and now spent his time washing off a stain that never disappeared. "Out, dammed spot!" cried Lady Macbeth, trying to wash away her crime. A more likable character, Don Quixote, is called the knight of "La Mancha," which means "stain" in Spanish – the stain of the traumas suffered in war and slavery by his father, Cervantes, who claims this paternity in his prologue.

In our work together, his tics were transferred to me; I became, like in a well-known French poem by Jacques Prévert, a veritable racoon.[19] Far from improving, his symptoms worsened; wash, wash, wash, until I told him, with some cynicism, that I expected he would soon wash the water.

That is when I woke up one morning with an urgent need to wash my hands. I blamed the honey on the toast I had with my quick breakfast. The sensation persisted for the rest of the day – out damned spot! – and water would not make it go away. The frenzied rhythm of my trips to the sink finally struck an archaic chord, which released the vitality of the transference. I told the patient about this, commenting: "I wonder whether it's not your hands that I am washing." He smiled; his tics loosened their hold and eventually disappeared.

Let us return to Bion's formulation. The vibrations of an archaic chord – which are also referred to by Descartes in *Meditations*[20] – had certainly penetrated the barriers blocking access to any possible other, after the rape that had to be kept secret from his parents. These vibrations caused me to create a screen resistant enough to transform them into words. I could have kept them to myself, as the neutrality recommended by my profession requires. But my words released the vitality imprisoned in his loneliness.

"Knock, knock, may I come in?" the symptom asks the analyst. According to Bion, this is "psychotic transference," lasting for the duration of the sessions in which an interference takes place. "Transference is transient," Bion says. He recognises such a moment in *War and Peace*, when Prince Andrei tells Pierre Bezukhov what he experienced on the battlefield of the Austerlitz battle: "That is sooth; accept it." What does he mean by that?

My pocket neurology manual refers to a remark about perception, borrowed by Freud from Ernst Mach. Perception, he says, is not at all passive, but looks for something in the other person that can serve as an anchor. My perception looked for something akin to the young man's symptom and found an experience of shame around the time when I was 8. It stepped in to validate his frantic cathartic activities, considered a pathology, since there was no other to provide an echo. The use of a transitive form outside the limits of syntax, as in "my handwashing of your hands," gave us access to an unconscious not repressed, but rather cut out, as there was no one to witness the child's terror.

"You're not very clean either," he could have told his analyst, who had come into contact with these pitiful things. Transference revealed a *folie à deux* – "foliadiou," as Martin Cooperman[21] pronounced it – and perhaps the presence of mirror neurons. Embryonic elements of speech, folded words, which shouted all at the same time in the dormitory, says Bion, had sparked a game of language and set time into motion.

Neurology and animism

Eccles discusses the question of free will and freedom by going back to the difficulty raised by Sherrington in his book *Man on His Nature*:[22] how to create free will without opposing cerebral function. As Sherrington puts it, we should not confuse the telephone wires with the messages they convey

(p. 222). Defying the scientific community, Eccles dares to imagine a field of probabilities applicable to interaction between synapses, involving elementary units of the psyche – "psychons" – devoid of energy. A 1981 finding by P. E. Roland illustrates this: in a state of deep relaxation, in a dark and silent room, when attention is focused on the end of a finger on which you imagine a touch stimulus, there is measurable neuronal activity in an area of the cerebral cortex. This phenomenon does not fit the description of a conditioned reflex.

According to Eccles, this phenomenon does not belong to the realm of classical mechanics. The interaction between the mind and the brain occurs through quantic probability, which links the motor cortical area to the will and its freedom:

> Recent experimental studies show that mental intentions preceding a movement are actually able to activate the cerebral cortex through the quantic selection of events producing different final results in identical initial conditions ... Such a situation cannot exist in a strictly classical process where a change in the final result necessarily implies a change in initial conditions.

Given his advanced age in 1994, Eccles has nothing more to lose and asserts that the mind is not the same thing as the brain, "contrary to the claims of materialists of every sort." He makes fun of the fascination with artificial intelligence: "At a conference at Yale, I asked Minsky from MIT, the most eloquent of its defenders, why he was announcing the existence of conscious super computers. 'To obtain bigger grants,' he said jokingly."

In this regard, in *Remarks on Frazer's Golden Bough*, Wittgenstein commented that so-called primitive people know more than the anthropologist, "for they are not as far removed from the understanding of spiritual matters as a twentieth-century Englishman." Frazer fails to see that "there is also something in us which speaks in favor of those 'savages'." This is when Wittgenstein formulates his famous aphorism: "One could almost say that man is a ceremonial animal."[23]

Based on this view of animism, Bion created the tool of "psychotic transference," to transform unthinkable "beta-elements" whose traces persist in our "sense impressions" into symbolic language, "the alpha-function"[24] Having stated, in *The Long Week-End*: "I died at Cambrai and at Amiens," where he survived by chance, he would admit, 75 years later, that in working with his patients, he was helped by the "forgotten of the Somme," whose ghosts came to assist him like guardian angels. And at the end of Book Two of *A Memoir of the Future*, *The Past Presented*, he answers one of them, who asks P. A., the psychoanalyst, if he is glad to see him: "I am indeed – but truth to tell I've always been afraid of meeting you" (p. 423). In fact, he had always been afraid to admit to himself that his freedom as an analyst – looked at askance by his colleagues – was inspired by this loyalty. My father's small moleskin war notebooks are haunted by the spectre of perpetual hunger and the imminent death of his comrades.

In *The Past Presented*, Man, the agent of the totalitarian power that has invaded England, asserts that the past "is of no consequence except as debris for collection and disposal"; then he exits, after telling the others to meet him in half an hour. In the meantime, P.A., the Psychoanalyst, is soliloquising and remembers the song he used to sing at the front:

> Oh my! I don't want to die, I want to go home! [...] That was true, we hoped that the ugly reality would not penetrate the joke armour-plate. The armour-plate of a tank was penetrable; we were bewitched, bemused, "probability-dazzled" cowards. "Probably" we would not be killed; "probably" we would survive to inhabit a new heaven and a new earth – "après la guerre." I did not know I loved life so much. I survived to foot the bill; [to pay] the bill for all those shells and tanks and bullets and the state of mind used to provide an armour more impenetrable than "gloire" [...]. I remember, am still penetrated by the memory of brave men whose name did not "live for evermore." "With whatsoever emphasis of passionate love repeated" the echo of their name [...] fades and dies. Why do I mind this grizzly, victorious lout? It is not death I fear, but the shame of knowing a few, only a few, of the multitudinous shabby failures.
>
> (p. 396)

Is this what also drives me to draw my patients into a zone haunted by ghosts? Joseph has recently left his room, where he was barricaded, surrounded by trash he could not throw away; he resumed his studies, interrupted years ago. He had lost his only brother, born ten years before him, and was living with this alter ego whose photograph was displayed on the living room mantle. When another boy asked him who the baby in the photo was, he answered: "It's me," even though he knew it was not him. When he was about 20, he was drawn into zones of quasi-time, "quasi hell, quasar time," as Bion calls them, where the ghost absorbed the living man. His analysis went on and on, without progress, without hope, punctuated by phone calls, even when I was in faraway countries – in which he told me he would soon be dead. While visiting his native home in a village, he took a huge stone and threw it into the well. The ghost's name was Pierre (the French word for "stone"). The way out of this gruelling situation was illustrated for us by a quasi-animistic ritual, which took place when I came back from talking with medicine men in South Dakota.

When Bion lost his entire crew near Amiens, he entered a time-space some babies know – those who stop nursing when their mother receives bad news. The baby may, if she – like Joseph's mother – remains haunted by the ghost of the departed, paralysed in a "space between two deaths,"[25] between actual death and symbolic death impossible to inscribe by means of funeral rites. In this intermediary space, time stops for lack of symbolisation, and causality does not apply. There is no use telling Joseph: "You are not well because your mother never stopped mourning your brother." He would have answered: "I know that, but what difference does it make?" What he was looking for was not the cause of his symptoms, but their target: to find an other with whom to come out of the solitude of his ghostly world, and bring peace to his brother's tormented soul by inscribing his name through a ritual gesture.

War and Peace

Tolstoy's novel is the inscription of catastrophes allowing no recourse to causality. Forty pages of the epilogue are dedicated to "the storm-tossed sea of history," which brings about experiences that "produce an effect incommensurable with ordinary human capabilities; and then the word CHANCE becomes superfluous."

To explore this theme, Tolstoy uses a character, just as Musil uses Ulrich, "the man without qualities,"[26] to testify to the total blindness characterising Kakania on the brink of World War I. Pierre Bezukhov is introduced in the role of the fool: the illegitimate son of a former favourite of Catherine the Great, he was educated abroad, influenced by the Enlightenment, and is leading a carefree life, governed by external events. His most remarkable quality is that he has none: he doesn't know how to behave in good society.

The first chapter, set in 1805, opens with the admonition addressed by Anna Pavlovna, maid of honour of the empress, to one of her guests: "Well, Prince [...] I warn you, if you don't tell me that this means war [...] I will have nothing more to do with you and you are no longer my friend." All her guests speak French. The Russian defeat at Austerlitz looms large on the horizon. General Mack has lost his Austrian army, and in Anna Pavlovna's drawing room Abbé Morio is discussing the proposed perpetual peace treaty. In this environment, Pierre begins to learn how to think. Tolstoy depicts him, when he arrives at the reception, just back in St Petersburg after a ten-year absence, as:

> a stout, heavily built young man with close-cropped hair and spectacles [...]. Anna Pavlovna greeted him with [...] a look of anxiety and fear, as at the sight of something too large and unsuited to the place. [...] Though he was certainly rather bigger than the other men in the room, her anxiety could only have reference to the clever though shy, but observant and natural, expression which distinguished him from everyone else in the drawing room.

The young man commits one act of impoliteness after another; he defends the lofty principles of the Revolution upheld by Bonaparte. But he atones for his offences by his friendliness and innocent disregard for mundanities. His father has called him back from abroad to choose a career, since at 20 he is still leading a dissolute life with no real purpose. At the reception, he meets his friend Prince Andrei, who is about to leave for the war in Austria against Napoleon, as an aide-de-camp to General Kutuzov.

The subject of the epic drama unfolding around them is everywhere: in the gunfire, in the galloping horses, in the crowd of soldiers, as well as on Kutuzov's sleepy face, as he sits without moving. At the Battle of Schöngraben, Bolkonsky – Prince Andrei – noticed:

> to his surprise [. . .] that no orders were really given, but that Prince Bagration tried to make it appear that everything done by necessity, by accident, or by the will of subordinate commanders was done, if not by his direct command, at least in accord with his intentions. [. . .] However [. . .] though what happened was due to chance and was independent of the commander's will, owing to the tact Bagration showed, his presence was very valuable. Officers who approached him with disturbed countenances became calm; soldiers and officers greeted him gaily [. . .] and were evidently anxious to display their courage before him.

This attitude resembles that of the analyst who finds himself entangled in the madness of war his patients bring to him. It is an attitude summed up by Cocteau in the phrase: "Since all these mysteries are beyond me, let us pretend to be their organizer."[27] But Bagration is not pretending, and makes his presence felt in a zone of catastrophe where symbolic and imaginary limits are surpassed.

At the end of *War and Peace*, Tolstoy abandons the concept of causality to make room for freedom:

> If history has for its object the study of the movement of the nations and of humanity [. . .] it too, setting aside the conception of cause, should seek the laws common to all the inseparably interconnected infinitesimal elements of free will.[28]

Serendipity

This new term invented by Horace Walpole (1717–1797), son of Prime Minister Robert Walpole, designates what Freud described in a letter to Jung as "the undeniable compliance of chance."[29] The term originated in a story translated from Persian: *The Travels and Adventures of Serendipity*.[30] The three princes in the story are the sons of a philosopher king in Ceylon, who sends them off to learn the customs of other peoples and complete their bookish education. On the way, their keen sense of observation allows them to record a multitude of details "by chance."

Without really paying attention, they noticed that the grass was short on the right, with blades of grass looking as if they were chewed here and there, great swarms of flies in some places, uneven traces of camel hoods, other traces of human hands and feet – and they would have ignored it all if another chance would not have brought them face to face with a caravan leader looking for a lost camel.

All these details then turn into clues that allow them to describe without hesitation the animal in question: blind in one eye, missing a tooth, limping and carrying a pregnant woman. This precision makes the man believe that they stole his camel, until it is brought back to him. Then they reveal the key to the puzzle. The short grass on one side shows that the camel only sees out of one eye; the chewed blades of grass indicate the space left by a missing tooth; the unevenness of the steps shows that the camel limps; and traces of hands beside traces of feet are those left by a pregnant woman who finds it hard to raise herself.

This fits the description of psychoanalysis of madness and trauma where the subject has disappeared with his image in the mirror, and the body records every little thing for survival in the midst of destruction. Hence the talismans that children grasp in their hands or carry in their pockets, in which they take refuge until they chance to meet someone for whom these things have meaning. When this happens, madness, *locura*, becomes, thanks to these unnoticed details, a means of healing, *la locura lo cura*, provided causal reasoning is abandoned, in order to let madness pursue its aim, *telos*, culminating in an encounter.

On this unprecedented path of transference, it becomes clear that these little things have become a refuge for the honour of those who have lost all identity, dissolved in a silence that keeps silent. In *A Memoir of the Future*, Bion invokes the word "Honours! a word which has been debased," already outdated in Don Quixote's time. He uses it to pass on his experience as an analyst and a soldier confronted with incomprehension:

> But just as it would be impossible to explain to anyone who had not been in action what it would be like to be a combat soldier or a [...] stretcher bearer, so it is impossible to describe to anyone [...] what it is to experience real psychoanalysis.
>
> (p. 516)

For honour is at stake in the relation between the analyst and the patient, who comes to him in a broken-down state. As Bion puts it: "I *would* be prepared to express an opinion in a psycho-analysis and to be held responsible for what I said. In that context there is evidence that a patient must respect himself" (pp. 529–530). What does he mean by that? A knowledge augmented by wisdom, which he illustrates by quoting the passage in *War and Peace* where prince Andrei tells Pierre: "It's sooth. Accept it."

The Battle of Austerlitz

In Book One, Tolstoy writes about the arrival of Pierre Bezukhov, to whom honour doesn't mean much. In Chapters 14–19 of Book Three, the Battle of the Three Emperors is being fought in a zone of catastrophe enveloped in fog, with no distinct contours or perspective. Space is described by contiguity without any gap and is swept by unforeseeable movements that thwart strategic reasoning. During the council of war held before the battle, Kutuzov is drawn out of drowsiness when the voices mingling Russian courage with Austrian precision fall silent. He says only: "I think the battle will be lost." During the fighting, he remains immobile, "in the same place, his stout body resting heavily in the saddle [...] yawning wearily with closed eyes," while all around him panic is spreading among the men fleeing for their lives.

When meaning disappears, things take over. Having just received a wound to the cheek, Kutuzov tells his aide-de-camp: "The wound is not here, it is there! [...] pointing to the fleeing soldiers." A little later, Prince Andrei leaps off his horse, "feeling tears of shame and anger choking him"; he runs to the flag, dragging it by the staff, until he is wounded and falls on his back.

When he opened his eyes, "he saw nothing. Above him there was nothing but the sky, the lofty sky, not clear yet still immeasurably lofty, with gray clouds gliding slowly across it." In the middle of the disaster, he was disconnected from events around him, and absorbed in an unknown impression:

> How quiet, peaceful and solemn [...] thought Prince Andrei, "not as we ran, shouting and fighting [...] how differently do those clouds glide across that lofty infinite sky! How was it I did not see that lofty sky before? And how happy I am to have found it at last! Yes! All is vanity, all falsehood, except that infinite sky. There is nothing, nothing but that. But even if it does not exist, there is nothing but quiet and peace. Thank God!"

Left for dead on the battlefield, he is saved by Napoleon, who comes across him and sends him to be treated by Baron Larrey, the surgeon of the French army.

Andrei was to relive this experience after speaking with Pierre Bezukhov on a raft crossing a river. He hears, once again: "It is true, believe it." Leaving the raft on which they had talked together, Prince Andrei:

> looked up at the sky to which Pierre had pointed and for the first time since Austerlitz saw the high, everlasting sky he had seen while lying on

the battlefield; and something [...] within him [...] suddenly awoke, joyful and youthful, in his soul.

Yet at the beginning of the novel, when the two friends were reunited in Anna Pavlovna's drawing room, honour had been a meaningless word for Pierre. Although he promised Andrei "On my honor!" that he would stop his wild partying, he went to meet his carousing companions, thinking that:

> all such "words of honor" are conventional things with no definite meaning, especially if one considers that by tomorrow one may be dead, or something so extraordinary may happen to one that honor and dishonor will be all the same! Pierre often indulged in reflections of this sort, mollifying all his decisions and intentions.

When Count Bezukhov died, it was learned that he had acknowledged his illegitimate son at the last minute. Pierre inherited his immense fortune, and married – as Swann says about Odette – a woman who was not his sort and who made him a cuckold. To save his honour, Pierre challenged her lover to a duel – he was a military man and drinking buddy from the old days. Pierre had never touched a firearm in his life. He shot blindly, wounded his adversary severely, left his wife in a fit of anger and fled to St Petersburg, setting out on an aimless journey, during which "he took no notice of what went on around him."

At a post station, he met "a short, large-boned, yellow-faced, wrinkled old man," on whose finger Pierre noticed a large cast-iron ring with a seal representing a death's head. The stranger addresses him, saying: "I have heard of you, my dear sir [...] and of your misfortune," in a tone that insinuated: "Call it what you please, I know what happened to you in Moscow was a misfortune." The stranger's gaze that never left him "was irresistibly attractive to Pierre" and drew him to the Masonic views held by the old man.

"Lesionella"

Illness produces lesions that are left to medicine to treat; according to French surgeon René Leriche's formula, "health is life lived in the silence of the organs." The problem starts with mental illness, where psychic suffering, equated with brain lesions, must be silenced. But there are injuries to alterity, such as the one just suffered by Pierre Bezukhov, which will not respond to such treatment. Despite his praiseworthy attempts to assuage human distress, the betrayal of those closest to him undermines his efforts. In the absence of any reliable alterity, he is lost.

Pierre Bezukhov's awkwardness and his refusal of social codes makes him Tolstoy's primary tool to explore social relations. He presents him in a phase of initiation where he is "the one who searches, the one who suffers and the one who asks." Moved by ideals that bring new meaning into his life, he undertook humanitarian activities, freed the serfs on his lands, and made peace with his wife, until "[again] he was overtaken by the depression he so dreaded." The assertion "I know [...] what happened to you ... I should like to help you" seems to him to be a trap from which his apathy allows him to escape and resume his search.

In *The Dawn of Oblivion*, Bion speaks of a diffuse fear that he feels during sessions, and compares the analyst's work to his own experience of going into action. When the character named Robin questions P. A. about countertransference: "Is it some unconscious fear?" the Psychoanalyst answers: "It is. [This] is one reason why we think analysts must themselves be analysed – there is [...] fear in a low key. Of giving the unwelcome interpretation" (p. 517).

Bion observes that:

> the analyst is engaged on an activity that is undistinguishable from that of an animal that investigates what he is afraid of: it smells danger. An analyst is not doing his job if he investigates something because it is pleasurable or profitable. Patients do not come to him because they anticipate some agreeable imminent event; they come because they are ill at ease. The analyst must share the danger, and has, therefore, to share the "smell" of the danger. It is your job to be curious about the danger – not cowardly, not irresponsible.

When Robin objects that the Psychoanalyst must hold himself in high esteem to speak this way, P. A. replies:

> I am trying to describe the job, not my fitness or otherwise for it. I have enough respect for the psycho-analyst's task to tell the difference between this social chat about psycho-analysis – or even a technical discussion of it and the practice of psycho-analysis. Anyone who is not afraid when he is engaged on psycho-analysis is either not doing his job, or is unfitted for it.

The diffuse danger Pierre Bezukhov senses is expressed in a phrase spoken during his initiation: "Love of death is not a cruel enemy, but rather more or less a friend," a notion he hastens to forget. Indeed, the manipulation of feelings through comforting words, and the confusion of tongues maintained by compassionate blah-blahs are not unfamiliar to psychoanalysis. Sometimes false listening goes on and on, without any access to unfelt fears, which only occurs when the analyst is touched in a way that makes him say, like Baudelaire in *Paris Spleen*: "I have more memories than if I'd live a thousand years."[31]

How is it knitted together?

To what type of memory do we assign that which is woven, through transferential interference, at the limit of an unconscious that has not been inscribed? Speaking of knitting, I am reminded of a song sung by Odette

Laure in 1955, which says something like: "I am knitting in a corner, I'm a halfwit, I'm a halfwit and I see naught. They act as if I was dead, as if I did not exist." But in fact, she sees all the things that others think are invisible.

Bion refers to a theory of conics developed by Girard Desargues, a seventeenth-century mathematician and architect contemporary of Descartes, who belonged to Marin Mersenne's circle in Paris. Desargues' theory inspired Pascal to write his "Essay on Conic Sections," at the age of 18. He also discovered, in projective geometry, that if two parallel lines intersect at infinity, they pass through the same point. In that regard, Bion points out that we do not have to understand the universe in which we live: "Even if we don't trouble with the 'universe', the not-us, we find that merely trying to know who 'I' am involves an intolerable amount of discovery [...] which as likely as not, we are right not to tolerate" (p. 491).

Thus, the repressed unconscious – in other words, memory based on forgetting – could be said to be a particular case of the cut-out unconscious constituted by images without reflection, intolerable to reason. In our practice, a mirror is created little by little, constituted by the interference "of primary elements, without reason, *aloga*," as Socrates says in *Theaetetus*,[32] knitted and unknitted constantly, until they "intertwine to create the *logos*, word and reason." But this testing process of repeated returns to square one serves, in fact, to pick up new elements to be interwoven, which are not always to the analyst's taste:

> If I meet a Not-me which nevertheless reminds me of Me, then I am likely to wonder what this object is. If it is a nice object, then [...] I have the pleasure of discovering what a nice person I am. If I do not like this Not-me [...] I am outraged; I do not like looking-glasses, sheets of water, novels, psycho-analysis ...
>
> (p. 489)

When he comes back from the brink of death, Prince Andrei does not join the ranks of the living. He has lost his wife, who died giving birth to their son, and has left the army to return to his tyrannical father's country estate. There, he looks after him and his son, frees the serfs, and plans to build a retreat on the property. When Pierre visits him, he becomes aware of his own depression, and their closeness allows him to relive the strange impression of serenity while he lay wounded among the dead and the injured: "But he knew that this feeling which he did not know how to develop existed within him," a feeling of joy and tenderness far from the love of death that had touched Pierre. Between them, trauma speaks to trauma, creating an interference that opens a sphere of trust – not of belief – in which a "transitional" subject, as Benedetti says, can emerge.

From the Battle of Austerlitz to Sebald's novel[33]

The transition from Tolstoy to Sebald's *Austerlitz* is carried out by "an association of uses," a term coined by Wittgenstein in his *Remarks on Frazer's Golden Bough*. Here, an association occurs through books carried in my backpack on a journey. In 1967, the narrator comes across a fair-haired young man in the waiting room of Antwerp Central Station, then meets him again by chance in other places in Belgium. He always carries the same backpack and he bears a resemblance with Wittgenstein, at least in the narrator's eyes.

The narrator is German. His family was involved in the Nazi regime, and he is unable to settle in his native country. He is a solitary traveller, like the other man, and maintains a close yet distant relationship with him until 1997. He visits him in London, in an institute of art history, located in Bloomsbury, behind the British Museum. The young man is a researcher, with a passion for the monumental architecture of the early capitalist era, like the Brussels Palace of Justice, and European railway stations, like Gare du Nord and Gare d'Austerlitz in Paris or Liverpool Street Station in London, a place near which they would meet again later, by chance. The narrator comments: "our paths kept crossing, in a way that I still find hard to understand" (p. 27).

This book, written without chapters, captivates the reader through uncanny details punctuating the young man's story. A monument, a dome, a forest landscape, a squirrel, windmills – what historian Aby Warburg called surviving images, *Nachleben*. They awaken in the hero intense emotions that remain a mystery to him. Little by little, they help him to decipher the story of his origins, since he does not know who he is: "He had quite often found himself in the grip of dangerous and entirely incomprehensible currents of emotions" (p. 34).

In 1975, the narrator returns to Germany intending to settle there permanently. After going "through a difficult period," he decides to go back to England. Sixteen years later, in 1991, fear of losing sight in one eye – like Kenzaburō Ōe's heroes – prompts him to consult an ophthalmologist in London. After the consultation, he decides to go into the bar of the hotel next door, the Great Eastern Hotel at Liverpool Street, where he runs into his old friend, once again by chance. Austerlitz takes up their conversation where it had been broken off twenty years earlier. He tells the narrator what he has found out about his life.

He arrived in England by train as part of a children's transport in 1939, when he was 4 and a half. He was given the surname Elias – that of the Welsh Calvinist preacher and his wife who took him in. His true identity was only revealed to him when he was 15, by the headmaster of his boarding school, because from then on he would have to write Jacques Austerlitz on his examination papers: "It appears [...] that this is your real name." But he has to keep it secret for the time being.

Now his foster parents are no longer there for him. The preacher is lying inert in a nursing home after his wife's death. The boy's education is taken over by his history teacher André Hilary, who has boundless enthusiasm for Napoleon, and who takes great interest in this unusual pupil:

> When I look back at André Hilary's performances today, I remember once again the idea I developed at the time of being linked in some mysterious way to the glorious past of the people of France. The more often Hilary mentioned the word *Austerlitz* in front of the class, the more it really did become my own name, and the more clearly I thought I saw that what had at first seemed like an ignominious flaw was changing into a bright light always hovering before me.
>
> (p. 72)

Most of his pupils were deeply impressed by Hilary's history lessons; his preferred topic was the Battle of the Three Emperors. Hilary gave the class an impromptu performance, switching from one role to another with astonishing virtuosity. The description of the battle is clearly inspired by Tolstoy.

"Austerlitz" is a folded word of which the adolescent is ashamed, since it has no meaning: "I had never heard of an Austerlitz before, and from the first I was convinced that no one else bore that name" (p. 67). The reader learns in passing that it was Fred Astaire's true surname. The history lessons stimulate the adolescent's intelligence, which flourishes, thanks to the limitless energy long restrained in arrested time. The quality of his essay on the concepts of empire and nation astonishes the teacher, who asks him if someone at home had initiated him into the study of history:

> When I answered Hilary's question I had some difficulty in not losing my command over myself, and it was in this situation, which I felt I could no longer endure, that I told him the secret of my real name. It was some time before he was able to calm down. He struck his forehead again and again, breaking into exclamations of astonishment, as if Providence had finally sent him the pupil he had always wanted.
>
> (p. 73)

By inscribing him in history, André Hilary encourages his pupil's vocation as a historian, which he supports unfailingly until he enters university.

After studying at Oxford and in Paris, Austerlitz becomes a truly learned man who spends his time in various libraries on the lookout for the memory of things, carefully noting the smallest details concerning places and dates. For him, "things are thoughts and thoughts are things." The narrator comments:

From the first I was astonished by the way Austerlitz put his ideas together as he talked, forming perfectly balanced sentences out of whatever occurred to him, so to speak, and the way in which, in his mind, the passing on of his knowledge seemed to become a gradual approach to a kind of historical metaphysic, bringing remembered events back to life.

(pp. 12–13)

The real question is one of temporality: "Why does time stand eternally still and motionless in one place, and rush headlong by in another?" (p. 100). At any moment, when he least expects it, he can suddenly see before him "images from a faded world" (p. 127).

When they visit the Royal Observatory in Greenwich, the narrator holds the place of the analyst, to whom Austerlitz expresses his revolt against the tyranny of time:

I have never owned a clock of any kind [...]. A clock has always struck me as something ridiculous [...] perhaps because I have always resisted the power of time out of some internal compulsion which I myself have never understood, keeping myself apart from so-called current events in the hope [...] that time will not pass away, has not passed away, that I can turn back and go behind it, and there I shall find everything as it once was [...] although that, of course, opens up the bleak prospect of everlasting misery and never ending anguish.

(p. 101)

His argument opposes the paradigms of classical physics and psychoanalysis. Pointing through the window to the river below, he reflects:

if Newton really thought that time was a river like the Thames, then where is its source and into what sea does it finally flow? Every river, as we know, must have banks on both sides, so where, seen in those terms, where are the banks of time?

The new paradigm of psychoanalysis of trauma and madness forces the analyst to displace the banks of time in order to access temporal spaces transmitted through generations. The narrator finally receives an enigmatic picture postcard from the 1920s or 1930s bearing the address of Austerlitz's house and proposing a date for a meeting. Beforehand, he regretted, like the analyst does, that he had been thoughtless, and he wishes he had done better:

Had I realized at the time that for Austerlitz certain moments had no beginning or end, while on the other hand his whole life had sometimes seemed to him a blind point without duration, I would probably have waited more patiently.

(p. 117)

The interior of Austerlitz's house is sparsely furnished and grey. After a while, Austerlitz takes up his story again.

The street of thought, *la calle del pensiamento*

In 1991, Austerlitz took early retirement from the university, intending to write. But little by little, "the entire structure of language [was] enveloped in impenetrable fog," so that he could no longer read or write, and worse still:

> I could see no connections anymore, the sentences resolved themselves into a series of separate words, the words into random sets of letters, the letters into disjointed signs, and those signs into a blue-gray trail gleaming silver here and there, excreted and left behind it by some crawling creature, and the sight of it increasingly filled me with feelings of horror and shame.
>
> (p. 124)

Walking through the city, he started to hear people behind him speaking foreign languages, and to see ghostly visions. He was irresistibly drawn to Liverpool Street Station, "one of the most sinister places in London, a kind of entrance to the underworld," standing on the site of Bedlam, the hospital for the insane built in the seventeenth century. Austerlitz discovers an abandoned waiting room in the station.

Reflecting that it had never occurred to him "to wonder about [his] true origins," in this place he recollects himself for the first time as a 4-year old child with his little rucksack, and realises "that it must have been to this same waiting room I had come on my arrival in England over half a century ago" (p. 137). His mind searches feverishly, filling with images of fortresses, mountains, forests of firs, clouds on the horizon, windmills – glimpsed unwittingly through a train window. He roams aimlessly through London and its cemeteries. In the bookshop of a "very beautiful woman," Penelope Peaceful, who solves crossword puzzles while listening to the radio, another coincidence takes the form of soft voices coming from the radio: two women are having a conversation about their common experience of a children's transport from Prague, going to London. For Austerlitz, this is a revelation: "only then did I know beyond any doubt that these fragments of memory were part of my own life as well" (p. 141). They weave themselves in with what was not inscribed, and impel him to go to Prague.

Like Austerlitz, a delusional patient had the impression of being on a stage without knowing his lines, in a part he used to perform perfectly: "I felt, said Austerlitz, like an actor who [...] has completely and irrevocably forgotten not only the lines [...] but the very part he has so often played" (p. 134). In a letter to Lou Andreas Salome, quoted by Bion, Freud says that in order to bring clarity to obscure and discontinuous things, one has to "bring to bear a diminution of the light," create "mole-like vision," and, Bion adds, focusing not on the mesh of the net, but on the holes. Austerlitz focuses on subdued colours, infinitesimal contrasts, intervals between spaces, countries, eras, books – a corpus providing the only body enabling him to tie together the fragments of his identity, and the stretches of time between meetings with his friend, who is questioning his own identity. A continuity is established between them, creating a relationship similar to that between Prince Andrei, who has just returned from the Battle of Austerlitz, and his friend Pierre, who is himself barely alive. Although everything is falsehood and vanity, "how quiet, how peaceful, it is true, accept it." The endless sky Andrei contemplates is the geometrical space where parallels meet at infinity.

Thanks to the presence of the narrator, Austerlitz can analyse the process involved in cutting out elements of history:

> how hard I must have tried to recollect as little as possible, avoiding everything which related in any way to my unknown past. Inconceivable as it seems to me today, I knew nothing about the conquest of Europe by the Germans.
>
> (p. 139)

When he arrives in Prague, he goes to the building that houses the state archives. There, a woman as serene and intuitive as Penelope Peaceful helps him to find a friend of his mother's, Vera, who was his beloved nanny while his parents worked – his mother as an opera singer, and his father as an official of the Czech Social Democratic Party. Austerlitz's walks with Vera, and the hours spent listening to her tell him about his early childhood, impart meaning to the strange impressions whose violence had made him lose consciousness and end up in a hospital on two occasions. He learns that his mother was deported to Theresienstadt, and his father disappeared in Paris.

With this knowledge, language can not only be rewoven, but can be augmented by rare words and neologisms, which are strewn throughout Sebald's text, while Austerlitz retrieves the Czech language he spoke until the age of 4. Things remember and speak to him. When photos "surface from oblivion [...] one has the impression [...] of something stirring in them, as if one caught small sighs of despair [...] as if the pictures had a memory of their own and remembered us" (p. 182).

In Mexico City there is a street called *la calle del pensiamento*. We accompany Austerlitz on the street of thought, carried along by the details of the things he photographs and by the strange voices that "were mysterious signs and portents." He says: "I saw myself transformed into a frightful [...] creature. A man beyond the pale" (p. 216).

In Chapter 20 of *The Long Week-End*, Bion has just come back from the front line in Flanders, arriving at Waterloo Station, to receive the Victoria

Cross. He walks in the city, wanting only to return to the front as quickly as possible. He has read the newspaper account of the war, describing the situation as "pretty good," saying the battle was won: "sounds all right." But he lost friends in this battle. He folds the newspaper: "Lying bastards!" he exclaims; he's had enough of forcing his facial muscles into a smile. The next day, he meets the others at Waterloo Station. Suddenly, they all burst out singing. But not Bion. He writes: "Never, never again ... No more singing: never. [...] We 'deserted' towards the Line" (p. 191). Yet this book was written in rhythmic tones, like a song that remained unsung until its author was 70.

Ricercar

Meaning "research" in Italian, this word is the title of a composition for harpsichord, improvised by Bach on May 7, 1747, in Potsdam, during a concert for the king at the Sanssouci Castle. When Frederick the Great learned that the Cantor of Leipzig would be attending, he gave Bach a theme on which to improvise: G, E flat major, G, A flat, B natural. Without the least preparation, Bach played a fugue which became, that same year, *A Musical Offering*, presented as a tribute to the king in 1748. He had composed the piece based on the acrostic *Regis Iussu Canto Et Reliqua Canonica Arte Resoluta*, "the theme given by the king, with additions resolved in the canonic style." Bach died two years later, in 1750, at the age of 65.

This acrostic is composed of words to which I attach particular importance. When research is initiated on order given by madness, *Regis Iussu*, resolution, *Resoluta*, comes about once the analyst improvises, in canonic style, *Canonica Arte*, on the first elements given to him. Sebald's style is musical, a fluid prose strewn with rare words that fit together like tiles, leaving no empty space.

A watercolour painted by Turner in 1841, *Funeral at Lausanne*, touched Austerlitz particularly, prompting the memory of his "last walk with Gerald in the early summer of 1966 [...] above Morges on the banks of Lake Geneva" (p. 110).

Gerald Fitzpatrick was his only friend from his boarding school days. He had lost his father, a pilot "shot down over the Ardennes in the last winter of the war" (p. 78). Gerald often invited Austerlitz to spend vacations in his family's peaceful home on the seaside near Barmouth, where his mother Adela was living with a sick uncle and a great-uncle who was a natural scientist. Gerald's great-grandfather, who had been a friend of Charles Darwin, then living in a nearby house, had transformed the Fitzpatricks' mansion into a veritable museum of natural history. *Funeral at Lausanne* reminded Austerlitz not only of the double funeral of Gerald's uncle and great-uncle, but also of Gerald's own funeral. He had become a pilot, like his father, and he crashed in the Savoy Alps:

and perhaps that was the beginning of my own decline, a withdrawal into myself which became increasingly morbid and intractable with the passage of time. [...] Like a tightrope walker who has forgotten how to put one foot in front of the other, all I felt was the swaying of the precarious structure on which I stood.

(pp. 117, 122)

Regis Jussu: the research is undertaken on orders. In analytic work, where voices intersect continuously with the traumas of the lineage, the analyst is summoned to participate in this research. He cannot answer: "I don't play that kind of music." The fundamental theme of *A Musical Offering*, which obeys the royal order, will be augmented by small increments: 1°, 2°, 3° ... 6°, inscribed in the score; the theme is transformed into a series of canons, until the final harmonic resolution. In the same way, in our analytic work, small elements that can take the form of dreams, voices or visions, on the part of both interlocutors, try to weave a time-space, until they find their resolution in an inscription. Austerlitz's obsession with railway stations looks like madness, until it is linked with Vera's narrative, when he finds her in Prague, at the end of his aimless wanderings in waiting rooms.

Parallel voices echo in an improbable dimension from which poetry and music emerge. In 1624, Claudio Monteverdi composed a brief dramatic cantata: "The Combat of Tancred and Clorinda," based on Canto 67, Book XII, of *Jerusalem Delivered* by Torquato Tasso,[34] in which the valiant knight discovers, when he removes her helmet, that he has unknowingly killed his beloved Clorinda, a fierce warrior from the Muslim camp. Clorinda comes to Tancred in a dream, to reassure him of her love: "Behold how fair, how glad thy love appears, And for my sake, my dear, forbear these tears." She tells him that he has sent her soul "[in] Abraham's dear bosom long to rest."

In the next Canto, Book XIII, verse 41, the Crusaders have to find wood to build the scaffolding they need to assail the walls of the city. The nearby forest, full of magic spells, pushes them back. Only Tancred dares to enter the woods. Cut off from the living, he wanders in the space between two deaths where Clorinda lies without a tomb. When he strikes a tree with his sword, blood streams from the cut and he hears Corinda's voice saying: "Enough, enough! Tancred, thou hast me hurt [...]. Cruel, isn't enough thy foe to kill, But in their graves wilt thou torment them still?" Her ghost comes to him in a dream, to profess her love. Only then: "of his dear love the relics sweet, As best he could, to grave with pomp he brought: Her tomb was [...] built of polished stone." The bark of the tree bears mysterious inscriptions, some in the Syrian language Tancred speaks, and the rest in an unknown language.

Clorinda cannot be buried before the mystery of this inscription is solved. In the afterword added to her book *Unclaimed Experience* twenty years after its first publication, Cathy Caruth recognises the unknown script to be

Meroitic, a still undeciphered language from Clorinda's native land. Having been a white child born to an Ethiopian queen, she was baptised and then abandoned, fed by a tigress and taken in by an Egyptian peasant. The bleeding wound speaks of a lost language, Caruth writes:

> Tasso's text raises the question: how are we to hear a language we cannot fully know? In his *Moses*, Freud asks what we can do in the face of traumatic experiences brought to us by the speaking wounds at the intersection of personal and world history. These questions arise each time we encounter the language of trauma. They cannot be connected to a single voice, and cannot be articulated in a single language. But it is imperative to remain open to this task, to its uncertainty, and to the power of literary resonances.[35]

Torquato Tasso went mad after he wrote his masterpiece. He had entrusted his manuscript to friends who refused to give it back, and ripped it apart with their envious criticism, adding the horrid threat of condemnation by the Holy Office for having endowed a ghost with speech, among other things. Enraged and justifiably paranoid, he was locked up in the Ferrarese prison, where Montaigne visited him when he was travelling across Europe.

As a child, Austerlitz also sees the shadows of his mother and father for a fraction of a second when he lies awake at night, and when he fears that he left them "through my own fault" (p. 45). These fleeting visions were considered superstitions by the pastor and were as unwelcome as Tasso's manuscript was by his friends. Austerlitz finds refuge in the cobbler's workshop, located near the manse. Evan, the cobbler:

> [u]nlike Elias [...] told tales of the dead who had been struck down by fate untimely, who knew they had been cheated of what was due to them and tried to return to life. If you had an eye for them they were to be seen quite often, said Evan. At first glance, they seemed to be normal people, but when you looked more closely their faces would blur or flicker slightly at the edges.

Evan has proof: a piece of black veil his grandfather has taken from a bier carried by small figures muffled in their cloaks. And Austerlitz adds: "and it was certainly Evan who once told me that nothing but a piece of silk like that separates us from the next world" (p. 54). Merely a piece of music heard just at the right time: *Regis Jussu*.

Cadence[36]

The French word for rhythm, *cadence*, comes from the verb *cadere*, "to fall;" it means "a fall." Something will be summed up in a *casus* serving to bring resolution to the case we are putting together to illustrate our practice. In a fugue by Bach, temporal tensions are resolved vertically, after the theme has initiated the question to which its harmonic resolution responds. Along the way, small cyclical canonic elements are inserted, requiring an adjustment, *ars, ararisko*, in the elements of time.

Austerlitz is put together like music. The element that creates the tension is the theme "Austerlitz Station," a name unknown to the child, until Hilary gives his surname a Napoleonic resonance. Vera will tell him that his French first name Jacques, uncommon in Prague, was given to him by his mother Agata, whose favourite composer was Jacques Offenbach (p. 154).

At the end of the novel, the orchestra deploys all its instruments: Sebald sings the names of medicinal herbs "for all sorts of recalcitrant conditions" (p. 271); the names of monsters "prepared" by Honoré Fragonard, the painter's brother, displayed at the museum of veterinary medicine in Maisons-Alfort – the sight of which makes Austerlitz lose consciousness and wake up at the Salpêtrière Hospital, next to the Austerlitz railway station (p. 269). In the Jewish section of the Montparnasse Cemetery, he deciphers on a memorial plaque the words *morts en déportation*, and reads on a tombstone the name Hirsch among those who "had died after being deported in 1944." He then reflects that about a dozen years after that date, he had lived in Amélie Cerf's apartment, Hirsch in German, during his first stay in Paris as a researcher: "Was Amélie Cerf [...] perhaps the last surviving member of her tribe?" (p. 260).

After his trip to Theresienstadt, where we hear, as a counterpoint, Hannah Arendt's voice on totalitarian systems (pp. 239–244), Austerlitz gets hold of a copy of a propaganda film recorded by the Nazis in 1944, which made the camps look like a Potemkin village, in preparation for the visit of a Red Cross commission. When he slows the speed of the tape trying to catch a glimpse of his mother's face, the merry polka of the soundtrack is suddenly transformed into a funeral march. At the end of the novel, all these voices find resolution in the melodies played by the five members of a circus troupe that had set up its small tent behind the Austerlitz station:

> I still do not understand [...] what was happening within me as I listened to this extraordinarily foreign nocturnal music conjured out of thin air, so to speak, by the circus performers with their slightly out-of-tune instruments, nor could I have said at the time whether my heart was contracting in pain or expanding with happiness for the first time in my life. Why certain tonal colors, subtleties of key, and syncopations can take such a hold on the mind is something that an entirely unmusical person like myself can never understand.
>
> (pp. 272–275)

During his second trip to Prague, Vera gives him a photograph – rescued from the totalitarian chaos – which possibly shows his mother on the stage of a provincial theatre (p. 182). Later, when he is about to set out for the

Pyrenean foothills, after hearing that his father, exiled in Paris, could have been interned in the camp at Gurs in 1942, he gives this photograph to the narrator, along with the key to this house in London, telling him that he could stay there whenever he liked, "and study the black and white photographs which, one day, would be all that was left of his life" (p. 293).

Erased traces

The book ends with a much more brutal collapse, that of the new national library, which Austerlitz – insatiable reader and constant visitor of the Bodlein in Oxford, of the British Museum Library and of the old national library on rue Richelieu – considers to be "an utter absurdity, something that must have been devised [...] on purpose [...] to exclude the reader as a potential enemy [...] as if [he] were on business of an extremely dubious nature" (p. 280). Austerlitz's hostility to the "pharaonic President's Grande Bibliothèque" is further exacerbated when he learns that:

> on the waste land between the marshaling yard of the gare d'Austerlitz and the Tolbiac Bridge where [the] library now rises, there stood until the end of the war an extensive warehousing complex to which the Germans brought all the loot they had taken from some forty thousand apartments of the Jews of Paris [...] interned at Drancy before deportation, from 1942 onwards. In [this] Austerlitz-Tolbiac storage depot [...] over five hundred art historians [...] were employed day after day, in fourteen-hour shifts, to [...] sort the goods. More than seven hundred train loads left [...] for the ruined cities of the Reich.
>
> (pp. 288–289)

In a manner of speaking, Austerlitz has given the narrator his rucksack, from which he has never parted since he left Prague with the children's transport. He also gave the narrator the gift of time, which he knows how to stretch out, like he did with the tape of the film, to bring to life the living dead, like Colonel Chabert.[37] The hero of the Balzac novel Vera gave him from her mother's collection (p. 282) had extracted himself from the mass grave of those fallen in Napoleon's Battle of Eylau. Our patients also pass their backpacks to us, as well as stretched out time which resonates with similar moments in our own history, whose script, although different than theirs, can produce harmonic tones when chords vibrate in sympathy.

Socrates tells us in the *Phaedrus* that the one who is duly out of his mind, "*to orthôs mamenti*, the one who is right to be mad" and who performs as a fool, may benefit from an analysis of the soul, *psyche*, to emerge as a subject of history, *istoria*. When he meets the narrator for the last time, Austerlitz is about to take a train at the Austerlitz station, on the day of a strike. He sets out in search of his father and his French friend Marie de Verneuil, a historian like him, whom he had met at the National Library on Rue de Richelieu. True resolution consists in the birth of a subject. Now he uses a different tone; he is the "I."

The true object of Austerlitz's research concerns transference as an interference with the narrator, at the intersection of personal history and History, striving for an inscription that will set time in motion:

> I feel, almost physically, the current of time slowing down in the gravitational field of oblivion. It seems to me then as if all the moments of our life occupy the same space, as if future events already existed and were only waiting for us to find our way to them at last [...]. And might it not be [...] that we also have appointments to keep in the past, in what has gone before and is for the most part extinguished, and must go there in search of places and people who have some connection with us on the far side of time, so to speak?
>
> (pp. 257–258)

Sebald is a theoretician of timely interferences, like those that enable the analyst to join in the dance.

In *War and Peace*, after a hunting expedition at the Rostovs, Natasha dances in the little wooden house of "Uncle [...] a distant relative [...] a man of small means," who joined the hunters without being invited (p. 925). To everyone's surprise, it was thanks to his dogs that they caught the wolf and the hare they were chasing. He invited Nicholas and his sister, who didn't know him, to spend the night at his house. That evening, music was played and songs were sung to the sound of a balalaika. To everyone's surprise, the old uncle took up a guitar and invited Natasha to dance: "Natasha threw off the shawl from her shoulders, ran forward to face 'Uncle', and setting her arms akimbo also made a motion with her shoulders and struck an attitude." Everyone present is stunned: "Where, how, and when had this young countess educated by an emigre French governess, imbibed from the air she breathed that spirit and obtained that manner which the [French dances] would, one would have supposed, long ago have effaced?" (p. 957).

What does Tolstoy want to convey? In the hunting scene, he displays the extraordinary richness of a vocabulary that is about to disappear. His pleasure in using this language culminates in the force that takes hold of Natasha and prompts her to execute dance movements she never learned, that would soon become obsolete – like the skills of crafts becoming outdated, but transmitted through generations, no one knows how. In our own craft, we need an immense vocabulary, and tales and songs, since we cannot simply groan when we encounter foreclosed zones of History.

Vasily Grossman: *Life and Fate*[38]

The subject of this novel – written in 1960 and published in Switzerland as a samizdat draft in 1980 – is illustrated in the fate of the book itself. Sent to the KGB by Grossman's colleagues from *Novi Mir*, the literary journal of the Soviet Writers' Union, the manuscript, the used carbon paper and the typewriter ribbon were locked up in 1962 at the Lubyanka. Grossman died two years later. Thanks to microfilm of copies hidden by true friends, the manuscript crossed the Iron Curtain with the help of Andrei Sakharov in the 1970s. What is at stake for Grossman is the truth, *alètheia*, that which cannot be forgotten, and is indissociable from freedom. Written at the start of the 1950s, after the Night of the Murdered Poets, when Stalin ordered the execution of Jewish writers,[39] the book testifies to the parallel between the two totalitarian systems, a comparison Hannah Arendt[40] made at the same period.

In his book, Grossman describes the Battle of Stalingrad (August 1942– February 1943), with Tolstoy's Battle of Austerlitz as a backdrop. Grossman witnessed the battle as a journalist. A convinced Bolshevik, he had hoped that the war would put an end to Stalin's regime of terror. In the 1930s, he witnessed the programmed famines in the Ukraine, his native region. When the Nazis carried out the Holocaust by Bullets there, in which his mother was killed, he realised that they were Jews, and blamed himself for not having taken her with him to Moscow. In Chapter 17 of *Life and Fate*, the long letter addressed from the Ukraine to physicist Viktor Strum by his mother – whom his wife had refused to take into their home – gives a poignant testimony of her everyday life, and the increasing torments endured by Ukrainian Jews until their extermination. Like his hero, Grossman had first chosen the world of science. He was a chemical engineer, but turned to literature as early as 1935. And like his hero, he did not speak Yiddish, because the official ideology condemned community-centred life.

The book fights on all fronts, against the Nazis and against the creation of a "new man" who has rid himself of his ancestors. I caught a glimpse of such a psychological war in a classroom of the Maison des sciences de l'homme where we were giving our seminar. Marc Augé, president of the EHESS, had invited Vietnamese philosopher Tran Duc Thao to give lectures there. Born in Hanoi in 1917, Thao had received a scholarship to study in France, entered the École normale supérieure (ENS) in 1939 and came in first at the *agrégation* exams. Author of *Phenomenology and Dialectical Materialism*, he greatly impressed the young Louis Althusser. Back in Vietnam in 1951, he held important government positions and played an advisory role in education, until he was required to make his self-criticism in 1958 for having distanced himself from the official ideology.

The lecture I was attending was given before six people. Tran Duc Thao discussed predation: when a cat leaps on top of a mouse, he must have a permanent image of the mouse in his brain – a hallucinated image. He had been sent back to Paris from his country with a one-way ticket, no money, and he died soon afterwards. I blamed myself for not having gone beyond the intellectual dimension of what he was telling us.

Vasily Grossman shatters this abstract framework by portraying the doubts of Soviet physicist Viktor Shtrum when he receives his mother's letter, sent from the ghetto the day before her murder:

> Never, before the war, had Viktor thought about the fact that he was a Jew, that his mother was a Jew. [...] the century of Einstein and Planck was also the century of Hitler. The Gestapo and the scientific renaissance were children of the same age. [...] There were moments when science seemed like a delusion that prevented one from seeing the madness and cruelty of life.
>
> (pp. 78–79)

In Part II of the book, the critique extends to the pseudoscience of historical materialism which "has rejected the concept of a separate individuality, the concept of 'a man', and operates only with aggregates" (p. 79). But Shtrum has a hard time believing that this is happening, even when his daughter, still a schoolgirl, shows him proof of Stalin's crimes.

At the end of 1942, when the Battle of Stalingrad is fought, Shtrum is on the verge of despair. Just then he suddenly makes an important scientific breakthrough that occurs to him by chance – like a "fairy gift," as Erwin Schrödinger said when he conceived his quantum equations. Filled with joy, Shtrum reveals his discovery at a lab meeting where a woman colleague informs him that "almost all the names of Jews have been crossed off the list of the Ukrainian Academy [of Sciences]," including hers. Shtrum has trouble believing her: "My dear woman, have you gone mad?" he answers, unaware that the same fate awaits him (p. 344). Preoccupied with his discovery, which had "arisen from the depths," he marvels at the fact that he cannot associate it with any determinism: "there had been room in his head for [many things]. [...] All this was what had given birth to the theory; from where there [is] no consciousness, only the inflammable peat of the unconscious" (p. 333).

Life and Fate is a cathedral of our times, whose epic dimensions leave room for chance. In contrast to the love of Humanity, it praises the "private kindness of one individual towards another, a petty, thoughtless kindness; an unwitnessed kindness" (p. 392). When Grossman wrote his novel, and when he submitted it through the channels of the hierarchy, he knew that his life was at stake, that he would be the target of "a hunt to destroy what is human in man." He spoke from the place Bion held when he said: "I died at Amiens, at Ypres, at Cambrai." Grossman died in Moscow in 1937 when he signed a petition in support of the trials prosecuting old Bolsheviks, and in 1953 when he wrote a confession for having published, in serial form, in the *Novy Mir* magazine, the first part of his novel *For a Just Cause*, violently attacked by Pravda.

Daphnis and Chloe

In *Attention and Interpretation*,[41] Bion notices that in a patient's delusions, there is a "splitting of time [...] where a moment in time has been stretched out to cover an enormous space, like a piece of elastic" (p. 39). The exploration of these out-of-time spaces is not morbid; it aims, rather, at enabling survival outside this zone of death, starting with a "renaissance."

Grossman portrays such a survival in an encircled house in a Stalingrad suburb, house 6/1, which is the target of German fire. Grekov, the commander of this point of resistance, is an exceptional fighter, close to his men, and rebelling against the political commissar sent to re-educate him. Informers have denounced him to the Party when he complained about the kolkhozes not providing food. In the middle of the fighting, Grekov refuses to answer questions when he is interrogated. The commissar accuses him of being a kulak sympathiser as a pretext for demoting him, but he is soon evacuated, after what appears to be a stray bullet inflicts a light wound on his skull.

Headquarters sent a radio-operator named Katya to house 6/1. "Eighteen at the most ... I just hope the lads don't all pounce on her," Grekov thought, falling under her spell himself. She becomes attached to Seryozha, a young soldier inexperienced with women, and speaks with him of Dickens and of *The Charterhouse of Parma*. This is when the author interrupts the epic tale and opens a way out of arrested time, with a pastoral romance based on an Ancient Greek novel about the love between two foundlings, Daphnis and Chloe.[42]

In Chapter 60 of Part I, Grossman tells the reader:

> If the story of Daphnis and Chloe still touched people's hearts, it is not simply because their love was born in the shade of vines and under a blue sky. That story is repeated everywhere – in a stuffy basement smelling of fried cod, in a concentration-camp bunker, to the click of an accountant's abacus, in the dust-laden air of a cotton mill. And now the story was being played out again to the accompaniment of the howl of dive-bombers – in a building where people nourished their filthy sweat-encrusted bodies on rotten potatoes and water from an ancient boiler, where instead of honey and dream-filled silence there was only noise, stench and rubble.

But he says no more, and the reader must wait until Chapters 16 and 17 of Part II to discover the ending of the romance. The pastoral is the literary genre of warrior poets: Cervantes' *La Galatea*, Honoré d'Urfé's *Astrea*, Montemayor's *Diana* and Camões' *The Lusiads* were written by warriors, whose aim was the same as Grossman's: to affirm the triumph of a new life and of the given word. "It's all right. Don't be afraid. This is for life – if we live" (p. 401), Seryozha tells Katya during a bomb attack. The pastoral romance restores the symbolic dimension, in its essential fragility, when it is threatened by omnipresent treachery.

Grekov ordered the young soldier to go off on a mission, to be rid of him. But Seryozha disobeys orders and comes back, under shellfire, to be with the young girl in the cellar of the stronghold, which serves as a shelter. In the morning, Grekov comes down and sees them asleep in each other's arms, in the light of shrapnel fire, but does not wake them. Instead of lamenting his misfortune – like King Mark faced with Tristan and Isolde – he understands that something incredible has happened in this place doomed to certain destruction. The next day, the young man is ordered to leave the house:

> "I'm sending you back to [...] Headquarters," Grekov tells him. After a pause, during which Seryozha thinks, bitterly: "We're being expelled from Paradise. He's separating us like two serfs," the commander adds: 'That's all. [...] And the radio-operator can go with you. There's no need for her to hang around here with nothing to do. You can show her the way to HQ." He smiled. [...] Seryozha suddenly realized that never in all his life had he seen eyes that were so sad and so intelligent, so splendid, yet so human.
>
> (p. 402)

Those two would remain alive. We are on the eve of the great Russian offensive that, against all odds, was to regain the advantage. The house is razed to the ground. "I'm in command of a dead battalion" (p. 423), the officer sent to report on the outcome says. They are all dead, except the two heroes of the pastoral: "Those left alive were living."

Where is the exit?

Grossman mixes genres by making free use of the asyndeton, a figure of speech that makes connections where there aren't any. He goes from one chapter to the other without transition, and juxtaposes tragedy and comedy, daily life and centuries-old legend, the political dimension and minute details, the epic tale and a Greek pastoral romance, the foreseeable and the improbable. This inimitable mixing of genres portrays, in the midst of an apocalypse, a naïve love such as no one dares to speak of today, in an era when parents are given sex education courses by their children.

As we do in our work as analysts dealing with madness and trauma, the objective is to provide sense in situations where everyone says: "This makes no sense; we will re-educate your neurons and your behaviour scientifically." Grossman mixes the stakes involved in the Battle of Stalingrad with scientific stakes. After his discovery, Shtrum submits his paper to experts in Moscow and waits for their response, but encounters only silence, because his theory of particles contradicts Lenin's theory of matter. Accused of opposing the collectivist practice of science, his paper is ignored. He is expelled from his lab, his world shrinks, his relations with his friends fall apart. Expecting to be arrested any moment, he tells himself that it's the fate of so many others, and that everyone has to die. It is then, while this high-level scientist awaits death, that a phone call from Stalin gives him back his life. In the midst of generalised terror, Stalin says: "We must protect our scientists."

Through the voice of an SS officer, Grossman lists the four types of leaders at work in totalitarian regimes:

1. Simple, undivided natures [...] These people [are] full of slogans and formulae [...] They usually [live] in relatively modest circumstances. [...] Like schoolchildren, they get together in little groups to mug up [the fundamental texts].
2. The intelligent cynics [...] ready to laugh at [...] the ignorance of [...] men of the first category. They usually [live] more expansively.
3. Nine or ten men [holding] sway at the very top of the hierarchy, [who admit] perhaps another fifteen or twenty to their gatherings. Here [are] no ideals, nothing but [...] pitilessness.
4. The executives, people [...] indifferent to dogmas, ideas [...] and equally lacking in analytic ability.

(pp. 466–467)

Faced with "secret societies hidden in plain sight," as Hannah Arendt calls them, Grossman creates a myth by writing the epic tale of a war between two systems in which relations between people must constantly be deciphered if murder is to be avoided, except in the case of a trustworthy encounter, above suspicion since it occurs by chance. It is such an encounter that we are expected to have with patients who have been subjected to the double-talk of lawless agencies. They ask us for a promise on which to build a new loyalty, where it had become unthinkable. We are asked what constitutes our freedom, regardless of our affiliations.

Lacan illustrates the unconscious process using the Möbius band that keeps on turning above and below with no solution of continuity. What happens when it tears? Freud, who was familiar with Virgil, never said that the dream, "the royal road to the unconscious," was a highway on which those above, *superos*, lead him to the world below "to move the Acheron." The quote he uses as an epigraph in *The Interpretation of Dreams*, "*Si superos flectere nequeo, Acheronto movebo*" ("If I cannot bend the will of Heaven, I shall move Hell") is taken from Book VII of the *Aeneid*, in which Juno, blind with rage, shouts the famous verse at Jupiter. Of course, the Acheron is an illustration of repression. But sometimes Hell bursts into our sessions, as we shall see in Goethe's *Faust*, in which Mephistopheles takes the stage.

Notes

1   Schrödinger, E., *Mind and Matter*, Cambridge University Press, 1958.
2   Bion, W. R., *A Memoir of the Future*, Routledge, 2018.
3   Kandel, E., Schwartz, J. and Jessel, T., *Principles of Neural Sciences*, McGraw-Hill, 2000.
4   Kandel, E., *In Search of Memory*, W. W. Norton & Company, 2006.
5   Braudel, F., *The Mediterranean and the Mediterranean World in the Age of Philip II*, University of California Press, 1996.
6   Sebald, W. G., *Austerlitz*, Bell, A. (Trans.), Random House, 2001.
7   Grossman, V., *Life and Fate*, Vintage Classics, 2006.
8   Coates, S., *September 11: Trauma and Human Bonds*, Routledge, 2003.
9   Koselleck, R., *Futures Past: On the Semantics of Historical Time*, Columbia University Press, 2004.
10 Eccles, J., *How the Self Controls the Brain*, Springer, 2012.
11 Van der Kolk, B., *The Body Keeps the Score*, Penguin Books, 2015.
12 Musil, R., "The Enthusiasts," in *Theater*, Rowohlt, 1965, German edition. See *infra* Seminar 11 on Robert Musil.
13 Freud, A., *The Psychoanalytic Treatment of Children*, Imago Publishing, 1946.
14 Van der Kolk, B., *The Body Keeps the Score*, op. cit.
15 Kuhn, T. S., *The Structure of Scientific Revolution*, University of Chicago Press, 1996.
16 Seksik, L., *Le cas d'Eduard Einstein*, Flammarion, 2013.
17 Breuer, J. and Freud, S., *Studies on Hysteria*, Forgotten Books, 2012.
18 Laub, D., "Reestablishing the Internal Thou," in *Psychoanalysis, Culture and Society*, No. 8, Macmillan, 2013.
19 Prévert, J., "Inventaire," in *Paroles*, Gallimard, 1976. An enumeration of things, where *raton laveur*, "raccoon," is frequently repeated throughout.
20 Descartes, R., *Discourse on Method and Meditations*, Dover Philosophical Classics, 2003.
21 Davoine, F., *Wittgenstein's Folly*, Hurst, W. (Trans.), YBK Publishers, 2012.
22 Sherrington, C. S., *Man on His Nature*, Macmillan, 1941.
23 Wittgenstein, L., "Remarks on Frazer's Golden Bough," in *Wittgenstein: Sources and Perspectives*, Luckhardt, C. G. (Ed.), Cornell University Press, 1979, pp. 19–20.
24 Bion, W. R., *Cogitations*, Karnac Books, 1991, p. 134.
25 Lacan, J., "Antigone between Two Deaths," in *The Seminar of Jacques Lacan: The Ethics of Psychoanalysis*, W. W. Norton & Company, 1997.
26 Musil, R., *The Man Without Qualities*, Alfred A. Knopf, 1995. See *infra* Seminar 11 on Robert Musil.
27 Cocteau, J., "The Wedding on the Eiffel Tower," in *Modern French Theatre*, Benedikt, M. and Wellwarth, G. E. (Eds.), E. P. Dutton & Co, 1964.
28 Tolstoy, L., *War and Peace*, Maude, L. and A. (Trans.), W.W. Norton & Company, 1966, p. 1349.
29 Freud, S. and Jung, C. G., *The Correspondence between Sigmund Freud and C. G. Jung*, McGuire, W. (Ed.), 1909, letter April 16.
30 Merton, R. and Barber, E., *The Travels and Adventures of Serendipity*, Princeton University Press, 2004.
31 Baudelaire, C., *The Flowers of Evil and Paris Spleen*, Dover Thrift Editions, 2011.
32 Plato, *Theaetetus*, Liberal Arts Press, 1955.
33 Sebald, W. G., *Austerlitz*, Bell, A. (Trans.), Modern Library, 2001.
34 Tasso, T., *Jerusalem Delivered*, Esolen, A. M. (Trans.), Johns Hopkins University Press, 2000.

35 Caruth, C., *Unclaimed Experience: Trauma, Narrative and History*, Johns Hopkins University Press, 2016, p. 139.
36 Cadence: portion of a Baroque musical piece left to improvisation.
37 De Balzac, H., *Colonel Chabert*, Book Jungle, 2009.
38 Grossman, V., *Life and Fate*, op. cit.
39 Rubinstein, J. and Naumov, V., *Stalin's Secret Pogrom: The Postwar Inquisition of the Jewish Anti-Fascist Committee*, Yale University Press, 2001.
40 Arendt, H., *The Origins of Totalitarianism*, World Publishing Company, 1951.
41 Bion, W. R., *Attention and Interpretation*, Karnac Books, 1984.
42 Longus, *Daphnis and Chloe*, Penguin Classics, 1989.

3 Seminar 10: 2005–2006
J. W. von Goethe (1749–1832)
Madness against cognitive distortions

The algebraic opposite of the moral order

Under the general heading "Madness and the Social Link," our seminars continue to look to books that examine this relation in a never-ending present. One of these works is the little book re-edited regularly at troublesome moments in our history: *Discourse on Voluntary Servitude*,[1] written at the age of 18 by La Boétie, who became Montaigne's friend "because it was he, because it was I." We also turn to another little book: *La mémoire courte*[2] by Jean Cassou, who translated *Don Quixote* after World War II. *La mémoire courte* (*Short Memory*) was published in 1953, after prosecution of collaborators began, bringing condemnation to some and amnesty to others.

Jean Cassou witnessed the events of a whole century. He was born in Spain in 1897, the son of an Andalusian mother and a French father who died when his son was 16. After studying Spanish literature in Paris, he published a novel in 1923, *L'Éloge de la folie* (*In Praise of Madness*), was chief editor of the magazine *Europe,* played an active role in the Front Populaire government in 1936, joined the Communist Party and then left it in 1939, after the signing of the German-Soviet Nonaggression Pact. He was named Director of the National Museum of Modern Art in 1940, but was quickly divested of his functions by the Vichy regime, and joined the Resistance in September 1940, as part of the Group of the Museum of Man. He evaded the Gestapo and fled to Toulouse, where he was arrested in August 1941 and freed in 1943. After being seriously wounded in August 1944, he regained his post as Director of the National Museum of Modern Art in 1945, a position he occupied until 1965, before becoming Director of Research at the École pratique des hautes études. He died in 1986.

La mémoire courte was published in 1953. Cassou could not condone amnesty. To him, it meant forgetting and falsifying memory. A new world cannot simply be built on the ruins left by the two world wars, saying simply *Good-Bye to All That,* the title of a book by Robert Graves.[3] Graves was the friend who took the poet Siegfried Sassoon to be treated by

William Rivers at Craiglockhart. Without the work of inscription performed by Graves and Sassoon, no goodbye is possible, madness teaches us, in the zones where time is arrested. In 1953, François Poncelet was inducted into the Académie Française; he was to take the seat of Philippe Pétain, and to pay tribute to him. He solved this dilemma by conferring blame and praise on both illustrious opponents, General de Gaulle and Marechal Pétain, in his acceptance speech.

But an "irreducible residue" remains: "The dead died for what?" Jean Cassou's question cannot be conjured away by a policy of "dead dog going down the stream," to use the phrase coined by André Tardieu in 1909. So we are left to deal with the dead, because Folly brings them back, speaking as "a woman" in Erasmus' *Praise*, and saying that they can't be ignored because they have a long memory, a memory without oblivion, Bion says.

Cassou is well read: a long memory is what Aeneas refers to when Dido blames him angrily as he is leaving her. They first met after Aeneas had wept – *sunt lacrimae rerum* – at the sight of Juno's Temple; Aeneas fell in love with the queen, who was a widow. Forgetting his mission to establish Rome in Latium, Aeneas rules over Carthage dressed as a Phoenician prince, because Dido, persecuted by her brothers, had fled the Phoenician city of Tyre. Mercury brings Aeneas a message from Neptune, to remind him of his mission. When Aeneas is preparing his ships for his departure, Dido makes a desperate scene, in Book IV, after "blazing through the entire city, raving like some Maenad, *incense per urbem bachatur*." She assails the "traitor, *perfide*":

> Can nothing hold you back? Not our love? Not the pledge once sealed with our right hands? Not even the thought of Dido doomed to a cruel death? [...] Pity a great house about the fall [...]. If only you'd left a baby in my arms – our child – before you deserted me! Some little Aeneas playing about our halls, whose features at least would bring you back to me [...] I would not feel so totally devastated, so destroyed.[4]

Dixerat, she has spoken, and he, *ille*, "warned by Jupiter now" to make haste to reach Italy despite his desire, remained speechless for a moment, "his gaze held steady." Then he answered in a few words: "Ego *te*, I ... you have done me so many kindnesses [...]. I shall never deny what you deserve, my queen [...] while I can recall myself and draw the breath of life" (verses 331–336). This is the half verse, *dum memor ipse mei*, which Cassou placed in exergue, in Latin, at the start of *La mémoire courte*: the words of a traitor to queen Dido.

And he opens his little book with the terrible assertion: "This traitor was right, today Frenchmen have a short memory." This time, the traitor is Philippe Pétain, who spoke these words in 1941. Cassou takes the memory of betrayal from the mouth of the traitor. At the end of that year, Cassou was imprisoned in the military prison in Toulouse, where he composed from memory, and in secret, his *33 Sonnets of the Resistance* – since there was nothing to write with in his cell.[5] These sonnets, published underground in 1944, testify to the will of a man who is not content with short memory and would agree with Bion's statement that "the man who cannot be a friend to his friends – including those who died – cannot be the enemy of his enemies."

The Riom trial held between February and April 1942 was fabricated by Pétain as a pretext to explain how it is possible to become a friend of the enemies of one's enemies. The accused were Édouard Daladier and Léon Blum, the first made prisoner in Germany and the second sent to Buchenwald. The idea behind the trial was to find scapegoats for the 1940 defeat by blaming it on the Front Populaire government, because Pétain had been Minister of War in 1934. A proponent of the Maginot Line, he had refused to increase conscription, even though the number of enlisted men in Germany was twice as high. Maginot himself died before the King of Belgium let Guderian's army enter his country on May 10, 1940 and cross the Ardennes forest – reputed to be impenetrable – as if the air force did not exist. The infantry remained the backbone of the fighting.

At the Riom trial, the judges were in allegiance with Pétain, but events turned against him because Members of Parliament spoke convincingly and foreign journalists covered the trial. Indeed, the proceedings became the trial of Marechal Pétain. Given this turn of events, Hitler ordered the trial to be suspended, since the reason for it had been to bring Frenchmen the proof of their responsibility in setting off the war. As far as de Gaulle was concerned, France was in London. After the war, the legislative and legal decisions of the French State enacted between 1940 and 1945 were declared null and void, opening the door to amnesty for those who had collaborated to various degrees with the occupiers.

This year's seminar deals, once again, with "memory that does not forget," and produces a particular type of transference in which madness abolishes previous and subsequent oppositions, from within and from without. This memory puts the analyst on the spot with questions like: Are the enemies of my enemies my friends? Is the opposite of a moral order immoral? These dilemmas in logic are the weapons of madness against the confusions created by perversion. A remark made by Jean Cassou summarises this battle which we also fight in psychotic transference: "But what is this Resistance if not again and again the stirrings of a conscience which has said no to the obvious and sides with the improbable and the impossible" (p. 47).

"The refined tone of extraordinarily good company"[6]

Contrary to the waffling language of politicians or the cynicism of double-talk, this expression of de Crébillon the younger alludes to that superlative form of conversation which enables talk without content, as long as a certain tone is maintained. We get an idea of such talk when we hear Delphine Seyrig in *Last Year at Marienbad* or Dario Fo in satirical theatre using *gromalat*, gibberish that could be any language, depending on the intonation. Erasmus used wordplay when he dedicated *In Praise of Folly, Moriae Encomium*, to his friend Thomas More, author of *Utopia*, "Nowhere Island." The function of folly in this book is to shatter the refined tone of the extraordinarily good company, the tone of analysts who speak in ready-made phrases, approved by their extraordinary schools.

Written in 1515, Thomas More's *Utopia*[7] describes places where the ill and the mad are cared for "without the walls of towns," in their suburbs, *suburbana e arum*. The relation between the fools and the inhabitants of Utopia resembles those in the Sotties, where the Fools are prompted by Mother Folly[8] to give free reign to delirious tirades of admirable virtuosity against the abuses of the world:

> They take great pleasure in fools, and as it is thought a base and unbe-
> coming thing to use them ill, so they do not think it amiss for people
> to divert themselves; and, in their opinion, this is a great advantage to
> the fools themselves; for if men were so sullen and severe as not at all
> to please themselves with their ridiculous behaviour and foolish sayings,
> which is all that they can do to recommend themselves to others, it
> could not be expected that they would be so well provided for nor so
> tenderly used as they must otherwise be.

We recognise the reference to the serious mindedness that diagnoses an emotional illness in the "unmotivated laughter" of the patient who makes fun of his therapist, whose dissonances he has detected. Babies are also equipped with such a lie detector, enabling them to distinguish a sincere smile from a forced smile on a face with unsmiling eyes. Narcissistic psychoses, which analytic dogma has long excluded from transference, attack the analyst's narcissism when he fears the unknown Bion described, surfacing when unknown zones in himself start to resonate.

William Rivers, Bion's teacher encountered through his analyst John Rickman, came to certain conclusions about this point by connecting it to the neurological experiments he conducted with Henry Head on nerve regeneration. He applied these experiments to his work in analysis with traumatised war veterans. At first, during an initial "protopathic" period, the pain following the cutting of a nerve is extreme. Then, during a subsequent "epicritic" period, there are identifiable thresholds of pain as regeneration occurs. According to Rivers, the process is similar in transference, where the destruction of alterity is intolerable at first, and then shows more or less pronounced fluctuations as regeneration of language occurs in transference. Pat Barker's *Trilogy*[9] also describes the process of Rivers' self-analysis in relation to war traumas existing in his lineage.

The stranger questioned by Oedipus,[10] when he arrives at Colonus where he will die, says: "The spot thou treadest on is holy ground [...]. Such, stranger, is the spot to game unknown, But dear to us its native worshipers" (verses 63, 64). This describes the sacred spaces Oedipus has entered, about which the Choir of elderly citizens says: "whose name no voice betrays [...]. And as we pass them with averted eye, We move hushed lips in reverent piety," *aderktôs, aphonôs, alogôs* (sightless, voiceless, wordless) (verse 131). Here, the "protopathic" is at work – the "*pathos formel* saturated with energy" Aby Warburg invoked in his madness. It touches the analyst beyond the realm of words, in zones he learns to explore to gain access to events cut out of History by the double-talk of scoundrels.

Tartuffe

The inspiration for Molière's play came from a Spanish short story translated by Paul Scarron under the title *The Hypocrite Impostor*, to which Molière added a political dimension.[11] Omnipresent from the start of the play, Tartuffe only makes his entrance in the third act, reciting the mantra of the pious: "Laurent, lock up my hair shirt and my scourge, And pray for freedom from each carnal urge. If anyone comes calling, say I have gone To share my alms with the poor souls in prison" (Act III, Scene 2). Just as Vasily Grossman, in his naivety, exposes hypocrites when he entrusts the manuscript of *Life and Fate* to them, Orgon's foolishness is in fact a weapon.

In this light, I reread *Tartuffe* from a political perspective, realising that Orgon, who is usually considered a dolt, was intended by Molière to be "an authentic fool," as the Sotties would call him – a fool who reveals "secret societies hiding in plain sight" such as the Company of the Blessed Sacrament or the Cabal of the Devout, which raged against the play. Staged simultaneously with the publication of Pascal's *Provincial Letters* in 1657, which ridicules the Jesuits, the play displays for all to see the depravity hidden behind rigid religious rites. But Dorine, the maid, is not fooled; she tells the impostor just what she thinks of him, in the tradition of the judgements of the Sotties: "For I could see you nude from top to toe Without your pelt setting my cheeks aglow" (Act III, Scene 2).

Thus, Orgon is a fool who must let his folly do its work, to bring to light the betrayals of the man to whom he has given everything: his possessions, his daughter and – not quite but almost – his wife, until the last act of the play, in which Tartuffe wants to throw him out of his own house. The controversy about *Tartuffe* forced Molière to rewrite his play several times after repeated prohibitions, in 1664 and 1665, although the king had given his verbal agreement to the play before leaving for Flanders. The play's triumph in 1666 intensified hostilities. In the meantime, Molière had written and staged *Don Juan*. In 1669, he wrote a preface to *Tartuffe*, in which he defended the play by means of an analysis of perversion that could not be more pertinent for us today.

He started by attacking the taboo that prohibits laughing at impostors:

> The marquises, the precious ladies, the cuckolds, and the doctors have suffered the portrayal in peace, and have even made a show of being amused [...]. But the hypocrites could not take mockery [...]. It is a crime they could not forgive, and they all took up arms against my comedy with a frightful furor. [...] they are too politic for that and know too well how to get along in the world to unveil the depth of their soul. Following their praiseworthy custom, they concealed their private interests with the cause of God. [...] They insult me piously and damn me from charity. [...] [They] thrust onto their side truly worthy people [...]. That is what obliges me to defend myself.

The name of God can be a cover for the name of any idol presiding over any cause.

Then Molière becomes more insistent, when he condemns the crimes perpetrated by perversion:

> If the mission of comedy is to correct men's vices, I fail to see why some should be privileged. In the State, this is [...] much more dangerous [...] and we have seen that the theatre is a great force for correction. [...] We are willing to be wicked, but we will not be ridiculous. [...] To me, it seems enough to make known the criminal motives [of this morality]. [...] There is nothing so innocent that men cannot stain it with crime, no art so salutary that they cannot reverse its intentions, nothing so good in itself that they cannot turn it to bad uses. Medicine is a beneficial art and everyone respects it as one of the most excellent things we have, yet there have been times when it became odious and often it has been made into an art for poisoning men.

What he is attacking is "true excellence" being corrupted, and "the malice of the corruptors."

Like Hannah Arendt and Vasily Grossman, Molière defends his freedom to judge in situations where freedom is stifled. Right at the start of the play, Dorine mentions the political battles Orgon had fought before Tartuffe came on the scene: "During the war, he seemed quite sage, And in serving his prince, showed some courage, But now he's become an absolute fool Since he gave himself up to Tartuffe's rule" (Act I, Scene 2).

The "war" she refers to is the Fronde, a series of civil wars (1648–1653) during the period when Anne of Austria governed France as regent for her minor son Louis XIV, until the Prince de Condé and the Cardinal de Retz forced her to flee to Rueil and then to Saint-Germain-en-Laye. Ever since then, Orgon has been hiding a box containing compromising documents entrusted to him by a friend. Tartuffe has taken the box, intending to give it to the king. In the last scene of the play, he makes his entrance with a police officer – suggesting an arrest by the police – but the situation is suddenly reversed; the police officer arrests the informer and restores Orgon's honour:

> I need not explain to you my reason. Calm yourself, sir, after passions of such heat. We're ruled by a Prince who's a foe to deceit, A prince whose eyes can read what the soul has writ, And who can't be fooled by a hypocrite.

The box is returned unopened, and the scoundrel is unmasked.

Now, the question is how to distinguish between the aporias of madness and the dissonances promoted by perversion.

Goethe: rendezvous with the devil

In the 1960s, Paul Watzlawick and other members of the Palo Alto School[12] discovered that "paradoxical injunctions" – Gregory Bateson's double bind – drive people crazy. For instance: "I love you and rape you; be free, it's what I want; go ahead, desire it – it's an order." Analysts displaying such behaviour sparked the birth of anti-psychiatry in England, led by R. D. Lang, and inspired Ken Loach's *Family Life*.[13] In this context, the aim of madness is to cause a reliable alterity to emerge, while the contradictory injunction intends to destroy it. But it would be useless to tell the young girl in the movie: "Of course you went crazy, you are stuck in a double bind." In that case, what is there to do?

Paradoxes can also be sources of freedom: "I refuse to join a club that would accept me as a member," Groucho Marx used to say. The medieval Theatre of Fools enacted by the Marx Brothers attempts to create a new social link rooted in the symbolic order: *sumballein* in Greek means "to gather together," the opposite of *diabellein*, "to disperse." The Devil is an expert in attacks on the link. Therefore, in our clinical work, it is important to distinguish clearly between the masked madness of perversion and madness that creates disorder, because they have contrary aims.

In Gounod's *Faust*,[14] the devil appears when the scholar wants to kill himself with poison and cries out: "Satan, come to me!" and Mephistopheles arrives at once, saying: "Here I am!" Thanks to an elixir of youth, the aged doctor is transformed. The opera portrays him as a marvellous young man (pot-bellied in many versions). Faust changes from a Pico della Mirandola who knows everything that could be known in his era, and especially how to talk to the devil, into a vulgar libertine: "Pleasure will be mine, So will young mistresses." Indeed, his young mistress Marguerite is driven insane, and imprisoned for killing her child. These events are played out in the opera against a background depicting the revelry of Walpurgis Night in the Harz Mountains. In the kitsch opera of the Second Empire, collaboration with the devil creates a musical unease signalled by a quarter-tone. The Devil is in the details.

Goethe worked with the devil all his life, going so far as to seal the manuscript of *Faust, Part Two* for posthumous publication. Not because it was scandalous or blasphemous, but because it was illegible. Later, the authors of Gounod's libretto, Barbier and Carré, created for the most performed of the French operas – along with Bizet's *Carmen* – an almost likeable Mephistopheles, although not quite a secular figure. He is anticlerical, but needs the clergy to exist. The two also collaborated when Offenbach wrote *Orpheus in the Underworld*, in which Eurydice is a silly girl who betrays Orpheus with a shepherd, forcing Pluto to send her to the Underworld.[15] But Hades is not Satan, if we keep in mind a required characteristic of *diaballen*: the attack on the given word and the proffered vow.

Doctor Faust did, in fact, exist in the early sixteenth century, and inspired a long literary tradition. He was a famous astrologist and alchemist, invited to the courts of Charles V and Francis I. It was indeed said of him that he had signed a pact with the devil. A biography of this man was written in German and translated in England, where Christopher Marlowe (born in 1564 and assassinated in 1593) read it, before writing his play *Doctor Faustus*, staged in London in 1588. Goethe drew his inspiration from it, as well as from a puppet show on the same subject, to write his play in 1775 and then publish *Faust, Part One*[16] in 1808.

The Prelude on Stage at the beginning of the play introduces the theatre director, *Direktor*, the poet, *Dichter*, and the buffoon, *Lustige Person*, eager to talk about folly: "Be brave, and show them what you've got, Have fantasy with all her chorus, yes, Mind, Reason, Passion, Tears, the lot, But don't you leave out Foolishness." In the tradition of *Till Eulenspiegel* – a German novel published in Flanders in 1515, from which Charles de Coster drew his inspiration in 1867 to write *The Legend of Ulenspiegel*[17] – the Lustig is a folkloric figure, originating in the Theatre of Fools as well. Madness is a tool that becomes indispensable as soon as the devil makes his appearance.

The Prologue in Heaven, which follows the Prelude, reveals a pact between God and Mephistopheles, concerning the ascetic Doctor, a servant of God. Mephistopheles tells God: "If you give me permission first, I'll lead him gently on the road I set." God, who has heard stranger things, is confident of the outcome and replies: "A good man in his darkest yearning Is still aware of virtue's ways." He has given his permission: "Well and good [...]! Divert this spirit from his source, You know how to trap him, lead him, On your downward course" (verse 325). And He adds: "Those like you I've never hated. Of all the spirits who deny, it's you, the jester, who's most lightly weighted" (verse 339). Had Goethe sensed the arrival of tyrants worse than the Devil, who would surpass him in the practice of cognitive dissonances?

Let us take the "benign" example of an addict to drug use and trafficking. A man who came to see me used drugs from morning to night, and had no intention of stopping. The rationale he used was: "It can't be so bad, even children take it." I tell him that if he wants to work with me, our rigorous research admits of no drug use at all. I will see him free of charge until he stops using and selling, because I don't want the dirty money from his deals. And then I add this extravagant request: "I want you to give me your word of honour." To my great surprise, this quixotic formula touches him deeply: "And what if I want to give myself my word of honour?" I lose my temper and answer: "I could care less about a promise you make to your mirror, since I'm here. I am the one who is asking." After he left, I asked myself where I had gotten that phrase, other than from my childhood, when we used to say it and spit on the ground to seal our pact. The fact is that he stopped using and we were able to work together. I was not the censor who preached that it is evil to use drugs, but I suggested that he use tools other than those of public opinion. As if we carried, since childhood or even before that, two fragments of speech that joined together. I am borrowing this image from the etymology of *sumballein*, the fitting together of two shards of broken pottery, owned by a host who gives one to his visitor, so that after their death their descendants can recognise each other – the opposite of the forged currency of double-dealing and corruption.

Narr/Tor

Faust, Part Two was published after Goethe's death in 1832. Faust and Mephistopheles are summoned to Augsburg, to the Emperor's court. The Emperor, like all emperors, has lost all his money, of course. In Act I, at his request, Mephistopheles enters the "realm of the mothers" in order to bring back the "ideal form" of beauty. Mothers, Goethe says, are: "Goddesses, enthroned on high, and solitary. No space round them, not even time: only To speak of them embarrasses me. They are The Mothers!" (verses 6213–6216). From their realm, Mephistopheles brings back Helen of Troy and Paris. Faust falls in love with Helen, and wants Mephistopheles to look for her in the Underworld. But Satan is forbidden to enter the Greek Underworld. This is what happens next: in Act III, Faust and Helen have a child who will die; Act IV depicts a battle between the Emperor and some feudal lords whom Mephistopheles defeats; and in Act V, Faust cultivates the land the Emperor gave him as a reward for his services, and dies, his soul saved by Marguerite. The mystic choir ends the play with the verse: "Woman, eternal, Beckons us on" (Act II, verse 12110).

Unlike "daimons" – *daimones*, as the Greeks call them – Mephistopheles is a cold monster: "Truly, I don't feel a thing! It's winter in my body" (verse 3848), he says at the end of *Faust, Part One*, during Walpurgis Night. As we go from the intimate world of the first *Faust* to the macrocosm of the second, madness is still present. The court jester *Narr* dies of having drunk too much – until he awakens from his drunken stupor. The place he left empty is filled by Mephistopheles, calling himself *Tor*, "Mephistor." This is where Goethe contrasts two types of madness: that of *Narr*, who narrates and taps people on the nose, and that of *Tor*, who sows discord, mixes you up and makes you dizzy with his cognitive dissonances. Jonathan Swift made this opposition in his *Digression on Madness*, between the Fool and the Knave. This is where we find a way to differentiate between the enigmas created by madness which open a third dimension in a binary world without relief, and paradoxical injunctions which imprison you in that world through submission.

Mephistopheles, seated on the left of the Emperor, listens to the Chancellor's speech on the state of the empire:

> Here one steals cattle, there, a wife [...] And boasts of it for many a year [...]. The judge, in pomp, on his high cushion, Meanwhile there grows a furious roar, From swelling tides of revolution. [...] No rights are left for us, not one. [...] Men seize the pillows from your bed, Even the bread from your table's gone.
>
> (Act II, verses 4787–4875)

The public is not fooled: "Two rogues there – already known – Fool and Dreamer – so near the throne [...] – The Fool plays – the Wise Man speaks, in time" (verse 4953). He capitalises on negativity. Mephistopheles has won: Faust has done everything necessary to be damned. In a scene that could not be more timely, he meets his friend Wagner who, for the good of mankind, is constructing an artificial man in his laboratory – a homunculus bringing together all the newest scientific knowledge available. His praiseworthy intention is to eliminate procreation, an "idle foolery," and replace it with life that does away with chance: "But we'll laugh at Chance itself, yet, And brains, with thoughts to celebrate, In the future, a Thinker will create." Faust too desires the good of mankind. On the lands the Emperor gave him for defeating the feudal lords, he drains marshes, displaces populations, kills Philemon and Baucis because they refuse to leave their hut, and then dies, his soul saved at the last minute.

From worry to boredom

The publisher of *Faust, Part Two* used verse numbers consecutive to those of *Part One*, published twenty years earlier. At the end of the play, Faust is dying after having used his political power to kill a lot of people. Like in medieval theatre, abstract concepts are embodied by women who visit him to cause him torment: Want, Guilt, Care and Fate. Having become blind, like Oedipus, before he dies he speaks words that echo those in *Part One*, addressed to the present moment: "Ah, stay a while! You are so lovely!"

(Act I, verse 11583). The clock stops, the hand falls, and the chorus says: "All is spent."

Mephistopheles destroys the past and the future: "Past! A stupid word. Then why? Past and pure naught, complete monotony! 'There, it's past!' What's to read into it? It's just the same as if it never lived." When Faust had asked him: "Who are you?" he had answered:

> I am the spirit, ever, that denies! And rightly so: since everything created, In turn deserves to be annihilated: Better if nothing came to be. So all that you call Sin, you see, Destruction, in short, what you've meant by Evil is my true element.
>
> (Act I, verses 1338–1344)

But he fails to annihilate the past, because a host of Angels, one lovelier than the other, appears, intent on thwarting his plans. After showering him with roses, the Angels enact an angelic-paedophile musical comedy worthy of Monty Python, which makes a fool of him – bringing to mind the fitting title of Ben Johnson's comedy *The Devil Is an Ass*.[18] Mephistopheles' body is "bathed in fire" as he watches them swarm around him: "You, the tall lad, you could make me love you, The priest's pose doesn't really suit you, So show a little lust, and look hereon! You would be more modestly naked too." While he becomes more and more excited, the choir of angels "[carries] away the immortal part of Faust" (Act II, verse 11825).

Mephistopheles understands that he has been tricked: "How then? – Where did they vanish to? You took me by surprise, you adolescents. Now with what they've salvaged from the tomb, As their own prize, they've flown off the heaven." He is seized by boredom: "But whom could I complain to, anyway? [...] I've mishandled it all disgracefully, A common lust, an absurd passion, Swayed the hardened devil foolishly" (Act II, verses 11835–11840).

The etymology of "ennui" is *odium*, hate, experienced as lack of affect. Mephistopheles' official profile might read: "Profession: devil, expert in negations of all kinds, supplier of illusions and world champion of manipulation, disguised as intelligence." A perfect description of the banality of evil. In truth, he is a dolt who compensates for his shortcomings by his hold on souls, persuading Faust to do what he wants him to by using temptations that evaporate one after the other. His madness is perverse, *Torheit*, locked in the logic of cause and effect.

The statue of Philippe Pinel in front of the Salpetrière Hospital in Paris – which I see regularly on my bus route – showing him freeing the mad from their chains, is a perfect image because it escapes the hold of causalistic chains that diminish the psyche, inside the skull or in a structure impervious to transference. This is where Erasmus' madness, *Narr*, turns around and challenges the analyst when, inevitably, the latter finds himself in the role of the devil.

Having embodied Mephistopheles at such critical moments, I can tell you that something major is at stake here: the birth of a transitional subject who tries to exist outside the zombie-like state to which he has been relegated, provided the analyst can say in what way he has acted like an ass. All kinds of tricks can be tried, but if the analyst, like a boar on a farm, faces the mob that has gathered, a first mirror can emerge for events without any witness, subjected to negation and often ignored by analysts. Yet Freud, in his *Moses*,[19] and when his books were burned in Berlin and he himself was threatened with the same fate, declared the aim of psychoanalysis to be historical truth. His warning preceded that of Jean Cassou in *La mémoire courte* fifteen years later.

Marc Bloch: facing cognitive dissonances

A short memory is what the psychiatrists and psychoanalysts attending a conference at the Bonneval Hospital on September 28, 1946 could be said to have had. Lacan's opening address, "Remarks on Psychic Causality," was later published in *Écrits*.[20] In it, he accomplished the prodigious feat of not mentioning the war, except in five lines in which he speaks of himself, completely ignoring the tens of thousands of mad patients who starved to death in psychiatric hospitals.[21] It's a pity that he had not read the little book which had just been published in 1946 by historian Marc Bloch (1886–1944), entitled *Strange Defeat*.[22] Written between 1940 and 1942, the book has three chapters: "Presentation of the Witness," "One of the Vanquished Gives Evidence" and "A Frenchman Examines His Conscience."

The witness, Marc Bloch, introduces himself as "a Jew" and "a born fighter" of Alsatian origin. His ancestors fought in the wars of 1793 and 1870. Having been an information officer in World War I, he volunteered for service in World War II, at the age of 54, when he was the father of six children. He called himself "the oldest captain in the army." Assigned to Fuel Service, he witnessed the disaster after the invasion of Belgium on May 19, 1940. This is where the testimony in the first chapter of *Strange Defeat* ends. Bloch's Paris apartment was ransacked and his books were sent to Germany. He taught in Montpellier in precarious conditions, threatened by the anti-Jewish laws. He went into hiding in 1942, when the Germans invaded the Free Zone. His story is reminiscent of Jean Cassou's, but has a tragic ending. Being one of the leaders of the Resistance in the Lyon area, he was imprisoned in Montluc Prison, tortured by Barbie and his gang, and killed in a ditch on June 16, 1944, with 29 other Resistance fighters. He took the young boy trembling next to him by the arm affectionately and told him: "Don't worry, son, it doesn't hurt," before being shot first.

"One of the Vanquished Gives Evidence" invokes cognitive dissonance to explain the reasons for the defeat: "Whatever the deep-seated causes of the disaster may have been, the immediate occasion [...] was the utter incompetence of the High Command" (p. 25).

> Our leaders, or those who acted for them, were incapable of thinking in terms of a *new* war. In other words, the German triumph was, essentially, a triumph of intellect – and it is that which makes it so peculiarly serious.
>
> (p. 36)

Bloch goes on, becoming more precise: "They relied on action and improvisation. We [...] believed in doing nothing and in behaving as we always had" (p. 49). "Unfortunately, our leaders were not drawn from among those who suffered least from a hardening of the arteries" (p. 50).

> The story goes that Hitler, before drawing up his final plans for the campaign, summoned a number of psychologists to his headquarters [...]. I cannot vouch for the truth of this, but it does not seem altogether beyond the bounds of probability.
>
> (p. 54)

Bloch analyses the absence of the air force as voluntary servitude to cleverly worded propaganda.

In "A Frenchman Examines His Conscience," Marc Bloch goes beyond the military sphere to look for reasons for the disaster, invoking the distortions produced by the adulterated use of popular sayings:

> But here I find myself [dealing] with an entirely different order of problems which belong strictly to the world of thought. It was not only in the field that intellectual causes lay at the root of our defeat. The destiny of the People is in their own hands, and I see no reason for believing that they are not perfectly capable of choosing rightly. But what effort has been made to supply them with that minimum of clear and definite information without which no rational conduct is possible? [...] None. In no [other] way did our so-called democratic system so signally fail.
>
> (pp. 143–144)

Bloch condemns – like Hannah Arendt does in *The Origins of Totalitarianism*, written at the same period – the "mental laziness" consisting of reciting ready-made ideas that confuse, for example, murder with self-defence:

> If we turn back on ourselves [and] keep [our] eyes lazily shut to the facts, we shall be lost. Salvation can only be ours on condition that we set our brains to work with a will, in order that we may *know* more fully, and get our imagination moving to a quicker tempo.
>
> (p. 149)

He calls upon the *thumos*, human vitality in Ancient Greek – "of a people paralysed by fear which produces boredom, apathy or, on the contrary, fanatical obedience." Indeed, it is *thumos* that inspires the prophetic visions of those who explore the memory of the future in zones of arrested time.

Alexis de Tocqueville

Marc Bloch was a historian specialising in the Middle Ages; in 1924, he published a famous work entitled *The Royal Touch*.[23] I would have liked the opportunity to sit down with this founding father of our School, the EHESS, and discuss the prophetic talents that often serve as a reason for hospitalisation. In his book *The Danger of Words*,[24] psychiatrist Maurice O'Connor Drury, Wittgenstein's disciple, presents a series of cases – without disclosing any names – that nowadays are considered suitable for drug treatment or electroshock. He then goes on to describe men and women whose political vision marked their epoch and made them famous.

Alexis de Tocqueville (1805–1859) was one of these visionaries who, a century earlier, showed a prophetic inclination at the end of his *Democracy in America*,[25] as if he could step out of the present and see the time before his birth and the time after his death as a continuum. Much like Marc Bloch, he asks himself "what kind of despotism democracies are prone to," and he foresees Europe's future (Vol. II, Chapter 6):

> I think then that the species of oppression by which democratic nations are menaced is unlike anything which ever before existed in the world: our contemporaries will find no prototype of it in their memories. I am trying myself to choose an expression which will accurately convey the whole of the idea I have formed of it, but in vain; the old words "despotism" and "tyranny" are inappropriate.

Since he can't name this new thing, Tocqueville launches into a methodical description:

> The first thing that strikes the [observer] is an innumerable multitude of men all equal and alike, incessantly endeavouring to procure the petty and paltry pleasures with which they glut their lives. Each of them, living apart, is a stranger to the fate of all the rest – his children and his private friends constitute to him the whole of mankind; as for the rest of his fellow-citizens, he is close to them, but he sees them not – he touches them, but he feels them not; he exists but in himself and for himself alone; and if this kindred still remain to him, he may be said at any rate to have lost his country.

The emergence of totalitarian systems is part of what he foresees:

> Above this race of men stands an immense and tutelary power, which takes upon itself alone to secure their gratification, and to watch over their fate. That power is absolute, minute, regular, provident, and mild. It would be like the authority of a parent, if, like that authority, its object was to prepare men for manhood; but it seeks on the contrary to keep them in perpetual childhood: it is well content that the people should rejoice, provided they think of nothing but rejoicing. [...] it provides for their security [...] directs their industry, regulates the descent of property, and subdivides their inheritances – what remains, but to spare them all the care of thinking and all the trouble of living?

Tocqueville foresees bureaucratic omnipotence:

> It covers the surface of society with a net-work of small complicated rules, minute and uniform, through which the most original minds [...] cannot penetrate, to rise above the crowd. The will of man is not shattered, but softened, bent, and guided: men are seldom forced by it to act, but they are constantly restrained from acting: such a power does not destroy, but it prevents existence; it does not tyrannize, but it compresses, enervates, extinguishes, and stupefies a people, till each nation is reduced to be nothing better than a flock of timid and industrious animals, of which the governments is the shepherd. [...] The people [...] console themselves for being in tutelage by the reflection that they have chosen their own guardians.

We now come to the question of freedom and can clearly see that the version Tocqueville gives us is an update of La Boétie's *Discourse on Voluntary Servitude*: "By this system the people shake off their state of dependence just long enough to select their master, and then relapse into it again." This system Hannah Arendt calls "without precedent," which murdered Marc Bloch and Freud's sisters, already existed in embryo. We will come back to it in the next seminar, when we consider Robert Musil's *The Man Without Qualities*,[26] written in 1930, during the rise of Nazism, and left unfinished at the death of the author during his exile in Switzerland in 1942.

Notes

1 De la Boétie, E., *Discourse on Voluntary Servitude*, Hackett Classics, 2012.
2 Cassou, J., *La mémoire courte*, Fayard, Mille et une nuits, 2001.
3 Graves, R., *Good-Bye to All That*, Anchor Books, 1985.
4 Virgil, *The Aeneid*, Fagles, R. (Trans.), Viking Press, 2006, Book IV, verses 305–330.

5 Cassou, J., *33 Sonnets of the Resistance and Other Poems*, Arc Publications, 2005.

6 De Crébillon, C. P. J., *The Wonderings of the Heart and Mind*, Geo & Alex Ewing, 1751.

7 More, T., *Utopia*, Dover Publications, 1997.

8 Davoine, F., *Mother Folly: A Tale*, Stanford University Press, 2014.

9 Barker, P., *Regeneration*, Penguin Books, 1992.

10 Sophocles, *Oedipus at Colonus*, Dover Publications, 1999.

11 Molière, *Tartuffe*, Dover Thrift Editions, 2000.

12 Watzlawick, P. and Weakland, J., *The Interactional View*, W. W. Norton & Company, 1997.

13 Loach, K. (Dir.), *Family Life*, 1972.

14 Gounod, C., *Faustus* (opera), 1859.

15 Offenbach, J., *Orpheus in the Underworld* (opera), 1858.

16 Van Goethe, J. W., *Faust*, Oxford World's Classics, 2008.

17 De Coster, C., *The Legend of Ulenspiegel and Lamme Goedzac … in the Land of Flanders and Elsewhere*, CreateSpace, 2013.

18 Johnson, B., *The Devil Is an Ass*, Oxford University Press, 2000.

19 Freud, S., *Moses and Monotheism*, Vintage Books, 1955.

20 Lacan, J.,"Remarks on Psychic Causality," in *Écrits*, W. W. Norton & Company, 1966.

21 Von Bueltzingsloewen, I., *L'Hécatombe des fous*, Flammarion, 2007.

22 Bloch, M., *Strange Defeat*, Hopkins, G. (Trans.), Oxford University Press, 1949.

23 Bloch, M., *The Royal Touch*, Routledge, 2015.

24 O'Connor Drury, M., *The Danger of Words*, Routledge, 1973.

25 De Tocqueville, A., *Democracy in America*, Reeve, H. (Trans.), Nabu Press, 2010.

26 Musil, R., *The Man Without Qualities*, Alfred A. Knopf, 1995.

4   Seminar 11: 2007–2008
Robert Musil (1880–1942)
The birth certificate of phantoms

In *The Man Without Qualities*, Musil says of war that it "arises (like crime) from all those things that people ordinarily allow to dissipate in small irregularities."[1] Long before him, speaking of "the Serene Peaceful State of being a Fool among Knaves," in his Digression on Madness, Swift distinguishes the Folly praised by Erasmus[2] from perversion, just as Goethe opposes Narr – the Fool – to Tor – the Knave. The literary works we present draw attention to madness as it fights perversion, so as to incite thinking about events that have been falsified or erased.[3] The work of madness is to inscribe in the past memory cut out in the present.

In his book *In Search of Memory*,[4] biologist Eric Kandel grounds his search in trauma. His intellectual autobiography starts at the age of 9, when he had to flee from Vienna with his parents in 1938 and immigrate to the United States. He studied in Brooklyn and was interested, at first, in history, literature and psychoanalysis. At Harvard, he met Anna Kris, the daughter of psychoanalyst Ernst Kris (1900–1957), also born in Vienna and exiled in New York, whom Lacan had criticised for his presentation of a clinical case in which the patient eats "fresh brains" after his sessions.[5]

Well past the middle of his autobiography, Kandel opts for studying biology. At Columbia, he studies the brain "neuron by neuron." Looking for one that is large enough to examine under his microscope, he chooses the Aplysia, a sea slug whose quick reaction to danger and limited number of neurons allow him to observe how it remembers and how it forgets hammer blows to its tail. Kandel's research aimed at defining different types of memory: learning, declarative memory, long-term memory, and immediate memory with its disorders.

Kandel refers to the studies of Spanish histologist Santiago Ramón y Cajal (1852–1934), who recreated the observation of neurons from drawings – since painting had been one of his early passions. He felt that a freehand drawing of an observation provides a clearer image of a neuron than a photograph since the drawing shows living neurons. He had studied anatomy with his father, who taught it to him using bones dug up from a cemetery. Through drawing, he sought to infer the properties of living cells by using dead cells. We might ask if the situation is not reversed today, when we treat living neurons as if they were dead souls.

But this only succeeds in creating ghosts, and is what inspired the title of this year's seminar: "The Birth Certificate of Phantoms." Therapies aimed at undoing neurological connections encourage ghosts to come back from their dissociated time, whereas in all cultures ghosts aspire to die and be put to rest thanks to ceremonial rituals. They come back in the hope of never coming back, instead of being forced, along with those they haunt, to carry out an exhausting task.

Time as a political problem

We must stop regarding madness as something negative, since its purpose is positive, as August Comte, inventor of positivism, asserts. Based on the experience of his own "cerebral episode," he proposes "a subjective theory of the brain," considered as "an organ through which the dead act on the living."[6] According to him, the course of madness follows the upheavals of history, as shown by the works discussed in this seminar. They point to the coexistence in one and the same field of madness confined in asylums and madness that engenders a "political self,"[7] such as the king's jester in Shakespeare's plays, the Fool in Medieval theatre, and other literary fools, for whom Time is a political problem.[8]

The word "folly" does not always designate madness. It can also refer to small castles built on the outskirts of cities, or musical compositions for harpsichord and lute, such as the well-known theme of "Follies of Spain." The word comes from *follis*, "bellows," as well as "foliage." Adam de la Halle[9] wrote *Le Jeu de la feuillée* – *feuilles* means "leaves" in French – translated into English as *The Play of Madness*. One of our earliest musicals, it was performed in 1276 in Arras, in the province of Picardy. The title alludes to a leafy branch indicating the presence of a tavern where one can lose one's head, and also to a shed made of foliage, constructed for fairies during the feasts celebrated in May. The play also presents the raving madness of the *Dervé* – "the mad" in the language of Picardy – and that of the poet from Picardy who, under the name Adam, is just as crazy when he wishes to leave his good city of Arras for Paris. In reality, the author, Adam de la Halle, accompanied the Count of Artois to Naples, and died there in 1288.

The action of the play unfolds in the time-space of those "outside of time," and answers the call of fairies Morgane, Maglone and Arsile on June 3, after the pagan celebrations of the month of May. We have already encountered the call of beings from the beyond, like the ghost of Beloved in Toni Morrison's novel, like the dead conjured up by Bion, Pat Barker, Strindberg and Jean Cassou, like the millions of victims of the final solution making themselves heard in Hannah Arendt's *Eichmann in Jerusalem*. These writers, Freud tells us, are "valuable allies, for they are apt to know a whole host of things between heaven and earth,"[10] which our institutes of psychoanalysis have difficulty grasping.

Robert Musil also answers a call of this kind. Like Bion, he was decorated during World War I, which, he says, "came upon him like an illness." After being educated in military boarding schools, he became an engineer and then a writer, like Vasily Grossman. His first novel *The Confusions of Young Törless*, published in 1906, describes "budding dictators" who form small groups of torturers in classrooms. He also plays on the various meanings of the word "madness": that of the Fanatics in his play *The Enthusiasts* (*Die Schwärmer*)[11] and that of the assassin Moosbrugger and of Clarisse in *The Man Without Qualities*.

The title of the first chapter of the novel dispenses with the notion of causality at once: "From Which, Remarkably Enough, Nothing Develops." The first sentences of the book illustrate Ulrich's insistence on precision – he is a man of science like Musil, and will attest to it throughout the book:

> A barometric low hung over the Atlantic. It moved eastward toward a high-pressure area over Russia without as yet showing any inclination to bypass this high in a northerly direction. The isotherms and isotheres were functioning as they should. [...] It was a fine day in August 1913.

A year later, war broke out. The action of the novel takes place in this interval, in a country called Kakania, where the elite come together to organise a remarkable movement called the "Parallel Campaign," from which nothing developed.

In Chapter 2, entitled "Where Did the Man Without Qualities Live?" we learn that he has rented "a sort of little château," a small castle he is renovating with his father's money, since, as the title of the next chapter asserts, "Even a Man Without Qualities Has a Father with Qualities." A law professor, Ulrich's father is only revealed to the reader through letters his son does not answer. His last missive was a telegram that, "drafted [...] with meticulous care by his father himself, informed him [...] of his own death" (p. 714). One of the subjects his father debated with other jurists was whether or not dangerous madmen should be treated like animals.

This question is taken up directly in Chapter 18 through Moosbrugger, the character who savagely assassinated a prostitute in a delusional fit. At the psychiatric hospital where he is confined, he will be visited by Clarisse, who is quite crazy too. She is married to Walter, who plays the piano like mad. Both of them are childhood friends of Ulrich, who has not seen them for several years; when he goes to their house at the start of the novel, he finds them both at the piano, lost in a musical hypnosis, "faces flushed, bodies hunched, their heads jerked up and down while splayed claws banged away at the mass of sound [...]. Something unfathomable was going on: a balloon, wavering in outline as it filled up with hot emotion" (Chapter 14, p. 45). An astounding description of music lovers in Kakania.

Later the reader learns that Clarisse stubbornly refuses to have a child with Walter (Chapter 38, p. 155). She is the daughter of a famous painter who abused her sexually when she was an adolescent, as Freud was astounded to discover happens so often. If Musil had finished the book, she would have ended up in a Venetian psychiatric hospital, after the Viennese hospital where he had first sent her to explore the case of Moosbrugger, which was making headlines: "While [...] people of course sighed over such a monstrosity, they were [...] more deeply preoccupied with it than with their own life's work" (Chapter 18, p. 68).

This 34-year-old journeyman carpenter has been hospitalised several times before. But his kindness, his love of justice and his disarming smile had caused him to be "declared [...] normal just as often as [...] not accountable for his action." He had started out in life as an orphan shepherd, "and his poverty was such that he never dared speak to a girl" (p. 69). His case was debated by men of law, who regarded it as an instance of "diminished responsibility," and psychiatrists, "more timid professionally," who:

> certify as really insane only those persons they cannot cure – which is a modest exaggeration, since they cannot cure the others either. [...] These [are the] lesser patients whom the angel of medicine treats as sick people when they come to him in his private practice, but whom he shyly leaves to the angel of law when he encounters them in his forensic practice.
>
> (Chapter 60, p. 262)

The problem stems from their narrow-minded recourse to causality.

The probable man exhausts the sphere of the possible

The category of the possible is essential for Musil. It was already present in Pindar's *Third Ode*, addressed to Hieron of Syracuse on the occasion of the Python Games: "O my dear soul, *philia psycha*, do not crave immortal life, but exhaust the field of the possible."[12] The context is the birth of Asclepius, son of Apollo, and a mortal woman, Coronis. "In love with what was distant [like] many others [who] have felt that passion," she betrayed the god with a handsome stranger. Artemis avenged her brother using a sharp arrow, but when Coronis is placed on the funeral pyre, Apollo "snatched the child from the corpse" and took the future demigod of medicine to Chiron the Centaur, who taught him "to be a healer of the [...] maladies of men [with] gentle incantations, soothing potions [or] with surgery" (verses 50–55). This was the parentage of a line of physicians that includes Hippocrates, an Asclepiadean from the school of Kos.

As we all know, excess, *Ubris*, sets *Nemesis* in motion, to restore to men their fair share, *Nomos*. Asclepius too is subject to this law: "But even skill is enthralled by the love of gain. Gold shining in his hand turned even that man, for a handsome price, to bring back from death a man who was already caught" (verses 55–60). Zeus struck both of them dead. Hence the warning: "Do not crave immortal life, my soul, but exhaust the field of the possible."

To exhaust the field of the possible, Musil creates an experimental subject, meticulous and precise, a mathematician like him, whom his friend Walter has nicknamed "the man without qualities" (p. 58). But Ulrich is not disembodied. He is a trained athlete, a passionate and quite wealthy man, although he admits that he lives beyond his father's means. He is always busy thinking. Now he has decided to be, for a year, "a person who does nothing at all" and who "attaches no more importance to what is than to what is not," considering that "[to] pass freely through open doors, it is necessary to respect the fact that they have solid frames." Chapter 4 opens with this statement, followed by: "But if there is a sense of reality [...] then there must also be [...] a sense of possibility" (pp. 10–11).

This also applies to the analyst, who has to pass through the doors of transference in the treatment of madness and trauma, which, although they have long stood open, hang on to the solid frame of brain disease and psychotic structure, cemented to the foreclosure of the name-of-the-father. Does this place Ulrich in the position of the analyst? Why not? If we are to believe Musil:

> Such possibilities are said to inhabit a more delicate medium, a hazy medium of mist, fantasy, daydreams, and the subjunctive mood. Children who show this tendency are dealt with firmly and warned that such persons are cranks, dreamers, weaklings, know-it-alls, or trouble-makers. Such fools are also called idealists by those who wish to praise them. [...] But the possible includes not only the fantasies of people with weak nerves but also the as yet unawakened intentions of God.
>
> (p. 11)

Such children are often precocious analysts.

According to Bion, the analyst must enter the time-space of madness and trauma without desire and without memory. This is how Musil has Ulrich enter the year in suspense before the imminent catastrophe. After trying three roads that might lead to becoming "a great man" – the army, the engineering profession and research in mathematics (Chapters 9–11) – he finally gives up. But he is not altogether coherent in his decision-making:

> Today he is still far from being consistent. [...] it remains doubtful whether he would accept a slap in the face with [...] detachment ... The chances are that he would first hit back and then on reflection decide that he shouldn't have.

What Aby Warburg calls the seismograph of his soul detects the prodromes of a world war.

A chance event, his being aggressed one night by three hooligans who beat him up, leads to his encounter with a new mistress he nicknames Bonadea, for she helps him up and takes him home in her cab. At the same time, he realises that this "rage and scorn [are] a spontaneous materialization of free-floating hostility" (p. 21). He detects:

> this condition of vague atmospheric hostility with which the air of our era is charged, and when it suddenly comes to a head in the form of three strangers who lash out like thunder and lightning and then afterward vanish again forever, it is almost a relief.
>
> (Chapter 7, p. 22)

Chapter 7, entitled "In a Weak Moment Ulrich Acquires a New Mistress," is followed by a chapter describing the atmosphere in Kakania, a now "vanished [state] that [...] was, after all, a country for geniuses, which is probably what brought it to its ruin" (p. 31). "And in Kakania, at least, it would only happen that a genius would be regarded as a lout, but never was a mere lout taken – as happens elsewhere – for a genius" (p. 29). Still, there were constant cognitive dissonances: "In this country one acted [...] differently from the way one thought, or one thought differently from the way one acted" (p. 30).

These dissonances reflect what the title of Chapter 16 calls "A Mysterious Malady of the Times." How did it happen? Musil wonders:

> So what has been lost? Something imponderable. An omen. An illusion. As when a magnet releases iron filings and they fall in confusion again. As when a ball of string comes undone. [...] As when an orchestra begins to play out of tune ...

You could not identify anything in particular, but everything was a little warped (p. 56). This is what Ulrich's sabbatical allowed him to detect, with "a hint of aversion," in a resonance similar to that observed in psychotic transference.

Always the same story

Part II of the first volume is entitled "The Like of It Now Happens." The man without qualities had qualities, but was indifferent to them; he "consists of qualities without a man" (Chapter 39). At the end of the book, in Chapter 121, Ulrich refuses Paul Arnheim's proposition to join his business firm. This "man of consequence," a prestigious figure of the Parallel Campaign, is a German modelled after Walther Rathenau, industrialist, writer, politician, and a friend of Max Warburg, Aby's brother.

He was assassinated in 1922 by a far-right extremist group because he was a Jew. The future-in-the-past haunts the present of writing, in the roaring twenties which did not yet know that they were an interwar period.

In those years, "the malady of the times" was searching for a fool, to make itself heard. When he started his novel, in 1930, Musil was 50; he saw Hitler rise to power, along with the tormentors of Young Törless. He also heard the bombastic speeches, "reeking unbearably of humanitarianism," and the slogans of the fanatics, which made him think that "basically, the first thing to do is exclude the soul from all human relations where it doesn't belong." And what is the soul? "It is easy to define negatively: it is simply that which sneaks off at the mention of an algebraic series" (p. 106). This definition is radically opposed to the objectives of the Parallel Campaign, whose ultimate aim is "the union of soul and economics" (Chapter 26).

Ulrich receives a letter from his father suggesting that he contact a "great cousin," the muse of the Campaign. He does so after much hesitation, badgered by:

> all the well-meaning people who knew they were related [...] "There's a woman you must get to know." It was always said with that marked emphasis on the "you" intended to single out the person addressed as exceptionally well-placed to appreciate such a jewel, and which can be [...] a cloak for the conviction that he was just the sort of fool for such an acquaintance.
>
> (Chapter 22, "The Parallel Campaign, in the Form of an Influential Lady," p. 93)

The fool, *Narr*, that Goethe opposes to the *Tor*, collides with the anti-Semitic fanaticism Aby Warburg saw coming in his madness, and which Musil – in peril with his wife Martha, née Heimann, while he was writing the novel – embodies in the group, hostile to "the Jewish mind," to capitalism, to socialism, to rationalism, to parental authority, to psychology, and so on, which drives young Gerda, the daughter of Leon Fischel, to attack her father's Jewishness (Chapter 73).

Musil himself was treated with hostility in 1935, at the International Congress of Writers for the Defense of Culture, held in Paris at the Maison de la Mutualité, where he was the Austrian delegate – fearlessly. He had fled Berlin to return to Vienna, and by coming to Paris "he had not feared that this act of independence would attract the wrath of the Austrian government."

Edouard Roditi, who was present at the Congress, gives this account:

> He was shouted down for having dared to associate communism with fascism, and enraged the audience even more when he defended the freedom of opinion of artists and writers, who must not expect "any assistance from the State, which, whatever its political form, has

recourse to culture only as a weapon that it uses to achieve its own mysterious ends."

Roditi adds that he was barely allowed to finish his address, because on top of what he was saying, this troublemaker didn't fit in: he had a sporty look – like Ulrich – he was too well dressed, he stood out in "this caricature of the Parallel Campaign, in other words, the caricature of a caricature."[13] Two years later, in Vienna, Musil gave a lecture entitled "On Stupidity."[14]

Musil was inspired by the well-known figure of the Fool – *Narr* – who confronts the Knave – *Tor* – when he wrote Chapter 28, entitled "A Chapter That Can Be Skipped by Anyone Who Has No Very High Opinion of Thinking as an Occupation." In this chapter, which Bion surely did not skip, we encounter his "thoughts without a thinker in search of someone to think them." Ulrich has the following thought:

> one can quite distinctly perceive in oneself a faintly nonplussed feeling that one's thoughts have created themselves instead of waiting for their originator. This nonplussed feeling refers to something that many people nowadays call intuition [...] and they think they must see something supra-personal in it; but it is only something non-personal, namely the affinity and kinship of the things themselves that meet inside one's head.
>
> (p. 116)

When he joins the Parallel Campaign at his cousin's incitation, Ulrich has the impression of being in a pasteboard world, the world of "shadows of fleetingly-improved men" that Judge Schreber saw in his delusions. Madness does not denounce, but shows that the mysterious malady of the times is, in fact, stupidity. Ulrich observes:

> So the times had changed, like a day that begins radiantly blue and then by degrees clouds over, without having the kindness to wait for Ulrich. He evened the score by holding the cause of these mysterious changes that made up the disease eating away genius to be simple, common stupidity.
>
> (Chapter 16, pp. 56–57)

This phrase that Musil repeated at the start of his lecture can be borrowed by all those who try to unmask appearances, revealing the ambient stupidity.

Psychotic transference

Musil's language is precise. "The precise man" records things we are in the habit of not seeing, and makes them visible – like the war that no one sees coming. Musil relies only minimally on imagination; instead, he takes the rigor of his reflection all the way to the sensitive chord he touched just before his death in 1942, as we will read later.

When he receives a telegram announcing his father's death, Ulrich travels to the family mansion where he meets his sister Agathe, whom he has not seen since they were children. After changing out of his travelling clothes, he finds her dressed like him, in a "loose lounging suit of soft wool [...] almost a Pierrot costume" (Book 2, Chapter 1, p. 734). They enter the room where the body of their father lay. A strangely intimate love is born between them, almost ghostlike. It brings to mind Musil's older sister Elsa, who died in infancy four years before he was born in 1880. In his *Diaries*, he admits that she "fascinates" him: "In truth, fascination is not the word; this sister interested me. I asked myself how things would be had she lived, if she would be the one I felt closest to. Would I put myself in her place?"[15]

From the start of the first volume, a ghostly presence is felt, a strange "impression," embodied in Chapter 18 by a sensational news item. The murder of a prostitute by Moosbrugger fascinates Clarisse. Ulrich thinks:

> How shall we translate [this]? [...] It is playacting, but like all playact-
> ing it tries to say something, of course [...]. Imagine, if you will, what
> it is to have a heavy world weighing on tongue, hands, and eyes [...]
> and inside nothing but an unstable, shifting mist; what a joy it must be
> whenever someone brings out a slogan in which one thinks one can rec-
> ognize oneself. What is more natural than that every person of intense
> feeling get hold of this new form before the common run of people
> does? It offers that moment of self-realization, of balance between inner
> and outer, between being crushed and exploding.
> (Chapter 34, "A Hot Flash and Chilled Walls," pp. 137–138)

The murdered woman haunts Clarisse's delusions like a ghost.

Moosbrugger rejects the term "sex crime" to qualify his deed, because of his aversion for women, whom he considers unfathomable. He analyses the moment when "thoughts are things and things are thoughts" that come to taunt him. Has he tried to change them into signifiers by taking literally Lacan's formula: "the signifier is the murder of the thing"?[16] This is what he asks himself in Chapter 59, entitled "Moosbrugger Reflects":

> When he was feeling on top of things, Moosbrugger paid no attention
> at all to his voices and visions but spent his time in thinking because he
> had always been impressed with the word. He thought better than other
> people because he thought both inside and outside. Thinking went on
> inside him against his will. He said that thoughts were planted in him.
> (p. 258)

Psychiatrists show no interest in the richness of the words he uses, which are borrowed from local dialects. And they are even less interested in the words that, for him, are not inscribed in a signifying chain, and which pounce on him threateningly:

> It had happened that he said to a girl, "Your sweet rose lips," *Rosen-lippe*, but suddenly the words gave way at their seams and something upsetting happened: her face went gray, like earth veiled in a mist, there was a rose sticking out of it on a long stem, and the temptation to take a knife and cut it off, or punch it back into the face, was overwhelming. Of course, Moosbrugger did not always go for his knife; he only did that when he couldn't get rid of the temptation any other way.
>
> (p. 259)

In Chapter 87, "Moosbrugger Dances," he dances on the brink of his execution, which doesn't matter to him: "He was daydreaming like a youngster: a man they had locked up so often he never grew older" (p. 427). According to the Vedas,[17] a sacrifice is required to come out of confusion, but such a rite occurs in a symbolic context, while Moosbrugger is desperately alone.

Clarisse cannot grow older either. She has been dancing this dance since the night her father came into her room, and now she is intent on saving Moosbrugger. In the *Posthumous Papers* – the sketches for the novel at the end of Volume II, she does everything in her power – even risking her sanity, and persuades Ulrich to use his influence to bring this about. In these *Papers*, Ulrich was named *Anders*, the Other, the name Hannah Arendt's first husband adopted. When the psychiatrist at the hospital where Moosbrugger is confined asks Clarisse, in a joking tone, when she comes to see the murderer: "My dear lady, of what concern is [this] to you?" (II, p. 1639), she answers: "Perhaps the patient is here because he is standing in for someone else" (II, p. 1634). The "someone else" is a murdered youth: Moosebrugger, the prostitute or herself when she was raped by her father, an event that she describes to Ulrich with the precision characteristic of traumatic memory, in Chapter 70, entitled "Clarisse Visits Ulrich to Tell Him a Story" (p. 314).

Musil could have condensed the action into twenty pages: Moosbrugger is executed, Clarisse goes mad, street riots cause the disintegration of the Parallel Campaign, and World War I breaks out. Why did he need nearly 2,000 endless pages? He wants to lead the reader not to the end of a story, but to dissolution – *Los* in German, *luô* in Greek – called *déliaison* by Pierre Janet. When there is no end to cognitive dissonances that annul the truth and betray intelligence, words fall apart, for Clarisse as well.

The segments concerning Clarisse's madness are in Volume II of the book, the portion published posthumously. In sketches written at different times, the mission she has taken on is transferred to her alter ego, *Andres*.

She doesn't want to save the world, but rather liberate it, redeem it – *Erlösung* means redemption – by means of words freed from their usual meaning. In an early sketch, she has left for Italy and is staying on the Island of Health, where Ulrich is summoned to join her: "One does not gather up one's insights [...] when like her one is growing into ever-new catastrophes. [...] Clarisse began to express her life in poems." She wanted to:

> free words from their grammatical bonds. She gave Ulrich three words and asked him to read them in any order he chose. [...] Clarisse called this the chemistry of words. [...] She worked with exclamation points or underlining. God!! red!!! goes! [...] This placed in Clarisse's hands the responsibility for a monstrous irresponsibility. [...] But Clarisse's decline progressed more rapidly than Ulrich could follow.
>
> (II, pp. 1564–1565)

These unpublished chapters show that Musil was familiar with psychotic transference: it is a crazy, ageless girl who theorises that which takes place on the brink of catastrophe. In her uncertainty, Clarisse forces Ulrich to enter her delirium, so as to create a social link when everything is dissolving. The urgent need to destroy dissonances in order to create words woven into a reliable chain of signifiers leads, here too, to the murder of the things, which Moosbrugger has taken literally. Clarisse asks Ulrich "to go into the pond with her and kill himself. [...] This was a little too much" (p. 1566). Indeed, in the Vedas, the Hymns on Sacrifice recognise the need to offer up one's own person, and discard it at the same time, since one will not be there to reap the benefits of the sacrifice. That is why a substitute[18] is required, but Clarisse does not find one.

One of the early sketches describes Clarisse's hospitalisation in Venice. When a strange man trapped her in a gondola:

> Clarisse suspected the trap being set for her [...]. But this suspicion had no value for her, no causal valency. [...] It's unreasonable for me to go along. But my madness is merely that I fall out of their general order and my causality isn't theirs. [...] When they entered the building, she divided the rest of her jewelry [...] among the matrons, who accepted them, seized her, and strapped her to a bed. Clarisse began to cry, and the matrons said *"poveretta!"*
>
> ("The Island of Health – Uncertainty," p. 1577)

Hölderlin's Diotima

Musil writes that "Clarisse crystallizes elements of her era" that ordinary causality does not perceive. In the meantime, the Parallel Campaign is becoming bogged down in speeches exhorting the masses to express their discontents, preferably nonsense. Its first objective, on the initiative of His Highness Count Leinsdorf, "who never rises so high as when he does not know where he is going," had been to celebrate, in 1918, the seventy-year jubilee of the reign of Franz Joseph, in order to outdo the thirty-year jubilee of the German Emperor, planned for 1914. To that purpose, brilliant minds come together at the salon of Ulrich's cousin, whom he has nicknamed Diotima, "in reality [...] Ermelinda [...] and in truth [...] just plain Hermine" (p. 93), wife of Vice-Consul Tuzzi in the Ministry of Foreign Affairs, "who looked like a leather steamer trunk with two dark eyes" (p. 104).

Her alias reminds the reader of Diotima in Plato's *Symposium*,[19] "the stranger of Mantinea" invoked by Socrates when he is asked to speak about love. A prophetess, she postponed by ten years the outbreak of the plague in Athens – though the disease did not spare Pericles. It is through Diotima that Socrates informs us about the birth of transference in a context of trauma and madness: Eros is the son of *Poros*, passage or porosity, and of *Penia*, scarcity or poverty – that of the traumatised men whom Socrates, a veteran of the Peloponnesian War, attended to on the battlefield, thanks to his porosity. Their general, Alcibiades, testifies to this definition of transference in such cases, when he arrives completely drunk at the end of the Banquet. He saw Socrates, from atop his horse, looking after his companions, and fell madly in love with him after the latter attended to his physical and psychological wounds. Much to his dismay, Socrates did not give in to his repeated advances. He was not a therapist willing to sleep with his patients.

Diotima appears again in Friedrich Hölderlin's novel *Hyperion*,[20] as a woman with whom he had been madly in love. Hölderlin was born in a little Swabian town in1770. He lost his father when he was 2, and his stepfather when he was 9. Four of his younger sisters also died during his childhood. He studied to become a parson but his faith was insufficient, so he became a private tutor. In 1796, he was hired by a Frankfurt banker of Huguenot descent, and fell madly in love with his wife, Susette Gontard. This forced him to leave his position in 1798, but he kept writing to Susette and meeting her secretly until 1800, when he saw her for the last time.

This period was marked by intense literary activity, starting with the novel *Hyperion*, published in 1797. In the novel, Susette becomes Diotima. In January 1802, Hölderlin is hired as a tutor by the Hamburg consul in Bordeaux. There, he learns that Susette is gravely ill. In May, he leaves the city in a state of frenzy, and sets out across France on foot to join her. When he arrives in Stuttgart, he learns that she has died. Forcibly admitted to a Tübingen clinic in 1806, he spent the last thirty years of his life in the house of a Tübingen carpenter, continuing to write poems until his death in 1843.

Hölderlin's hero Hyperion is a Greek of the eighteenth century, inspired by the French Revolution to take up arms against the Turks to free Greece – as Byron would do later. (Byron died during the Siege of Missolonghi in 1824.) Hyperion befriends Alabranda, a revolutionary who draws him into combat, and he falls in love with Diotima, but leaves her to return to armed combat. After being wounded at Mistras, the ancient Sparta, and becoming sickened by looting and massacres, he decides to return to Diotima, but learns that she is dead – the situation that would play out in Hölderlin's life five years after the publication of the novel.

The Diotima who animates the Parallel Campaign in Volume I of *The Man Without Qualities* is given this pseudonym by Ulrich jokingly: "[As] a classical beauty on the plump side, [she] corresponded to [the] Hellenic ideal of beauty, with a bit more flesh on her [...] to soften those strict classical lines" (p. 112). In a peremptory tone, she asserts without hesitation: "I like the company of women. They don't know anything and are unfragmented" (p. 112). In Volume II, the meeting between spiritual twins Ulrich and Agathe introduces another dimension. This meeting is no doubt based on the Greek myth of Hyperion, who married his sister Theia, with whom he had three children: the Sun, the Moon and the Dawn.

Breaths of a summer day

Book 2 of *The Man Without Qualities* is not an adjunct to Book 1. Far from the furore of the Parallel Campaign, it opens the doors of time to a bucolic poem. In that passage, *poros*, a little girl appears:

> he remembered a detail from his childhood. [...] It was the little girl who had only two qualities: one, that she had to belong to him, and the other, the fights with other boys this got him into. And of these two things only the fights were real, because there was no little girl. Strange time, when he used to go out like a knight errant to leap at some boy's throat, preferably when the boy was bigger than he [...] and wrestle with the surprised enemy! He had collected quite a few beatings ...
>
> (II, Chapter 3, "Start of a New Day in a House of Mourning,"
> pp. 748–749)

On the brink of the two wars, joined together in a fold of time, the reference to Dulcinea is clear. A feminine agency emerges when the law of men collapses, unheeded. She belongs to Ulrich like Diotina to Hölderlin, and to Musil his little sister dead before his birth. For Cervantes, Dulcinea is literature, which inspired Musil to write, just before he died in Geneva on April 15, 1942, impoverished and forsaken, a new version of a fragment that marks the completion of his novel:

A noiseless stream of weightless drifting blossoms, emanating from a group of trees whose flowering was done, drifted through the sunshine, and the breath that bore it was so gentle that not a leaf stirred. [...] Spring and fall, speech and nature's silence, life and death, mingled in this picture. Hearts seemed to stop, to have been removed from their breasts, in order to join this silent procession through the air. "My heart was taken from out my breast." [...] Time stood still, a thousand years weighed as lightly as the opening and closing of an eye. [...] But if [...] you attain the highest selflessness, then finally outer and inner will touch each other as if a wedge that had split the world had popped out!

(II, pp. 1382–1387)

In the folds of time, the wedge that separates tears from laughter can also pop out, as we will see in the next seminar on François Rabelais and Yvette Guilbert.

Notes

1 Musil, R., *The Man Without Qualities*, Wilkins, S. (Trans.), Alfred A. Knopf, 1995, p. 1756.
2 Erasmus, D., *Praise of Folly*, Aeterna Press, 2015.
3 Arendt, H., *Thinking Without a Banister: Essays in Understanding, 1953–1975*, Schocken Books, 2018.
4 Kandel, E., *In Search of Memory*, W. W. Norton & Comoany, 2006.
5 Lacan, J., "Response to Jean Hyppolite's Commentary on Freud's *Verneinung*," in *Écrits: A Selection*, Fink, B. (Trans.) W.W. Norton, 2007.
6 Arbousse-Bastide, P., "Auguste Compte et la folie," in *Les Sciences de la folie*, Mouton, 1972, p. 68.
7 Tweedy, R. (Ed.), *The Political Self*, Karnac Books, 2017.
8 Davoine F., *Mother Folly: A Tale*, Stanford University Press, 2014.
9 De la Halle, A., *The Play of Madness*, Mermier, G. R. (Trans.), Peter Lang Publishing, 1997.
10 Freud, S., *Delusions and Dreams in Jensen's Gradiva*, S.E. 9, Hogarth Press, 1907.
11 Musil, R., *The Confusions of Young Törless*, Penguin Classics, 2001; *The Enthusiasts*, PAJ Publications, 1983.
12 Pindar, *Olympian Odes. Pythian Odes*, Race, W. H. (Ed., Trans.), Harvard University Press, 1997, verses 21–62.
13 Roditi, E., "A Glimpse of Robert Musil," *BOMB Magazine*, winter, 1986.
14 Musil, R., *Precision and Soul: Essays and Addresses*, University of Chicago Press, 1995.
15 Musil, R., *The Musil Diaries 1899–1941*, Mirsky, M. (Ed.), Basic Books, 1998.
16 Lacan, J., "The Function and Field of Speech and Language in Psychoanalysis," in *Écrits: A Selection*, Fink, B. (Trans.), W. W. Norton & Company, 2007.
17 Malamoud, C., *Cooking the World: Ritual and Thought in Ancient India*, Oxford University Press, 2000.
18 Malamoud, C., *Cooking the World*, op. cit.
19 Plato, *Symposium*, CreateSpace, 2013.
20 Hölderlin, F., *Hyperion*, Archipelago, 2008.

5   Seminar 12: 2009–2010 François Rabelais (1483–1553) and Yvette Guilbert (1865–1944)

Mirroring madness

We are used to saying that madness is at once the symptom showing what cannot be said, and the research tool needed by erased elements in catastrophic zones, which strive to find inscription. Hence the paradoxical nature of our practice: these elements may be known in the official history, without being part of the transmission. Bion warns that the analyst must remain wary of the "everyone knows that" attitude. Of course everyone knows, but if "that" is not validated by another, the subject of that historical truth cannot emerge. On "that" point, it is identified with the event whose inscription can only occur through the interference of transference. This year, the books I propose for our research are *The Fourth Book* by François Rabelais[1] and *The Song of My Life* by Yvette Guilbert.[2]

Yvette Guilbert

We have all seen her portrait painted by Toulouse Lautrec, wearing a green evening gown and long black gloves. In her autobiography, she describes the poverty of her childhood, which resembles a Zola novel or a Maupassant short story. Both these writers were her admirers as well as examples in her "search for truth," undertaken after the 1870 Franco-Prussian War. She remembers: "From the earliest of my memories [...] I see only pictures of wretched poverty." Her mother comes from a middle-class family in the North of France, and her father is the son of Normandy farmers. He is a carouser and a gambler, forces his wife to earn an income for the family, ends up leaving her, and dies in 1884. But he has passed on to his daughter a taste for Offenbach's tunes, and for the singing cafés – *cafés concerts* or *caf-concs*, very popular at that time – where he took his mistresses.[3]

During a four-year period when the family enjoyed unexpected prosperity thanks to an innovation of her mother's in the making of hats, her workshop was flooded with orders and Yvette could be given an education in a boarding school. But after this flourishing period, poverty returned. "*Petit trottin*" (young girl scurrying to bring dresses and hats to wealthy ladies) – she criss-crossed the streets of Montmartre, Clichy and Ménilmontant to deliver the garments sown by her mother. From the time she was 12, she says: "I earned my bread." After her mother sent away the workers in her atelier, "we used to get up at seven [...] and worked on till eleven at night, to earn five francs a day between the two us."

When she became a seamstress herself, she discovered "the meanness of certain rich women when they get a chance of sweating a penniless seamstress." When she was 16, she became a salesgirl at Printemps, the first Parisian department store. Since then, she writes:

> I have always kept a special fondness for all those who sew. I love them. It is to the Parisian working girl that I owe the root of my talent, for it is from her that I learned life, the lot of poor girls who have no one to protect them.

Yvette and her mother often suffered from cold and hunger. Still, Yvette could count on her mother's integrity and unfailing support: "By the time I was eighteen, I had learned of every masculine trick, of every trap laid by men. Although my body remained pure, I felt my soul in danger and my mind soiled."

Two men encountered by chance are responsible for the new direction her life was to take. First, Charles Zidler, who would later open the Moulin Rouge. He spoke to her on the street, offering to hire her. Her mother did not agree, but Zidler sent them theatre tickets and her mother gave her permission to go with a friend. When they attended the performance, a theatre critic sitting beside them noticed the pertinence of Yvette's comments and suggested that she should take acting lessons. This time her mother said yes. She learned the profession by performing in boulevard theatres, grew tired of the intrigues that went on, and decided to try being a singer. She asked Zidler for advice and he encouraged her again: "You might as well starve doing something amusing." Her first performances were catastrophic. In Lyon, she was shouted off the stage by audiences that chanted "Where's her bubs?" to a simple beat.

But she persisted: "I knew I was *more intelligent* than they, and I could become anything I chose. Yes [...]. It was my intelligence that came to my rescue every time and pieced together my broken courage." She knew she was "not pretty" and didn't have the right look for the times: "Tall, thin, flat, with a long, slender neck, a big turned-up nose, a large mouth with thin lips." At the Eden concert hall where she made her debut, she was nicknamed "the funny telescopic lady." She worked on her repertoire, she composed *"La Pocharde"* ("The Drunk Woman"), and on the banks of the Seine, at a bookstall, she came upon a little leaflet of songs that included *"Le Fiacre"* ("The Carriage") and *"L'Hôtel du Numéro 3"* ("The Hotel at Number 3") – which she later sang – written by Xantof, whose real name was Léon Fourneau, but Russians were in fashion then. She "created a *silhouette* contrasting with everything that had been done before: that of 'the red-haired lady dressed in green satin with long black gloves.'" She was well read and endowed her satire of the belle époque with its prestigious ancestry:

> Ah! Juvenal! Little did you guess that in the music-hall [. . .] you would live again in me and that my black gloves were made of the same stuff as the thongs of your famous whip! Ah, what should I have done without the perverts of my time?

In 1889, she was singing at the Eldorado, where Madame Charcot sent her husband to entertain a newly arrived Viennese student. The young Sigmund Freud fell in love with a Renaissance song by Eustache Deschamps (1340–1404), *"Dites-moi que je suis belle"* ("Tell Me I'm Beautiful"), and with the singer, with whom he kept up a correspondence that lasted until his death in London 1939. In 1890, Zidler hired her to perform at the Moulin Rouge, where she shared the spotlight with La Goulue, the famous can-can dancer, and "Valentin the Boneless," famous for his rubbery limbs. Two years later, her concerts in Liège and Brussels were an enormous success. Zidler predicted she would now embark on an international career, which in fact came into being as early as 1893 in Europe, and then in the United States, where she would travel regularly. There, she met Max Schiller, a German Jew whose Romanian parents had fled to Berlin to escape anti-Semitism. She married him in 1897.

Admired by Alphonse Allais, Pierre Loti, Francis Jammes, François Coppée, Pierre Louÿs, Victorien Sardou and many others, one day she was summoned by Charles Gounod, who asked her to sing the "King of Thule" aria. He then seized her arm and told her firmly: "I forbid you ever to take a singing lesson – no professor whatsoever." And when she objected, he added:

> No, no! Somebody would "manufacture" you a voice, a register, and you could never get out of it. As you are now you have every voice, without having one at all; on the contrary, go on speaking in song as you are doing – that spoken song is your "marvel."

For her, he set to music Jean Richepin's cruel and poignant poem *"La glu"* ("The Trap"). Another triumphant tour of the United States followed. But now disaster befell her.

In 1899, her career was suddenly interrupted when she had a kidney removed at home, developed septicaemia and needed other surgeries that forced her to leave the stage for six years. She described this period as "six years of martyrdom," during which she expanded her repertoire to include medieval songs. She was fed up with audiences that "saw only impropriety" in her songs, "while I meant them as a bitter attack against the matrimonial farce, the Parisian *ménage à trois*" that brought fame to playwright

Feydeau. She confessed having been afraid to sing *"Le p'tit cochon"* ("The Little Pig"). Like Bion when "he was about to go into action in a session," she was afraid, since this song was "a slap in the face to thousands of my listeners."

She had to negotiate with censors. The Police Prefecture authorised her song *"Les vierges"* ("The Virgins") after the refrain was replaced by meaningful coughing that greatly amused the audience. At the centre of her repertoire were the young girls left out in the street and driven mad – Charcot's hysterics. And she deplored the fact that "a type of humour considered clever by a certain audience filled the public with dismay in the music hall."

This "certain audience" hears the singer's revolt against the humiliation of women by "forbidden love," the humiliation of the drunkard, of the morphine addict, and of all the women haunted by "The macabre dance of the fetuses" aborted in secret – a song composed by a song writer "who delighted audiences at the Chat Noir," a famous cabaret in Montmartre. At the café-concert, this song brought her "an aborted kind of applause, of course." Despite attempts to trivialise the matter: "Adultery is a well-established custom; people have got accustomed to it [...] the women clapped with the palms of their gloved hands hollowed – the men went ahead, they had nothing to fear – and the girls instinctively held themselves in."

During her convalescence, her "second career" started with research on French *chanson*, with the help of experts on medieval history such as Gaston Paris and Joseph Bédier, "who became beacons to light the blind, such as myself." She learned Latin "to give the lines rhythm in accordance with the original stresses," and once she had recovered, she wrote "this cry from my heart" entitled "In Truth I Tell You." This long poem is a manifesto: "Never be discouraged, never be discouraged at having to learn." For her, time was set in motion again, its rhythm covering two pages that end with the lines:

> There is a time for everything ...
> A time when we are disgusted with the present
> A time that says: How about the past?
> A time that is silent and brings us the dread of Time
> And a time that commands: Work! Work!! Work!!!
> And that is the good time.

Between 1900 and 1927, she "assembled her tools with care and patience": 60,000 songs from the period between the eleventh and nineteenth centuries, as well as medieval songs and Mysteries, which made up her second repertory.

She refused to be called a singer, preferring to call herself *diseuse fin de siècle*, an end-of-century *diseuse* (teller) with no illusions about her vocal capacities: "As for my voice – my singing voice – I have none, and yet I can express everything I intend." Especially "the monster," which in theatrical jargon means "the subject" – *monstrer* in Old French, meaning "to show" – such as a very old Eros, only twenty but used-up, jaded, gone haywire, loveless," portrayed in the song "*Eros vanné*" – which means both "tired" and "mocked." She wishes to augment language thanks to "a new style, an art of knowing how to say everything [...] without offence. [...] My skill in enunciating my syllables gave a completeness to my words with a clear-cut richness of colouring" (p. 178).

Since she was replacing her first repertoire with "the great and beautiful literature of the *chanson*," she was quite willing to leave her old style behind:

> It was on the shoulders of this notoriety, with the flavour of Rabelais and the bitterness of Zola that I was able to hang the Court train of my second effort, dedicated to "the science of a beautiful diction" which must be augmented by the capacity to light up or diminish words [...] to enlarge them or lessen them, to prolong them or to shorten them.

Her models are now "certain poets of the Middle Ages whose strange modernity so astonishing at times" makes her say: "Some mysterious power [...] impelled me towards them that I might learn the source of the satire of the Chat Noir of my early days" (p. 192). The reference to the Theatre of Fools is clear, this theatre that made fun of "politics with its puppets, its kings [...] its army leaders, its clerics [...] its favourites" (p. 194). "What treasures I have read! What strength there was in our primitive tongue; what power of suggestion in the truculent speech" (p. 192).

Jugglers are the ancestors of Offenbach and of the Chat Noir cabaret where Debussy and Eric Satie accompanied Aristide Bruant on the piano. One day, she shyly asked him if she could sing his songs. He answered: "Good heavens! With your talent and a heart that bleeds – go ahead, my dear." And she did. Her goal was not to teach a lesson to the gentlemen who laughed heartily before going off to meet their dancing girls, but rather to chronicle the sound of the century, amplified by that of centuries past. Her mission was to transmit the knowledge accumulated in language, passed down through the mouths of those ancestors, and now through hers.

After her convalescence, she went on another tour of the United States and Europe, as far as Constantinople. In 1915, she had to go into exile in New York with her husband, after she had been called "Frau Schiller, the *Boche*'s ally." There, she sang her new repertoire of medieval songs, met disciples of French medievalists and returned to Paris in 1922. Between the two world wars, Musil heard her in Brussels and remarked that "by not attempting to hide her age and by performing songs from different eras, she has not lost the richness of her youth," when as a *diseuse* – fearless – she used to tell her audience of old gentlemen what she thought of them. He saw her still strong fighting spirit as "a call to combat the insolent defenders of vice, by using her power to shock and the force of her aspirations."[4]

"To you, my very dear Freud, my true and loyal friendship"[5]

This is how Yvette Guilbert ended her letter dated March 14, 1931, in which she argued with her dear Professor Freud about the subject that concerns us. He never missed any of her concerts in Vienna, and kept her autographed photograph on his desk, where it can still be seen, at 19 Berggasse.

She wrote this letter in reply to Freud's letter dated March 8, 1931, in which he objected to her definition of her art:

> the obliteration of one's own person and its replacement by an imagined one has never quite satisfied me. It tells us so little, doesn't inform us how it is brought about, and above all it fails to explain why one person should succeed so much better than another in achieving what every artist allegedly wants.

The Freudian explanation invokes "repressed desires and traits that haven't had a chance to develop." As a result, "parts of [one's own person] are employed to represent the chosen character, and in this way find expression." When her husband, whom Freud calls "Uncle Max," translated the letter for her, its content ruffled her feathers.

We agree with her disagreement, as it brings to mind two paradigms of psychoanalysis: the one Freud adopted after abandoning his "Neurotica" – the psychoanalysis of trauma – and his own discussion in the *Gradiva*, *The Uncanny* and *Moses*, of an unconscious that is not repressed, but is connected to historical truth. By showing clearly in her performances "the banality of evil," Yvette Guilbert is the "passionate witness" Dori Laub refers to, about whom Hannah Arendt says that although "not wounded in his flesh," she can express everything through her tragic or comic style, from her position as a "horrified other."

Yvette Guilbert does not deny the traumatic sources of her experience: "My personal knowledge is that of all human beings who have experienced poverty, love, illness and all the other struggles against these dangers." But she does not agree with the notion of "traits that haven't had a chance to develop [as] repressed desires." She opposes the idea vigorously: "No, I don't think that what I express on the stage is a 'repressed' surplus."

She insists on making a clear distinction between her "I" and the "seismograph of her soul," the term coined by Aby Warburg, their contemporary, which imprints forms – *pathos formel* – expressed by the artist: "I could be the tsarina or Saint Francis of Assisi, when a text is given to me." And she declares again: "Embodying these characters requires before all else that I abandon my personality." Diderot's *The Paradox of the Actor*[6] agrees with her point of view:

> It's through the eyes that we learn most about the life of others. My eye is my great revealer. I see – I think – I conclude everything very quickly ... I don't have all the virtues or all the vices, but my sensibility, my painter's eye, help me to guess everything I don't know and to reveal everything I know.

She insists on her "physical" impressions and on "her habit of transferring" from the brain to the body everything she "shows" her audience. She shows "the monster" – "the subject" in theatre slang – to her public. Her phrase: "I see, I think, I conclude" also brings to mind Bion's "thoughts without a thinker," which find in the *diseuse* a thinker to think them. She might also have been taking Freud to task for abandoning his "Neurotica," when he turned away from the analysis of trauma in October 1897.[7]

In *Studies on Hysteria*, published with Josef Breuer in 1895,[8] a personal comment of Freud's regarding the case of Miss Lucy, who had olfactory hallucinations, is strangely similar to what his irreverent friend maintains. In a footnote, he wrote:

> I have had a very remarkable experience [...] which is still clearly before me. [...] I saw something which did not fit in at all with my expect-ation. [...] nor was I aware of my feelings of repulsion, which must [...] have been responsible for this perception producing no psychical effect. I was afflicted by that blindness of the seeing eye which is so astonish-ing in the attitude of mothers to their daughters, husbands to their wives and rulers to their favourites.

We might add the blindness of sons to their fathers, given Freud's admission in a letter to Fliess written on February 11, 1897: "Unfortunately, my own father was one of these perverts, and is responsible for the hysteria of my brother and those of several younger sisters."

Yvette Guilbert did not suffer from this blindness of the seeing eye when it came to her own father, whose compulsive gambling and addiction to mistresses constrained his wife and daughter to poverty. But she firmly refused Freud's interpretation involving repressed sexual fantasies:

> My soul (what I believe to be my soul) drives me to want to "be beauti-ful"; is it pride? I cultivate this in myself and I always strive to keep common human baseness out of "this soul." I have never had vices – I have lacked courage and had weaknesses. [...] On the stage I show myself divested of all falsehood. But that's not because these things are "repressed," no! no! They were never part of me. On the stage I become

what I want to become through the power of mental will. [...] Artists are very malleable ... I think it is what we have not yet been that helps us, in our art, to become it for our public. [...] Our frenzy comes from rage at seeing lies everywhere. This is what I struggled for all my life: the truth, I longed only for the truth – and the only truth I found here and there didn't last long.

The question of "historical truth" at the end of *Moses and Monotheism*[9] impels "old Freud," ill and exhausted – as he describes himself in a letter at the end of 1937 – to create "something new." He makes three attempts to write his *Moses* – in Vienna and then in London – unable "to efface the traces of the unusual way in which this book came to be written" and which returns "like an unlaid ghost." In 1938, when totalitarian regimes have gained favour, Yvette Guilbert writes to Freud, who is stopping in Paris on his way to London, telling him to "thank heaven" for having brought into his life "this admirable friend" – Marie Bonaparte – "who was able to soften the horrible truth of this barbaric adventure." On June 10, 1938, Freud answers her letter, saying: "Our beautiful Vienna is no more."

To "fight the danger" of the erasure of traces, both of them find "a new, unprecedented mode of expression" for the benefit of an audience that might consist of a single person, as Freud writes in his prefatory note to *Moses and Monotheism*, written in Vienna before March 1938:

> progress has concluded an alliance with barbarism [here and] in Soviet Russia. [...] So I shall not publish this essay. [...] Thus it may lie hid until the time comes when it may safely venture into the light of day, or until someone else who reaches the same opinions and conclusions can be told: "In darker days there lived a man who thought as you did."
>
> (p. 92)

This other whom madness looks for, driven by "rage at seeing lies everywhere," as Yvette Guilbert put it, was embodied by the author of *The Very Horrific Life of Great Gargantua, Father of Pantagruel.*[10]

Rabelais: "Better to write of laughter than of tears"[11]

Fools are recognisable by their babble and the mirror they hold up to the curious as well as to the indifferent, who don't care and whom they awaken from their apathy.

Pantagruel's fool, "whom he loved all his lifetime," is Panurge, "A cozener, drinker, roister, rover, and a very [...] debauched fellow, if there were any in Paris; otherwise [...] the best and most virtuous man in the world." In *The Third Book*, he has taken it into his head that he should marry, but he is afraid of being cuckolded, of falling prey to Yvette Guilbert's "Madame Arthur" with her "*je ne sais quoi*, indescribable something," which attracts a "multitude of lovers." In Chapter 9, Panurge asks Pantagruel for advice, and the latter encourages him: "Then marry, in the name of God." – "But, says Panurge, if my wife should make me a cuckold [...]. That is for me of a too sore prickling point." – "Then do not marry, quoth Pantagruel." In this exchange, with its quick back and forth, the rhythm is set by "contradictory iterations, the one part destroying the other" (Chapter 10). Having run out of arguments, the giant questions Panurge about his desire:

> Are not you assured within yourself of what you have a mind to? The chief and main point of the whole matter lies there. All the rest is merely casual, and totally dependeth upon the fatal disposition of the heavens.

Exasperated, Pantagruel suggests the "royal road to the unconscious."[12] But in Chapter 14, entitled "Panurge's Dream with the Interpretation Thereof," the results are less than satisfactory. Panurge is "angry [...] perplexed and very wroth" after having had a dream that started well, with "a pretty, fair, young, gallant, handsome woman, who [...] made much of me, as if I had been another neat dilly-darling minion, like Adonis." But he woke with a start when she "made jestingly pretty little horns above my forehead." The entire question has to be reconsidered. Pantagruel entreats him to seek advice from a prophetess: "What [...] harm doth the laudable desire of knowledge bring to any man, were it from a sot, a pot, a fool [...] or old slipper?" (Chapter 16). Laurence Sterne would later take up this argument in the chapter of his *Tristram Shandy* describing how a woman chooses a husband.[13]

In *The Third Book*, Panurge consults several experts: a theologian, a physician, a philosopher named Trouillogan – *trouille* is slang for "fear" – and old Judge Bridlegoose – and ends up being "counselled by a fool," the famous Triboulet, the court jester during the reign of Louis XII and Francis I. Pantagruel insists on the wisdom of listening to fools: "You know how by the advice [...] of fools, many kings, princes, states and commonwealths have been preserved, several battle gained, and divers doubts of a most perplexed intricacy resolved." One who is esteemed a fool, Pantagruel continues, is likely to:

> presage events to come by divine inspiration [...] departing from himself, [he] rids all his senses of terrene affections, and clears his fancies of those plodding studies which harbor in the minds of thriving men. All which neglects of sublunary things are vulgarly imputed folly.

The giant appreciates the sotties, the Theatre of Fools that has been delighting audiences since the fifteenth century: "The like we daily see practiced amongst the comic players, whose dramatic roles, in distribution of the personages, appoint the acting of the fool to him who is the wisest of the troop" (Chapter 37). This theatre of jugglers presided over by Mother Folly,[14] and explored by Yvette Guilbert, denounces the abuses of the era. Under the cover of jokes, Rabelais is doing the same thing.

Augmenting language

Rabelais published his *Pantagruel* when he was about 50, in 1532 – the age at which Cervantes published *Don Quixote*, and Sterne published the last Book of *Tristram Shandy*, whose "Shandeism" was inspired by "Pantegruelism." Rabelais, who was a fervent reader of Erasmus (1467–1536) and translator of Lucian (120–192), had to flee from his Franciscan monastery, which forbade the study of Greek for fear of bringing into question the Latin translation of the Bible. In the same period, Guillaume Budé (1467–1540), with whom Rabelais exchanged letters, advised Francis I, as an act of direct opposition to the Sorbonne, to create a College of royal lecturers. What was to be the Collège de France was founded in 1530, with the motto "*Docet omnia*" ("It teaches everything"). It did, in fact, teach Hebrew, Latin and Greek, then Arabic, mathematics and other disciplines. But this did not prevent Erasmus' translator, Étienne Dolet, from being hanged and burned on the Place Maubert in 1546.

In 1530, Rabelais received his diploma in medicine from the University of Montpellier, and established a medical practice in Lyon, where *Pantagruel* was published in 1532 under the pseudonym *Alcofribas Nasier*. The book was an instant success. Rabelais also became the father of two children, whose paternity he recognised in 1540. *Gargantua* – Pantagruel's father – was published in 1534 and *The Third Book* in 1545. The Sorbonne condemned Rabelais for the crime of heresy; knowing that the ecclesiastic judges were quick to sentence people to be burned at the stake, he fled to Metz, an imperial city, and returned to Paris in 1548, under the reign of Henry II, who had succeeded Francis I to the throne in 1547.

A first version of *Le Quart-Livre* (*The Fourth Book*), also censored, was published in the year of his return from exile, and was followed by a second version in 1552, a year before his death in Paris in 1553. His books were published despite censorship, thanks to "Royal Privilege" – licence to print given by the king – and to the protection of Cardinals Jean and Guillaume du Bellay, first cousins of the father of poet Joachim du Bellay (1522–1560).

In 1535, Rabelais became Jean du Bellay's personal physician and accompanied him to Rome on a diplomatic mission whose aim was to negotiate an agreement with the Pope for the divorce of Henry VIII from Anne Boleyn, the mother of Elizabeth I, and to repair the rift in the Anglican Church. Rabelais returned to Rome with Jean du Bellay several times. He was also close to a Court favourable to the Reformation – that of the king's older sister, Marguerite de Navarre, *la Marguerite des*

Marguerites – "the Daisy of Daisies" – author of a collection of short stories, *The Heptameron*,[15] and the mother of Jeanne d'Albret, who gave birth to the future king Henry IV. Close to those in power, Rabelais was aware of the imminence of the religious wars that started in 1562 and culminated in the St Bartholomew's Day massacre in 1572.

Rabelais' weapon against fanaticism is laughter, for whose sake he enriches and corrects his language constantly, even at the last minute, in the print shop. He creates typographical signs, adds accents, cedillas, apostrophes – as Laurence Sterne would do two centuries later. The "Gar" in Gargantua means "throat" – *gorge* in French – and is the root of words like "gargoyle." This local giant has left traces of his teeth, his steps, his turds, in a number of place names such as Mont Gargan in the Alpine valley of the Tarentaise. He was the son of Grandgousier and Gargamelle, both of them big mouths, in the double sense of the word, since his mother died of gorging on tripe. In Chapters 13 and 22 of *Gargantua*, Rabelais' linguistic genius flourishes, as the young giant invents countless games and witty descriptions of all manner of ass-wipes, to his father Grandgousier's delight.

Pantagruel, Gargantua's son, is originally an imp, King of the Dipsodes – the Thirsty people – who pours salt down the throats of drunkards to encourage their thirst. The publication of Pantagruel's *Horrible and Terrifying Deeds and Words* was preceded by five years of climate change in which draught sent a great many cachectic patients to the hospital, where Rabelais treated them while he wrote, fighting in both endeavours against the suffocation of speech. Although some critics disagree, Rabelais' language is not artificial. It springs from the oral tradition and should be read aloud to give it back the breath stifled by jargons. It is in Chapter 6 that Pantagruel meets the Limousin scholar, who comes from a region of Central France.

Taught to speak dog Latin, the scholar brings to mind the gibberish of our psychoanalytical schools. Descartes was aware of this when he wrote *Discourse on Method* in French, "so women could read it, as they are half the world." In the same way, Wittgenstein defended "the language of every day": "Is this language somehow too coarse [...] for what we want to say? And how is another one to be constructed? And how strange that we should be able to do anything at all with the one we have!"[16]

Pantagruel listens carefully to the scholar displaying his "newspeak," until he finally exclaims: "Prut, tut [...] what doth this fool mean to say? [...] But first come hither, and tell me whence thou art." The word "Lemovic" emerges from the scholar's rigmarole, and the giant takes him by the throat: "thou art a Limousin, and thou wilt here and by thy affected speech counterfeit the Parisians." The scholar "thoroughly conshit his breeches" and started to swear in his dialect. Pantagruel salutes the authentic speech of both high-born and low-born mouths: "Now [...] thou speakest naturally." And he concludes:

it becometh us to speak according to the common language; and [...] we should [...] strive to shun all strange and unknown terms with as much heedfulness and circumspection as pilots of ships use to avoid the rocks and banks [in the sea].

Rabelais refuses to "flay" language through snobbery. His psychotherapeutic advice to those who speak in jargon is to use everyday language, among themselves and with their patients, keeping a pleasant demeanour, instead of showing a mirthless countenance, impervious to laughter, and sinister, in the name of neutrality. The mirror of madness that Rabelais holds up to the reader is a detector of perversion – a word he uses often – and his babble is a seeking of alterity.

Triboulet, the fool

Rabelais counts on laughter to introduce the reader to his world. But starting in *The Third Book*, there are more frequent references to political events, as Panurge seeks advice from different sources. In Chapter 39, his consultation with Triboulet follows his meeting with old Judge Bridlegoose, who served loyally for forty years and in the end decided the outcome of his trials by a throw of the dice. Beaumarchais gave him an heir when he created Brid'oison, the senile judge who presided over the decision regarding the marriage of Figaro to Marceline. Thanks to his random judgement, the truth happens to be that she was Figaro's mother, and Bartholo his father.[17]

In 1897, Mallarmé read to Paul Valéry, in a toneless voice, devoid of emotion, his poem "A Throw of the Dice": "A throw of the dice will never abolish chance," written after his book *Igitur, ou la folie d'Elbehnon*.[18] This phrase, with its apparent redundancy, illustrates Judge Bridlegoose's throw-of-the-dice sentences. In such circumstances, which admit of no causality, we think of a verse written by Paul Verlaine, Mallarmé's friend: "Music first and foremost,"[19] since in catastrophic circumstances only rhythm may evoke a possible other.

Triboulet merely wags his head after taking the gifts brought by Panurge: a hog's bladder, a game bag, a wooden sword and a bottle of wine. He speaks few words: "By God, mad fool, beware of the monk. Buzansay hornpipe!" – Buzansay being a town where hornpipes are made – and his gestures are eloquent: a hard blow between Panurge's shoulders, the empty wine bottle put back in his hand, and taps on the nose with the hog's bladder.

Pantagruel plays the analyst in Chapter 46: "How [they] diversely interpret the words of Triboulet." He knows that the gestures of fools and jugglers are forbidden by the Church, which fears the return of pagan rituals,[20] yet he confirms this connection by linking Triboulet's "foolery" with the trances seen during the Bacchanalia in Antiquity. The wagging of the head is a sign of prophesying, like the "mystical pointing out of the

Pythian divineress" and the shaking of the head of the Menades, "demented prophetesses." Panurge goes on to say:

> He says you are a fool. [...] A mad fool, who in your old age would enslave yourself to the bondage of matrimony. [...] He says further-more, "Beware of the monk." Upon mine honour, it gives me in my mind that you will be cuckolded by a monk. [...] Moreover, he says that you will be the hornpipe of Buzansay, that is to say, well-horned, horrified, and cornuted. [...] whilst you think to marry a wise, humble, calm, discreet, and honest wife, you shall unhappily stumble upon one witless, proud, loud, obstreperous, bawling, clamorous, and more unpleasant than any Buzansay hornpipe.

Panurge agrees: "not that I would impudently exempt myself from being a vassal in the territory of folly. I hold of that jurisdiction, and am subject thereto, I confess it." And he takes the opportunity to speak of his preference in women: "my humour is much better satisfied and contented with the pretty, frolic, rural, dishevelled shepherdesses, whose bums [...] smell of the clover grass of the field, than with those great ladies in magnificent courts, with their perfumes of *maujoint*" – meaning "un-joined," as opposed to *benjoint*, "well-joined," the name of a real perfume. This is one of the rare times Rabelais refers to women's genitals. The only other such reference is in Chapter 28 in which they are called *"comment à nom,"* pronounced in sixteenth-century fashion as *"con-ment à nom,"* – *con* meaning "cunt." On the other hand, references to the male sex organs abound.

Panurge accepts Pantagruel's interpretations, and adds one of his own, about the empty bottle given back to him by "our unique morosoph." *Moria*, which means "madness" in Greek, allowed Erasmus to dedicate his *Praise of Folly, Moriae Encomium*, to his friend Thomas More, who was to be decapitated by Henry VIII. The empty bottle returned to him by the fool Triboulet prompted Panurge to consult Balbuc, the Oracle of the Holy Bottle: "Let us go thither, I beseech you. I will be to you an Achates [...] and heartily accompany you all along in the whole voyage [...]. 'Very willingly', quote Pantagruel." And he went off to ask his father for approval. Now the *Fourth Book* of *Heroic Words and Deeds* can begin.

Before accompanying them on the journey, let us come back to the rhythm of Triboulet's head-wagging. Rabelais invokes the *Cratylus*, mentioned in Chapter 37 of the *Fourth Book* – a text he had learned by heart before running away from his Franciscan convent with his friend Pierre Lamy. The words and deeds foretold in this text originated from the *Nomothètos,* the source of words, as close to nature, *phusis*, as possible, before they become conventional. According to Socrates, the name, *onoma*, is an instrument, *organon*, similar to a shuttle, *kerkis*, serving to separate, *diakrinein*, the warp and weft in the art, *technè*, of the weave, thanks to the rhythm set by the weaver: "Then, says Socrates, this giving of names [cannot] be the work of [...] chance persons, but only [of] an artificer of names, *onomatourgos* [...] not every man knows how to give a thing a name."[21] Triboulet is one of the few men who do.

This agency is needed when "the tool with the name is broken." The shuttle is out of service. "What will [one] do?" Wittgenstein asks, in paragraph 41 of the *Investigations*. "Perhaps [one] will stand there at a loss," or show to another the sign that "has become meaningless." It can happen that this other, who witnesses the catastrophe, shakes his head, initiating by this rhythm a language-game, in response to the broken tool. "In this way the [name] can be said to be given a place in the language-game even when the tool no longer exists."[22]

When language starts to speak on its own, without warp or weft, delusion looks for an other to re-establish the rhythm of the shuttle. Triboulet wags his head, Pantagruel says, "when violent impetuosity" – this is the physician speaking – is too great for "the weakness and imbecility of the bearing organ" (Chapter 45). Overwhelmed with sensations, language starts to spin like a radar, to look for the other with whom to name them in a language game. As long as no obstacle is met, delusional discourse is untethered and spins, in search of someone who can create an interference. When this happens, primary elements, without reason, *stoicheia aloga*, as Socrates calls them in the *Theaetetus*,[23] interconnect to produce *logos*, words and reason. Quoted by Wittgenstein in the *Investigations*, this passage testifies to catastrophic moments when speech and time have to be set into motion again.

The half shadow, *La Morne moitié*

When he went back to Cambridge from Vienna in the late 1920s after having abandoned philosophy for ten years when he returned from the war, Wittgenstein resumed his research, comparing it to a therapy. He then changed the last sentence of the *Tractatus Philosophicus* written at the front, from "Whereof one cannot speak, thereof one must be silent," to "... thereof one cannot help but show." Surviving forms emerge from the silence in search of an other who will enable their inscription. What exactly in this other responds when the tool with the name is broken?

In "The Graveyard by the Sea,"[24] Paul Valéry speaks of a "half shadow." This graveyard is the one where Georges Brassens wished to be buried, in Sète, a town in the South of France. Valéry wrote the poem in 1920, and quoted as an exergue, untranslated, the verses of the "Third Pythian Ode of Pindar": "Seek not, my soul, the life of the immortals; but explore the field of the possible." Valéry's poem starts:

> This tranquil roof pulsates above the pines
> With doves' sails fluttering beyond the shrines;
> While the indifferent noon forges the sea from fire:
> The sea will always recommence.

The seventh stanza reads:

> The soul laid bare to all the flares of solstice,
> I do uphold you, admirable justice
> And all the brightness of your pitiless blade!
> Pure, I return you to your premier place
> Look at yourself! ... But grant that light must trace
> Half shadows in its ever bleaker shade.

The pitiless weapons of the Great War have just fallen silent. The poem ends with the famous line: *"Le vent se lève, il faut tenter de vivre"* ("The wind awakes! To try to live is next!").

The surviving forms emerging from the disaster summon, in the analyst, a "half shadow" (*morne moitié*) – striving to reach the light – without which there is no relief, in the double sense of the word: contrast and easing of pain. The French word *morne*, "bleak," has the same root as "mourning." The radar of madness searches for this part of darkness, in the name of justice, to inscribe names on a grave. The analyst's duty is to give it its "primary place," without which mourning for the unburied dead becomes endless. In such cases, his work is not to relieve sexual repression, but, as Yvette Guilbert pointed out to Freud, "to bring to light" true impressions blocked out by perversion.

She spoke of this when she was 50, in the prologue to her autobiography,[25] entitled "My Fine Keyboard," in which she undoes the determinism of her social condition:

> What a splendid solution [...] to grow old. [...] When I came forth from my mother's womb, I had a long course to run, already traced out for me in the sealed book held by Fate. [...] Already in my unborn head was a keyboard marked "Intelligence." [...] Should I lose control of it? What should I be capable of doing with myself: drop of blood, shapeless egg that I was in the shelter of my mother's womb, what would be the outcome of my divine metamorphosis? [...] Oh, the glory of growing old, the magic of the accumulating years!

There follows a verbal cascade worthy of Rabelais:

> Human grammar, dictionary of light, arithmetic of the weights and measures of our endurances [...] of pretences, of poses, of tests of virtues, of the dance of hearts, alchemy of feeling, intercourse of bodies, sport of souls – to trudge on, to rush, to run, and to be buffeted by the cruel winds of poverty, of stupidity, of deceit, of covetousness, of lust, of hatred, of love, and glory, to arrive at last [...] at that zone where turmoil ceases, and then to recapitulate the struggles of the journey [...] – the barriers to be jumped, the mountains to be climbed, the

unworthy brothers on the road, their hands in their pockets when one cried to them for help [...] the robbers who stole your strength, those who took advantage of your virtues, of your weaknesses, of the traged- ies of your heart and of your body, those who spat on your soul, who sneered at your hard work, who cut your wings, with here and there balm for your wounds, a hand to hold yours [...]. What a marvel! Oh, the magic of the years! To live to be old, not to have died by the way, to have survived until the moment when Life at last allows you to read her book!

(pp. 11–13)

To those who sing off-key, the keyboard of her intelligence responds in terms similar to those of Gargantua's letter to his "Most dear son," in Chapter 8 of *Pantagruel*. "Work, work, work!" the singer says when she undertakes a second career. Pantagruel is asked to learn Greek, Latin, Hebrew, Arabic, cosmogony, history, law, medicine and the art of war, but above all he is advised to heed wise Solomon's warning that "Wisdom entereth not into a malicious mind, and that knowledge without conscience is but the ruin of the soul." Like a true psychotherapist, doctor of the soul, Rabelais spreads out language in his interminable word lists, to free it and give us the courage to face its shadows, like during the *Fastnacht* ushering in the Basel Carnival, when masked figures, called Larvas, invade the city to the sound of fifes and drums.

Prologue to *The Fourth Book*

In 1552, when Rabelais published the second version of *The Fourth Book*, he was presenting the reader with his testament, one year before he died. The context is the conflict of the Catholic Church with the Protestants, which Jean du Bellay tried to prevent in vain. Convened in 1545 at Luther's request, the Council of Trent, terminated in 1563, introduced the Counter-Reformation and sparked the European wars of religion. Rabelais, who was suspected of heresy, went into exile in Metz after the death of his protector in 1546. When he returned to Paris in 1548, he published the first eleven-chapter version of *The Fourth Book*, followed four years later by the sixty-seven chapters of the second version, dedicated to "the most Illustrious Prince and most Reverend Lord Odet, Cardinal de Chastillon," the older brother of Admiral Gaspard de Coligny, who was to be killed in 1572 during the St Bartholomew's Day massacre. Odet converted to Calvinism in 1562, and went into exile in England, where he was poisoned.

The author's prologue to *The Fourth Book of the Heroic Deeds and Sayings of Good Pantagruel* is addressed to "Good people." Rabelais makes a display of searching for them:

> Good people, God save and keep you! Where are you? I can't see you:
> stay – I'll saddle my nose with spectacles – oh, oh! [...] I see you. [...]
> You, your wives, children, friends and families are in as good case as
> hearts can wish; it is well, it is as I would have it [...]. For my part,
> I am [...] by means of a little Pantagruelism (which you know is
> a certain jollity of mind) [...] hale and cheery.

He then refers to the evangelist St Luke, a physician like him, whose word,
he says, "I obey and revere," and who derides "the physician neglectful of
his own health, 'Physician, heal thyself'."

After invoking the authority of the Scriptures, Rabelais seeks support
from the physicians of Antiquity, whose motto is *abios bios, bios abiotos*
("without health life is not life, it is not living life [...] only a languishment
and an image of death"). He tells us: "secure life to yourselves," standing
firm in the hope that heaven will grant this wish "because it is moderate
and mean." Then a little theatre is enacted between this world and the
beyond to convince the reader of the good reason for moderation, expressed
by the motto *mèden agan* ("nothing in excess"), inscribed above the
entrance to Apollo's Temple at Delphi.

The hero is a lumberjack named Couillatrix – *couilles* means "balls" –
who has lost his axe – *cognée* in French – and calls on Jupiter with
lamentations so loud that they are heard at the Security Council of the
Olympus which Jupiter just happens to have summoned about urgent
affairs, such as "conflicts between Persians, Turks, Syrians, Lybians, Tartars,
Muscovites, Germans, Saxons and Gascons" – a province in the South-West
of France. "What a devil have we below that howls so horridly?" the king
of the gods inquires impatiently. Exasperated, Jupiter asks Priapus for
advice: "What thinkest thou of it, say, thou bawdy Priapus? I have found
thy counsel just before now, *et habet tua mentula mentem* – your little head
has a good mind." A note specifies that *mentula* is a diminutive for *mens*, as
well as for the masculine sex organ, which in Priapus' case is far from little.

After debating about what kind of axe, *cognée, con-gnée* is lost, which is
indeed a word "equivocal to many things," since in it the word *con* –
"cunt" – makes itself heard again. The decision was made by the venerable
gods, amid fits of laughter, to send Mercury down, through "heaven's
wicket," to offer the poor fellow three axes, one of gold, one of silver and
one of wood, and give him two options: either he moderately chooses his
own, in which case he will be given the other two, or he chooses one of the
others, in which case the *ubris* of his desire will be punished by cutting his
head off with his own axe. The case was to set a precedent: "and henceforth
serve me all those losers of axes after that manner," a fate that would
befall, like in fairy tales, Couillatrix's greedy fellow bumpkins. After
instructing us on what the Middle Ages called "golden mediocrity," *aurea
mediocritas*, our psychotherapist allows us to read his book: "Now, my lads,
as you hope for good health, cough once aloud with lungs of leather; take

me off three swinging bumpers; prick up your ears; and you shall hear me tell wonders of the noble and good Pantagruel."

The two types of *cognées*, the one which pummels, *cogne*, in sexual intercourse, and the other that cuts off life, illustrate two types of transference. One deals with sexual desire, like in Clément Janequin's song – a poet quoted by Rabelais: "In the jolly game of shove, See the bonny ladylove; She won't admit it but I score, She wiggles and giggles galore," and the other deals with cutaway historical truth and with arrested time.

The madness of war

When time stops, poetic rhythm is inscribed in space, like Apollinaire's *Calligrammes* drawn at the front during the Great War. The poet, who received a head wound when a bullet went through his helmet the day he learned of his sweetheart's betrayal, was born in Poland in 1880. Guillaume Kostrowitzky enlisted in order to become a French citizen, and he fought on the same battlefields as Bion did. It was there that he invented the word "surrealism," revealed in a letter to Belgian writer Paul Dermée in May 1917.[26] At the same time, William Rivers discovered "psychotic transference," as Bion will call it, while working with young veterans like the poet Siegfried Sassoon.[27]

This is not to say that Rabelais was teaching future analysts lessons, but he was exploring the cognitive domains of madness and trauma in the wake of the conflicts dividing Europe. In the prologue to the 1552 *Fourth Book*, a first quandary is solved by Priapus before dealing with Couillatrix. Jupiter informs him that two lecturers at the Royal College, Pierre Ramus, a disciple of Plato, and Pierre Galland, a follower of Aristotle, "set together by the ears the whole university of Paris." Galland calls Ramus' theories "nonsense like Pantagruel's jocular books." The god doesn't know whose side to take, for "one is an old cunning fox" and the other "barks like a cur."

Priapus reminds him how on a previous occasion, he had resolved a dispute between a "fairy" fox and a just as "fairy" dog, the first belonging to Bacchus and the second to Vulcan: "Dog by his destiny was to take fox, and fox by his fate was not to be taken." After much sweating over the judgement, Jupiter had decided to turn them both to stone, and Priapus says: "[You] immediately got rid of your perplexity." The time of the episode is known: "This was the year of *couilles molles*, soft balls." Now Priapus suggests that the two intellectuals should be turned to stone, inasmuch as both are called Pierre, "stone" in French. This will serve to extinguish "the fire of faction, division, ballock sects, and wrangling among those idle bearded boys, the students." And their statues will be "an everlasting monument to show that those puny self-conceited pedants, ballock framers, were [...] condemned by you. *Dixi*, I have said my say." With these words, Rabelais tries to change the course of History, which is in danger of bursting into flames, ignited by the self-love, *philautia*, of fanatical egocrats.

After the prologue, we are en route for the Oracle of the Holy Bottle. Then we travel through Chapters 6 to 8, in which Panurge "bargains with Dingdong" to buy one of his sheep and ends up throwing it overboard, causing all the other sheep and the merchant to follow suit. Finally, in Chapter 9, we land on the triangular "Island of Ennasin," called "the Island of Alliances," where the noses of the islanders are shaped like an ace of clubs. The island is mentioned by Laurence Sterne[28] in the chapter "On Noses" in *Tristram Shandy*, in regard to an ancestor of the hero accused by his wife of having a short nose, not to say a short something else. But the great-grandson protested, saying that his great-grandfather's nose "was for all the world like the noses of all the men, women, and children [...] upon the Island of Ennasin."

Their strange alliances are formed through the surrealist association of random words:

> a man used to call a woman, my lean bit; the woman called him my porpoise. [...] I saw one calling his she-relation "my crumb," and she called him, my crust. [...] Now I could not [...] pick out or discover what parentage, alliance, affinity, or consanguinity was between them, with reference to our custom.

These alliances are the result of spontaneous encounters at a moment when a word catches another. Another example: "A wooden loggerhead said to a young wench, It is long since I saw you, bag. All the better, cried she, pipe. Set them together, said Panurge, then blow in their arses, it will be a bagpipe."

At the next stage of the journey, in the land of the Chicanous, in Chapter 13, Rabelais refers to Master Francis Villon (1431–1463). One of the travellers recounts the adventure of the Franciscan Friar Tickletoby tricked by the poet, who – when nobody knew what had become of him after being banished from Paris – had in fact, says Rabelais, joined a troupe of jugglers performing Sotties and Mysteries. Wanting to stage the Passion, he had asked Tickletoby to lend him some church attire. When the latter refused, because the Church considered jesters diabolical, the troupe disguised as devils attacked him, leaving him panting, "dragged about by [his] filly [...] scratching his bare breech all the way."

In Chapter 18, the fine crew is subjected to "a great storm at sea." "Half dead," Panurge transforms the cry of Aeneas, when he found himself in the same peril, unleashed by Juno. The verse: "*Ô terque quaterque beati*, O thrice and four times blessed are those who happened upon death [...] under the high walls of Troy."[29] becomes in Panurge's words: "O twice and thrice happy those that plant cabbages." Shaken by the storm, he bawls: "My heart's sunk down below my midriff. By my troth, I am in a sad fright, bou, bou, bou, bous, bous, I am lost for ever." While all around him are struggling to save the ship, "he sat on his breech upon deck, weeping and howling," through the five chapters the storm lasts. When the storm ends, the symbolic order returns, in Chapter 23.

The death of the great Pan

Pantagruel's fleet lands on the island of the Macreons, "ones much stricken in years," where old Macrobius, "whose name means 'the eldest'," shows them historical monuments, ruins of temples and ancient tombs bearing inscriptions and epitaphs in various ancient languages. Just as Yvette Guilbert, after the torment that almost cost her her life, explored the limits of language by deciphering medieval songs, the survivors of the storm at sea discover, at the confines of the known world, the country of forgotten ancestors.

The memory of their death, always accompanied by "great commotions," reminds Pantagruel, in Chapter 28, of the events recounted by Plutarch – who served as a priest at the Temple of Delphi in the second century – in his book *De Defect Oraculum* (*The Obsolescence of Oracles*), which Rabelais read in the French translation by Jacques Amyot (1513–1593). During a crossing between Greece and Italy, an Egyptian pilot heard a voice call out his name *Thamous*, three times. Finally, the pilot answered and "the voice [...] bid him publish [...] that the great god Pan was dead." When Thamous obeyed, shouting from the top of the ship's forecastle, "the words were hardly out of his mouth, when deep groans, great lamentations, and doleful shrieks, not of one person, but of many together, were heard from the land."

This mourning ushers in the schism between monotheism and polytheism – complete with the burning of witches and the massacre of pagans – a schism Rabelais bridges by resuscitating local deities: not only his amiable giants, but ancient serpentine divinities like Melusina, who will soon reappear in Chapter 38, among the "wild and bearded Chitterlings" fighting the bigotry of Shrovetide, who reigns on Sneaking Island and is a "flogger of little children" (Chapter 29). In 1924, Aby Warburg, like Rabelais, turned to animism in order to bridge the schism between medical and psychodynamic approaches to madness, and was released from Binswanger's psychiatric clinic after presenting his Lecture on Hopi Serpent Ritual.

Rabelais takes us on a journey that invites us to enter the "country of the marvel," the space of the madman in medieval literature.[30] Having started out from the prologue, where the Olympians try to resolve the eternal international crises that produce innumerable deaths, we have weathered the storm and have seen the calm return. During the journey, Pantagruel recreates the symbolic order by making a declaration of faith: "For all that we are, all that we live, all that we have, all that we hope, is him, by him, from him and in him. He is the good Pan, the great shepherd." Rabelais' audacious attitude in the face of bloody attacks is worthy of "the associations of practices" in animism, recommended by Wittgenstein, "on the model of free association in psychoanalysis."[31]

But there was more to come. After harpooning an enormous and "monstrous Physeter," a Moby Dick of the Renaissance (Chapter 33), a heroic-comic battle takes place between Shrovetide the Chitterlings and (Chapter 42). Pantagruel makes peace with their queen called Niphleseth ("phallus" in Hebrew), and celebrates the victory of life over the long faces of analysts who remain unmoved by patients whose life has withdrawn.

To raise time

We are heading towards the end of *The Fourth Book*, and salute on the way Chapters 55 and 56, often quoted in our seminars, in which Pantagruel heats up in his hand "frozen words" of various colours – the red ones coming from sliced throats – falling on the deck of the ship when it sails in a zone where the previous winter, the pilot informs them, there was "a great and bloody fight." We also leave behind Chapter 37, "a discourse well worth hearing about the names of places and persons," which makes reference to "the *Cratylus* of the divine Plato," at a time when the Ordinance of Villers-Cotterêts was signed into law by Francis I in 1539, to make French the official language, and when poet Joachim du Bellay published *La Défense et illustration de la langue française*, which led to the creation in 1553 of the Pléiade, a coterie of poets including Pierre de Ronsard, one of its founding members.

But they encounter a zone of arrested time just before they reach the end of their "extraordinary voyage." In Chapter 66, the ships sail near the Isle of Ganabin, home of "thieves, ruffians and murderers," Pantagruel explains. Xenomanes, the "great traveller," asks them: "Have you mind to go ashore there? – No. – You do well, indeed, for there is nothing worth seeing in the place." They are not fascinated by perversion. Only Friar John of the Funnels wants to land: "Believe me [...] let's rather land; we will rid the world of that vermin." But Pantagruel trusts his feelings: "I feel a pressing retraction in my soul, which like a voice admonishes me not to land there." Counselled by his *daimon*, no doubt of the same ilk as that of Socrates, he decides to have the gunner "fire the fun [...] to salute the Muses of this Anti-Parnassus [...] which made [...] a horrid noise." He does not care to converse with perverts. Where poetry is endangered, they make no stop and continue on their way.

In the previous chapters, before arriving at the island of perversity, it happened that the wind failed them; they were "becalmed and could hardly get ahead." This brought about a state of lethargy affecting them all, Pantagruel was slumbering, Panurge made bubbles and bladders with his tongue, Ponocrates tickled himself to make himself laugh, and the pilot was pulling maggots out of the seamen's noses. Only Friar John takes the initiative of asking "how to raise good weather." Panurge will repeat the question in Chapter 65: "Well then, Friar John asked 'la manière de hausser le temps en calme', how good weather might be raised." But also, since *temps* in French means "weather" and "time," Friar John's question could be: "How to raise time when it has been flattened in the proximity of perversion?"

Pantagruel answers: "I'll strive to give you satisfaction." He observes: "While we passed our time merrily [...] we have not only shortened the time of the calm, but also much disburdened the ship." But this explanation is incomplete. The true answer comes when they say "no" and refuse to land on the Isle of Ganabin, which, Hannah Arendt reminds us, many intellectuals find seductive. Then the wind picks up and the sails swell. Near the zones of hypocrisy and denial, fools impel us to look for a "higher sense," as Rabelais does at the outset, in the prologue of *Gargantua and Pantagruel*. The reading of his books is more than entertainment:

> And put the case, that in the literal sense you meet with purposes merry and salacious enough [...] you must not stop there as at the melody of the charming syrens, but endeavor to interpret "*à plus haut sens*," in a higher sense, that which possibly you intended to have spoken in the jollity of your heart.

"To raise time thanks to higher sense" is Rabelais' motto, later borrowed by Yvette Guilbert. I have taken you on a voyage aboard Pantagruel's ship, in search of the North-West Passage between two types of transference to which all three of them testify.

Giving higher sense also describes the transference that forces us to set out *On the Road* with Kerouac to make the great discovery of lands and events which have been erased from the map.

Notes

1 Rabelais, F., *Gargantua: The Fourth Book*, Urquhart, T. and Motteux, P. A. (Trans.), CreateSpace, 2015.
2 Guilbert, Y., *The Song of My Life: My Memories*, De Holthoir, B. (Trans.), G. G. Harrap & Co., 1929.
3 Brécourt-Villars, C., *Yvette Guilbert, l'irrespectueuse*, Plon, 1988.
4 Musil, R., "Yvette Guilbert," in *Essais, conférences, critiques, aphorismes et réflexions*, Seuil, 1984.
5 Freud, E. L. (Ed.), *Letters of Sigmund Freud 1873–1939*, Basic Books, 1961.
6 Diderot, D., *The Paradox of the Actor*, CreateSpace, 2015.
7 Freud, S., *The Origins of Psychoanalysis: Letters to Wilhelm Fliess, Drafts and Notes, 1887–1902*, Basic Books, 1954.
8 Freud, S. and Breuer, J., *Studies on Hysteria*, S.E. 2, Hogarth Press, 1895.
9 Freud, S., *Moses and Monotheism*, Vintage Books, 1955, p. 164.

10 Rabelais, F., *Gargantua and Pantagruel*, W. W. Norton & Company, 1991, Book II.
11 Rabelais, F., *Five Books of the Lives, Heroic Deeds and Sayings of Gargantua and His Son Pantagruel*, Urquhart of Cromarty, T. and Motteux, P. A. (Trans.), BiblioBazaar, 2009.
12 Freud, S., *Interpretation of Dreams*, S.E. 3, Hogarth Press, pp. 299–322.
13 Sterne, L., *The Life and Opinions of Tristram Shandy, Gentleman*, Wordsworth Editions, 1999.
14 Davoine, F., *Mother of Folly: A Tale*, Stanford University Press, 2014.
15 De Navarre, M., *The Heptameron*, Penguin Classics, 1984.
16 Wittgenstein, L., *Philosophical Investigations*, Ascombe, G. (Trans.), Oxford University Press, 1983, section 120.
17 Beaumarchais, P. *The Marriage of Figaro*, Broadway Play Publishing, 1991, Act III, Scene 16.
18 Mallarmé, S., "A Throw of the Dice," in *Poems and Prose Poems*, Hanson, J. (Trans.), Jim Hanson, 2016.
19 Verlaine, P., "Art poétique," in *One Hundred and One Poems by Paul Verlaine*, Shapiro, N. R. (Trans.), University of Chicago Press, 2000.
20 Schmitt, J. C., *La Raison des gestes dans l'Occident médiéval*, Gallimard, 1990.
21 Plato, *Cratylus*, CreateSpace, 2012.
22 Wittgenstein, L., *Philosophical Investigations*, op. cit., section 41.
23 Plato, *Theaetetus*, Jowett, B. (Trans.), Liberal Arts Press, 1955.
24 Valéry, P., "The Graveyard by the Sea," in *An Anthology*, Pollard, D. (Trans.), Princeton University Press, 1977.
25 Guilbert, Y., *The Song of My Life*, op. cit.
26 Becker, A., *Apollinaire. Une Biographie de guerre*, Tallandier, 2009.
27 Barker, P. *The Regeneration Trilogy*, Hamish Hamilton, 2014.
28 Sterne, L., *The Life and Opinions of Tristram Shandy, Gentleman*, op. cit., Book 3, Chapter 37.
29 Virgil, *The Aeneid of Virgil*, Humphries, R. (Trans.), Charles Scribner's Sons, 1952, I, verse 94.
30 Fritz, J. M., *Le Discours du fou au Moyen Âge*, Presses universitaires de France, 1992.
31 Wittgenstein, L., "Remarks on Frazer's *Golden Bough*," in C. G. Luckhardt (Ed.), *Wittgenstein: Sources and Perspectives*, Cornell University Press, 1979.

6   Seminar 13: 2011–2012
Jack Kerouac (1922–1969)
On the Road

Inscriptions not yet made

From early adolescence on, Jack Kerouac was dedicated to nurturing his
only passion: literature. He spent his time in libraries, and always carried
a notebook in which he jotted down things he might later use in his
writing.

At the New York Public Library, where he was a frequent visitor, we saw
the forty-metre scroll, left uncut, on which he wrote *On the Road[1]* in one
go, in a writing frenzy. This was not "automatic" writing – a term Kerouac
rejects, speaking instead of spontaneous prose.

Our subject this year, "what becomes inscribed when it had not been
previously?" designates an event impossible to transmit. Kerouac has kept
an impressive volume of correspondence. He wrote a great deal, since he
could not afford to telephone, and he kept copies of his own letters. He
wrote about his life and his ghosts.

Emergence of a ghostly figure

To introduce the reading of *On the Road*, I will recount a clinical story. At
the psychiatric hospital, Madam H was diagnosed with severe melancholia
after the death of her son-in-law. In the isolation room, she drew on the
walls with her excrement. She had married late, meeting her husband
through the personal ads. One day her husband refused to have their
daughter and her husband stay overnight in their house on the farm. They
had to sleep on straw in the shed. Their son-in-law died a few days later of
a serious infection. Madam H left her husband and took an apartment
overlooking the cemetery, where she could see her son-in-law's tomb.

When she came to one of our first meetings, she brought me a fragment
of paper torn from an envelope, on which she had drawn a simple little
flower, like those on the cheap wallpaper one saw in the bedrooms of the
1940s. Later she brought motifs drawn for needlepoint canvases used in
workshops that have now disappeared. When she left the hospital, she took
lessons given by correspondence, and throughout the seven years during

which we continued our sessions at the clinic, I was able to admire the progress of her technique in drawings of landscapes made with colouring pencils. In our last sessions, I started to see human forms appear. She left the therapy regenerated.

Her son-in-law liked to draw. She had kept his box of pastels, which she never used, but gave instead to her grandson. This transmission is part of an inscription making use of small things that gradually give access to human forms – in this case not through the "why" of her son-in-law's death, which we never uncovered, but through physical creation, done with her hands, which gave shape to his ghost and appeased his soul. Once this was done, she said goodbye to me.

Kerouac's performance

A film shows Kerouac reciting *On the Road* to the rhythm of a piano played by Thelonious Monk. Forms begin to take shape, starting from trifles: imaginary fragments, a voice, a rhythm, accents. The word "rhapsody" means sowing odes together. Plato uses the word to designate the work of the poet who puts together, for an audience, fragments of poetry from different cycles. A language game, Wittgenstein says, is also made up of a "facial expression, bodily posture and tone of voice."[2]

The film is improvised. Kerouac is standing while he reads. Thelonious Monk is hearing the text for the first time. The scroll is the road on which Kerouac started out in 1947, hitch-hiking at first, to go West. "Go West, young man, go West," as the Americans say. His first attempt was unsuccessful. He was hitch-hiking on a road where no one came by, and it kept raining. He gave up and went back to New York.

The original scroll was drafted without paragraphs, in three weeks, in April 1951, and was written "all in a rush, the hell with these phony architectures." Kerouac gives some details about his inspiration: "I had just gotten over a serious illness that I won't bother to talk about, except that it had something to do with the miserably weary split-up [with his wife] and my feeling that everything was dead" (p. 127). His father had just died. Six years later, the editor of Viking Press structured the text into four parts and into paragraphs, narrating four successive road trips. The first three had San Francisco as their destination: between July and October 1947, passing through Denver; in early 1949, through Louisiana; and in the spring of that year, through Denver again. The fourth road trip, described in the fourth part of the book, is Kerouac's journey to Mexico in 1950. He was able to make this journey thanks to the sales of his first book, *The Town and the City*.[3]

The death of his father – from stomach cancer, in 1946 – prompted the writing of the scroll. In the Viking edition, this event is replaced by the separation from his wife Edie Parker, whom he married in a hurry in August 1944, to get out of prison. He had been implicated in the murder of

David Kammerer by his friend Lucien Carr, whom he saw throw his knife in a sewer. The marriage didn't last long; by October, it was over, and was later annulled.[4]

The start of *On the Road* recounts the decisive meeting with the man who was to be Kerouac's companion on the road, Neal Moriarty, alias Dean Cassady: "he reminded me of some long-lost-brother. [...] And in his excited way of speaking I heard again the voices of old companions [of] my boyhood," so different from his "current" intellectual friends, Kerouac says. Dean's intelligence and even his "criminality" were "a wild yea-saying outburst of American joy; it was Western," far removed from his New York friends' "negative, nightmare position of putting down society and giving their [...] political or psychoanalytic reasons" (pp. 7–8).

When his father died, the terrible feeling "that everything was dead" brought back the death of his older brother, at the age of 9, when Jack was 4. A year after the publication of *On the Road*, in *Visions of Gerard*, he wrote: "I was not Ti Jean [...] I was Gerard, the world was his face." Gerard died after a long illness: "Gerard is dead and the soul is dead and the world is dead and dead is dead."[5] What is left is breath, which punctuates the narration of *On the Road*, a voyage undertaken to stay alive in what Gaetano Benedetti[6] calls a "death zone."

Breath regained

When Kerouac set out on the road for the first time and then had to turn back, as more and more time passed while he waited on the road, breath became his sole concern. I had this experience myself last April. Suffering from stomach cancer, I found myself in an intensive care unit as a result of septicaemia caused by the surgeon's error. I created little circles of air, of small capacity, that allowed me to re-establish the basic rhythm of life.

I shall give you two other examples of this vital rhythm. At the psychiatric hospital where I worked as a psychoanalyst, there was a young man who made concrete blocks in occupational therapy. While we talked, he always held one hand in his other hand, like Socrates in the Raphael portrait *The School of Athens*. In fact, he was feeling his pulse and showing me that he was alive. Ten years later, in my office, another patient who hardly spoke kept his eyes on my foot as I sat across from him with my legs crossed. I finally looked down and saw that my foot was swaying slightly. I told him that he was more concerned with the rhythm of my life than with what I was saying. "Yes," he answered softly.

In a death zone, we have to start with the pulse – a word Kerouac uses often – testimony that we are alive. The dream of a cell faced with death is a psychosocial dream, which ties the cell to others, beyond spoken and half-spoken words. In the film, Kerouac recites *On the Road* without pause, stopping only to breathe. His meeting with the pianist results in a "miraculous" improvisation that amplifies the syncopated rhythm of the jazz and of his own phrases.

When he first arrived in New York in 1939 to attend a school in preparation of entering Columbia University, he developed a passion for the jazz musicians he names throughout his book. The expression of this rhythm culminates in the performance, during his third stay in San Francisco, of a tenor horn player, Blowman, whose only passion is breath: "Blowblowblow!" (p. 201).

Break in continuity

As he reminds the reader at the start of almost all his books, Kerouac was born in 1922 in Lowell, Massachusetts, a textile industry town where his father owned a printing shop. His mother's maiden name was Lévesque; both his parents were of French-Canadian origin, immigrants from Quebec. Kerouac is a Breton surname. *Satori in Paris*, published in 1966, three years before his death, is the story of his unsuccessful search for an ancestor, Bris de Kervoack, who fought in Montcalm's army against the English in Canada, during the Seven Years' War between 1756 and 1763.[7]

The Franco-Canadian colony in Lowell spoke its own language, *joual*. Kerouac learned English at school and only became perfectly bilingual at 15. In Lowell, the rhythm of the Quebecois, Italian, Greek and Irish accents often took precedence over the meaning of words. In fact, the parents of some of his friends did not speak English at all. The music of his conversations with his older brother had an "angelic sweetness." Gerard transmitted to him his love for animals and defenceless beings, while he lay in his bed, or when he took him "on forgotten little walks," and they heard "that wind out on the cold canals of Lowell across the river."

In the spring of 1936, a catastrophic flood in Lowell destroyed the print shop, causing his father to go bankrupt. This kind and generous man, an enemy of injustice like Don Quixote, but also an ardent horse racing fan and lover of poker parties with no lack of drink, was forced to work for others, but not to give up drinking and gambling. The family's life in Lowell was disrupted by the constant need to move somewhere else, until they ended up in New York during the war; there, his mother worked in a shoe factory. After the death of his father – to whom the author had promised to look after his mother – and after his older sister married, Kerouac returned to live with his mother in Queens, until his death. He was everything to her, but he was not Gerard.

The *harmony* of the universe doesn't originate in the music of the spheres. The word is constructed from the root "ar," found in the Greek verb *arariskô*, "to adjust forcefully," and in *artus*, the Latin word for "limbs." In Vedic texts on sacrifice, Charles Malamoud tells us, the priest's knife severs the joints in the victim's limbs, while "articulating" the ritual words.[8] His scansion sets time in motion again, after it had been arrested in "an amorphous and anarchic interval without order."[9]

Harmony is broken in a nation, a city or a family by "attacks on linking" – Bion's expression – as is the case when one is betrayed by those he trusts. When Kerouac's father went bankrupt, he fell prey to Lowell businessmen whom he had considered his friends.

Writing America

Kerouac injected the accents of his "spontaneous prose" into the disharmony that had spread over America. He sacrificed his social status, much to his father's chagrin, because all he wanted was to become a writer, to bring home all those who had been strewn on the roads by wars and economic crises. The "beat generation" made him its herald, although he never considered himself a beatnik and was not interested in ideologies. Endowed with a "fantastic" memory, according to his friends, he was constantly writing it down in his notebooks. He witnessed the erosion of American ideals – from the period following World War I, which ended prosperity in Lowell, through World War II, followed by the Korean War and the Vietnam War. Kerouac's first book, *The Town and the City*,[10] describes this downfall through the saga of the Martin family, united in their small *town*, and then disintegrating after the bankruptcy of the father's print shop and the move to New York, the big *city*.

Like Cervantes, in whose footsteps he claims to follow – when the latter was roaming the Spanish countryside as a tax collector, in order to survive, after returning from ten years of war and slavery – "on the road" Kerouac met those who fell through the cracks of the American dream. A chorus of voices joins his, forming what we call "a plural body of survival." At the start of *On the Road*, Kerouac writes: "the only people for me are the mad ones" (p. 15). You have to be crazy to put unwelcome messages into circulation. Kerouac invents a new form of writing as a ritual to regenerate the destroyed social link.

His brother's death, rekindled by that of his father, made Kerouac understand the need for a tempo, a beat, when, as Hamlet says: "The time is out of joint." Mallarmé expresses this need in a sonnet dedicated to the Egyptologist Gaston Maspero, after the death of his wife. In the third stanza, the dead woman speaks:

> I am a soul longing to sit beside the bright hearth and
> To be brought back to life; all I need is to hear from your lips
> The murmur of my name repeated throughout the night.[11]

Kerouac lends his breath to forgotten names whose whispers come back to him with amazing clarity. Around the same time, in 1954, Mexican writer Juan Rulfo wrote his only novel – partly autobiographical – *Pedro Paramo*, the name of the narrator's father. Returning to his family's small town, he hears the whispers of voices that were silenced by this man's abuse and by the bloody Cristero War of the 1920s, which took a heavy toll on the writer's family.[12]

Kerouac's writing is not that of a leader, though he was seen as such by the *hipsters* – wearing their low-waist trousers on their hips – and by the "rucksack generation." The beat he finds in jazz is not a world view, but rather a heartbeat in "the rush of truth which chooses the words for its purpose." The truth of what he has to say is not circumscribed in explanations, but is expressed in a musical impulse coming from a "bottomless time."

On the Road cannot be classified as "psychiatric" writing, nor included with the automatic writing of the surrealists, although it uses the "ding ding" of the typewriter, which Kerouac had mastered very early in his father's print shop. Yet the content of the book is of the same nature as a delusion.

What is a delusion?

I can answer this question since I have had delusion in an intensive care unit. I spent a month there writing them down word for word, down to the last comma. I knew I was hallucinating, but this did not prevent me from seeing, at dusk – when babies cry as the day turns into night – in the helmet-shaped wall thermometer, the figure of Don Quixote who had come to visit me – hail, brother! – nor from glimpsing Dulcinea's mouth through the boxes of medication, and thinking that the files brought into my room were enormous envelopes addressed to me by people I knew. I hallucinated at night and I wrote during the day.

How is such a text put together? What is it made of? It is composed of word-things without metaphoric inscription. I am taken outside my room on a trolley. The elevator takes us down to the basement, where I was to see my ancestors. No one is there. The nurse prepares two candles; it is a bad sign. Fortunately, I am still alive and I find myself on a psychiatric ward from where we are taken outside, just as patients were at the hospitals where I worked, only to be brought back in again.

Our outing takes us into a village. In a pharmacy like Monsieur Homais' shop, where Madame Bovary stole her poison, two patients have come in to buy not arsenic, like she did, but strychnine. The pharmacist puts it in two paper pouches like those used for candy. One of them swallows the contents of his envelope, which he sets aside. The nurse, who has seen all kinds of things, tells me that he will be sick but will not die. Then I find myself in a cafeteria where I have a role to play. I know the answer to all these mysterious questions: this is madness and its writing, in the face of death.

Delusions tend towards writing whose phrases can be picked up with one's fingers, because they are made of word-things, and of the things themselves. Kerouac's scroll is concretely made of sheets glued together with Scotch tape, because he could not bear to change the pages on the typewriter. This is precisely what rhapsody means: material is pieced together for the sake of continuity. Faced with the hallucinatory messages addressed to me by radar signals, I grow tired and attempt to perceive an echoing signal. The radio wave is not random. It takes a very long time to grasp its message. It is a merciless memory that spares you no detail, down to the last comma. The words are carefully selected; you must not change them.

The agency at work insists. It is an exhausting experience, and when the delusion ends, the risk of suicide is great, because it provided support for your life. Afterwards, you wonder why it took so much of your time and you collapse. Yet when the delusion touches another person who can say "touché" like in a fencing match, the emergence of a word, a look, a gesture or a story creates the continuity of a trustworthy relationship that brings you out of reification.

Creating alterity

Kerouac fought against the perversity that treats people like things: "you'll understand," he tells his "wifey," at the beginning of his last book *Vanity of Duluoz*, "that my particular form of anguish came from being too sensitive to all the lunkheads I had to deal with ..."[13] Folly fights perverse stupidity by emitting waves – voices, visions, real or delusional sensations – that seek an obstacle against which to bounce off and be validated.

The analyst whose "seismograph of the soul" – a term coined by Aby Warburg during his episode of madness – alerts him to such uncanny signs must speak, contrary to the dogma summed up by a colleague in Berkeley, whose supervisor told her: "When your heart beats, shut your mouth." Neutrality prevents the seismograph from registering untold stories and allowing a new otherness to emerge, as is clearly seen in totalitarian systems at whatever scale, which always aim at the destruction of otherness. Attacks of a ruthless agency seek to do away with otherness, big or small. According to Lacan's concept of the big Other, the given word of the Other disappears, as does the little other in the mirror, because mirrors have been smashed. Yet "surviving images" appear on the edge of catastrophes, which can be said to be *akyral* – lacking the mirror symmetry of two hands. They have an uncanny quality, *unheimlich*, characteristic of ghosts walking through mirrors, defying optical laws.

Descartes himself became aware of this phenomenon on a November night in 1619, when he had three nightmares in his stove-heated room. He had been billeted near Ulm for the winter, during the Thirty Years' War, while serving in the army of the Duke of Bavaria. His first dream filled him with terror: he was chased by violent, netherworld winds that threatened to make him fall at every step, as his biographer Adrien Baillet recounts.[14]

This lurking death which haunted him could have been that of his war companions, as well as the phantom of his mother, who died soon after his birth.

Seventeen years later, he would write his *Discourse on the Method*, in which he refers to this episode: "like a man walking alone in the dark, I resolved to go so slowly and to keep looking around me so warily that even if I didn't get far I would at least be sure not to fall." His *Discourse* constitutes a personal psychotherapy, for he does not wish "to teach the method that everyone must follow [...] but only to display how I have tried to direct my own."

After leaving the army, Descartes set out on the roads of Europe. Like Kerouac, like Cervantes, he was a knight errant, until he settled down in Holland:

> as soon as I was old enough to emerge from the control of my teachers, I spent the rest of my youth travelling, visiting courts and armies, mixing with people of different temperaments and ranks [...]. For it seemed to me that I could find much more truth in the reasonings that people make about matters that concern their interests than in a scholar's closeted reasonings about theoretical matters. In the former case, if a person judges wrongly he will soon be punished for this by the upshot; whereas in the latter case there are no practical consequences [...] except perhaps that the further his conclusion are from common sense the prouder he will be of them.[15]

Kerouac's desire to travel was sparked by his meeting with Neal Cassady in early 1947. Neal shared his passion for writing and for reading. Earlier, in 1942, he had joined the Merchant Marine, as a tribute to his Breton origins relentlessly alluded to by his father. Jack took with him Tolstoy, Dostoevsky, Pascal and Homer. Neal was four years younger and came from a family broken up by the Crash of 1929. He had lost his mother at the age of 10 and had lived in Denver with an alcoholic father, who became a tramp. When they met, Neal had just been released from a reform school where he was sent after stealing dozens of cars, and had travelled to New York to get to know "real intellectuals." Kerouac was seduced by his passion for writing, as well as by his search for his lost father.

While drafting several versions of what would become *On the Road*, long before that famed month of April 1952, Kerouac "confessed" to Neal that he had had a mystical vision of fallen angels (as seen in stained-glass images). Such confessions often seal a new pact of loyalty in the face of the destruction of the social link by historical catastrophes. In the year of the *Anschluss*, 1938, Wittgenstein had also "confessed" to some friends in Cambridge that his family had Jewish origins. In 1929, at an interdisciplinary seminar on "personality investigations," psychoanalyst Harry Stack Sullivan, who treated schizophrenics, compared this need for confession to the analyst's avowals, which his patient needs at critical moments, and with the mutual confession made by young Indians of the Crazy Dog Society. Before setting out on the warpath, they each take an oath to fight until death if one of them is killed, and they seal their alliance by confessing transgressions of the law.[16] Sullivan then advised analysts to allow themselves to make some disclosures at critical moments.

Folly and writing

If one goes to the trouble of writing "what does not cease not to be written" – the Real, according to Lacan – one needs a very special interlocutor. In *The Flowers of Evil*, Baudelaire addresses his poems to the "hypocrite reader, my fellow, my brother."[17] In his preface to the second *Don Quixote*, Cervantes challenges the reader to admonish his jealous colleagues who paid a forger to destroy his work. But is this a reason to attach a psychiatric label to Don Quixote?

Kerouac did not escape this fate. After joining the navy in 1943, he rebelled against a petty officer and was diagnosed schizophrenic when he pretended to be mad. After his best friend from Lowell, Sammy Sampas – who was then a soldier (later killed in combat) – came to visit him in the hospital, Kerouac took up duty again on a Merchant Marine vessel whose mission was to build landing strips in Greenland. He narrowly escaped death when a torpedo sunk the ship next to his with its crew of 800 seamen.

He described himself as being "borderline." He was born in a house standing where a graveyard used to be, and he was haunted by the remorse of having wished Gerard dead the day his brother slapped him for destroying the Erector Set structures he had built, the only kind of play he was still able to enjoy. Later, true to the promise he had made his father to look after her, Kerouac always returned to live with his mother and spent the last ten years of his life with her, writing until the very end of his life.

In his adolescence, a famous trainer had noticed his prowess as a football player and had him recruited by Columbia University, where he studied on an athletic scholarship. But he left the university because of confrontations with the trainer, who humiliated him in public. It was then that he decided to pursue his dream of becoming a writer. In New York, at Edie Parker's apartment, which she shared with her friend Joan Vollmer, the muse of the beat generation, Kerouac met Allen Ginsberg, a student at Columbia, and William Burroughs, who married Joan and eventually killed her, in 1951 in Mexico. He escaped prosecution thanks to his influential relations, a tragic omen of what is now called "feminicide" in Mexico and Latin America – murders of women committed with impunity, and tied to drug trafficking.

Contrary to Burroughs, Kerouac did not brag about his addictions, nor did he take himself for a brooding author who needed drugs to write. In *Vanity of Duluoz*, he confesses that his need for intoxication sprung from his obsession with death, because death was what he had waited for during the first four years of his life, while his brother's life was in suspense. Established legend notwithstanding, at the end of his life Kerouac and his mother were not left to themselves like two abandoned drunkards. Three years earlier, he had married his third wife Stella Sampas, Sammy's sister – his Greek friend and football buddy in Lowell, who was killed in the war. Stella not only took care of him and his mother, but she also allowed him to write until the end. She is the "wifey" to whom he speaks in *Vanity of Duluoz*, a feminine agency emerging from the failings of the fathers' law, the Lady of his thoughts that Dulcina was for Don Quixote.

Paradoxically, Kerouac's "dropping out" started after the success of *On the Road*. Composed between 1948 and 1951, the final scroll was only published in 1957 by Viking Press, after many rejections, with the changes mentioned earlier. As soon as it came out, the book was made famous by a glowing review in *The New York Times*. In the meantime, Kerouac wrote 17 novels that were refused by Viking, which was holding out for another bestseller. Eventually, other publishers took over the publication of his works.

Expanding language

Kerouac was a master of "spontaneous prose." He named the totality of his prose the *Duluoz Legend*, wanting it to be known after his death as a complete oeuvre, like Proust's *Remembrance of Things Past*.[18] Duluoz was Kerouac's fictional alter ego, who polished language day after day, as he wrote. During the war years, André Breton was in New York, along with Marcel Duchamp, who had taken refuge there in 1915, and had created *The Bride Stripped Bare by Her Bachelors, Even*. But Kerouac denied being influenced by the surrealists' automatic writing, despite the uninterrupted typing of his scroll in the space of three weeks in April 1951. Soon after his death, the scroll was sold in London for $1.5 million. But its author had died in poverty, never able to fulfil his dream of buying a small farm in New Hampshire and bringing his family there.

Still, he never stopped writing. His language is a wind instrument that, by constant improvisation, seeks to discover what breath is capable of doing. The Latin word *follis* means "bellows." Kerouac causes air to twirl around the deadly petrification of perversion, like water spinning around a rock. He refused to be the guru of the "rucksack revolution," since he was not a teacher, but an "author," a word that comes from the Latin *augeo*, "to augment." Kerouac expanded language for two or three generations of people who experienced wars and economic crises. In 1917, 170,000 soldiers were being sent to France each week. The stock market crash of 1929 sent masses of people into the streets, in worn clothes, to line up in front of soup kitchens. After World War II, the GI Bill – of which he was a beneficiary – allowed young soldiers to pursue free university studies. But they had come back terribly changed, as they would be when they returned from the Korean War and the Vietnam War.

America as it once was could not go on forever. Kerouac invented a new writing style, in the same innovative spirit as that of Proust, to whom he compared himself without false modesty. Like Kerouac, Proust had refused all paid employment, but had not been obliged to do menial work, such as being a dishwasher at the university, writing dissertations for other students or working as a brakeman for the railroad.

Some fifteen years before his death in 1922, Proust isolated himself in a cork-lined room on Haussmann Boulevard, and then Rue Hamelin, to write *Remembrance of Things Past*, panting because of his asthma, writing, correcting and pinning up his "bits of paper." He was writing about the end of an era, that of the Faubourg Saint-Germain, swept away by the Great War. Proust, like Aby Warburg, foresaw the disaster to come. Both were born and almost died at the same period of the Franco-Prussian War. Aby, born in 1866, and his mother almost succumbed to typhus. Shortly after his birth in 1866, both Aby Warburg and his mother almost succumbed to typhus. Marcel Proust was born in 1871, and his father – a physician – was afraid that he would not survive, because of his wife's weakened state during the 1870 Siege of Paris, when food shortages were severe. This early trauma caused them both to develop, and never cease to trust, a very sensitive "seismograph of the soul," to use Warburg's term.

Kerouac knew that in order to "write" America, he had to depict as many people and experiences as possible, and not only those of others, but also his own. Like Proust, he never stopped writing, using his ever-present notebooks and his neatly classified letters, contrasting with his chaotic life. His phenomenal memory is traumatic memory, "without oblivion," as Bion would say. Both writers refused to let their editors make the slightest changes. When *The Subterraneans* was being published in 1958, five years after it was written, Kerouac answered the editor who asked him to remove his hyphens: "I would rather die than change the form of my work, which is my life," echoing Laurence Sterne's motto: "[to] live or write [...] in my case means the same thing." And he stuck stubbornly to his "Shandean dashes."[19]

The work of these authors inscribes the cut-out memory of trauma that forgets no detail and makes the rhythm of their phrases conform to their breathing. Kerouac gives hyperrealistic depictions of America's drifting without leaving himself out of the picture. One of his most devastatingly personal books is *Big Sur*, the name of the rocky California coast south of San Francisco, where he took refuge in 1960 in an isolated cottage belonging to Laurence Ferlinghetti, the owner of the City Lights bookshop in San Francisco, a meeting place of the beat generation. Written in 1961, this amazing book testifies to the terrible solitude to which fame had condemned him.

Ink in the blood

Kerouac was criticised for writing two books in traditional style: *Doctor Sax*, published in 1958 after earlier rejections, and *Vanity of Duluoz*, his last book, published in 1968. But in fact, in these works the rhythm is simply mastered more artfully. Since childhood, ink runs through his veins, literally; as he puts it, he has the ink of his father's printing shop in his blood. This had been clear since preparatory school and then at Columbia, where he wrote dissertations for wealthy students, as well as a manual for a French professor, all the while filling his notebooks.

His first texts, written on an Underwood typewriter, have been published under the title *Atop an Underwood*.[20] They are carefully classified, like his other notes. In 1943, in New York, he wrote a letter offering his services as a writer of synopses in the film industry. Like many of his subsequent texts, the letter started:

> I was born in Lowell, Mass., in March 1922 [...]. At the age of eleven I spent most of my time after school in my father's printing and editorial offices [...]. This early association with the printing and publishing business soon enough stained not only my blood but my hands and my face with ink.

Kerouac's scroll has the same shape as the rolls of paper on which his father printed the Lowell newspaper, in which he himself published film, jazz and sports commentary. Like the black Moleskine notebooks in which our fathers and grandfathers described their wars in flowing narrative with nothing crossed out, Kerouac's memoirs take us into a world recorded on things.

Doctor Sax begins:

> The other night I had a dream that I was sitting on the sidewalk [in] Lowell, Mass., with a pencil and paper in my hand saying to myself "describe the wrinkly tar of this sidewalk, also the iron pickets of the gate of the Textile Institute, or the doorway where Lousy and you and G. J.'s always sittin and don't stop to think of words when you stop, just stop to think of the picture better – and let your mind off yourself in this work."

G. J. was another Greek friend in Lowell, George J. Apostolos: "Just before that I was coming down the hill between Gershom Avenue and that spectral street ..." His dreams are haunted by ghosts who demand, so that his mind might speak to his soul, that his writing converse with the memories printed on the cracks in the tar. Such are a child's perceptions. These cracks were what he employed to enact his earliest traumatic impressions of his brother's illness and of his parents' poverty, without anyone suspecting. From then on, anything can happen.

Doctor Sax is a vampire. It's like reading *Harry Potter*: the fantasy world of a child who discovers evil, unhappiness, mediocrity and indifference, and refuses to be trapped in them, making them instead the material of his art. The life of this young boy, between the ages of 4 and 11, was marked by long moments of absorption in his surroundings; he set himself a kind of discipline: "'Take note, take note, well of them take note,' I'm saying to myself in the dream." He must remember everything to forestall denial, and find, in the jumble of unforgettable images which testify to his childhood, something that can help him to face the uncertainty of his own death and the bell that tolls since Gerard's death: *memento mori*.

Kerouac's ambition as a writer was, as he himself said, to make people see what he saw thanks to his sense of beauty, which he considered the ultimate degree of freedom. When he took up his pen to shape the impressions jotted down in his notebooks, he captured the social trends of his era, like madmen do, according to Harry Stack Sullivan, because they identify with the social link.

In 1943, LSD was synthesised in Basel by the Sandoz laboratories. Neal Cassady was part of the "liberation movement," but it is hard to say who was liberated from what. Contrary to Woody Allen's movie *The Purple Rose of Cairo*,[21] in which the characters step off the screen and mix with the spectators, the imagination-expanding machine does the opposite, swallowing up people's lives and making them actors in a script over which they have no control. For instance, Doctor Sax's script. Kerouac has often been identified with Dean Moriarty, his breakneck companion on the road. Yet Kerouac is different; in the guise of Sal Paradise, he opposes ideologies that devour people's lives. The publishers of *On the Road* feared that real people could be recognised behind the fictional characters: Allen Ginsberg is Carlo Marx, William Burroughs is Old Bull Lee. But for Kerouac, drawing on his life to write was the opposite of vampirising the lives of others.

The lost honour of childhood impressions

The Town and the City, written in 1945 and published in 1950,[22] looks at America with a child's eyes. The author's father is portrayed as the printer George Martin; one of his children, Julian, who was a twin, died, but "he's still taking care of us, even though we don't see him," says his mother Marguerite, an emigrant from Quebec. The first part of the book tells the story of this family with eight children, living in a big, slightly run-down house, filled with the good scent of vanilla, Kerouac's equivalent of Proust's madeleine.

In Chapter 8 of the second part, when the sudden news of the attack on Pearl Harbour comes bursting through the radio, the father remembers "that he had really felt the same way in 1917 [...] and it was all coming to pass again, the same stupid and violent unreality of things gone mad ..." In Galloway – alias Lowel – "the little kids ran out in the fields at dusk and yelled and screamed because they thought that Jap planes were going to come over any hour." The oldest son, Joe, enlisted in the air force:

> The great wartime wanderings of Americans were just beginning. Great troop-trains rumbled by in the night everywhere [...] and the rolling land at night, and weary harassed sleep in coach-cars, and the railroad stations again, and a hollow melancholy voice calling the names of place [...]. It was a railroad landing and the crowds of khaki-clad soldiers searching eagerly, or waiting casually, or singing and shouting ...

Trains filled with troops rushed towards an unknown destination:

> ... and thoughts, thoughts, thoughts in the night once more. [...] men and women went back and forth [...] walked around in absurd circles. It was like this, and it was more than that [...]. It was carried on night and day around the terrific cycloramas of the land and spread-eagling far overseas incredibly. No one could see it, yet everyone was in it, and it was like [...] the world itself, grown fantastic and homeless in war.

A veteran, like Kerouac's father, Wilfred Bion coined the phrase "thoughts without a thinker," which are "in search of a thinker to be thought." Alcide, who fought in World War I, never spoke about it, any more than Bion, who started to write about his war experiences in the last years of his life. So, the unthought thoughts of American people, strewn on the roads, found Kerouac to think them in writing, thanks to impressions recorded since his birth in 1922. Kerouac strove to bring them into existence using his notebook, which served as his material, while he sought another who could receive them. Speaking of these primary impressions, Bion has the infant ask: "How will I let myself out of this?" Out of these premature impressions recording the imminent break of the social link?

Normally, these impressions are filtered through the sound of reassuring words. They do not yet operate at the level of repression, but in the jumble of what Antonio Damasio calls body signals.[23] They resemble traumatic memories, which record the slightest variations, but they can be repressed if another is there to articulate them in a language-game. But a child left to himself, who notices a sudden change in his parents, gives up asking questions when he is confronted with their silence. The danger is that he will remain "stuck with" these impressions, which will constantly return in the present, awaiting someone who will confirm them through his own experience that resonates with them. Unless this happens, faith in the other is lost completely, and doubt as to the truth persists.

Kerouac became aware very early that it was urgent to note everything threatened by erasure. His notebook and pencil, the ink and paper he played with in his father's print shop, were his first means of inscription. This memory that precedes words is worthy of a presentation at a world summit of infants, to assert the sharpness of their perceptions. This might allow their future works to escape the fate of rejected manuscripts – one of which was *Swann's Way*, judged unworthy of the *Nouvelle Revue Française* by André Gide. Proust's madeleine left him indifferent. By contrast, when an analyst can enter into this special transference, the child in him comes to the aid of the child before him, who demands the right to speak, like the embryo on the first page of *Tristram Shandy*.

The dynamics of trauma inscription function like a succession of rough drafts with sharp, precise contours, with nothing blurred, looking for transference in the right place. Of course, one must find someone to speak to about all this, but whom? While "on the road," our patients met many psychoanalysts to whom they attempted in vain to show what they observed. Not surprising, since the absence of temporal sequence and causal relations repels the discursive thinking of the analyst, as long as he refuses to trust his own impressions and the coincidences interfering with what he is shown.

The images overlap, like the coincidence in *The Town and the City* when Kerouac's childhood intersects with the story of the veteran in a bar who shoots himself in the head, shouting: "War is me, I am the Spirit of 1914." The connection between the story of the child and that of the soldier is not obvious, except if we use the definition of trauma given by Claude Barrois and Jonathan Shay, analysts working with veterans: the betrayal of their families, of their superiors in the military, and of civilians who no longer recognise them.[24] This definition applies to a family or a nation as well.

Erasure of traces

The passage from the town to the city breaks the balance that had existed around the porch of the house, the print shop, the Meramec River, the language of the ancestors spoken with the neighbours, the polyphony of voices and accents. Moving to New York splits the family apart. A small native town with its joys and misfortunes is exchanged for an anonymous city – even if there was a strong desire to get away from this place where everyone knew everything about everyone else.

In the hospital where I was close to death, in my delusions I too was attempting to make people disappear. I saw myself in Macon, my home town on the Saône River, communicating directly with the river, the only reliable element over the centuries – where I was systematically erasing, one after the other, all the people walking on the bridge. This is how a child – a state to which my total dependency had brought me – attempts to do away with the catastrophes awaiting him.

For economic reasons, I too had to move to a drab city in Northern France, a city devastated by war, where people spoke with an accent foreign to me. My father had been offered a job there and my mother had to run a café for the first time in her life. The comments of the clients when I came in from school and crossed the room made me stiffen up like a puppet, like the figure connected to life support machines lying on the bed now. It took me a long time to remember the ordeal of that transition. It was I, not a murderous ideology, who had erased the traces. In this case, the erasure was a mode of survival.

The traces of what Kerouac cannot say are in his books. The war is ever-present with its aftermath of social disintegration. Kerouac never spoke of "his war" – the terror he felt on his way back from Greenland, when the ship next to his was torpedoed, killing 800 sailors, some of whom he knew. This erased narrative resurfaces in the form of a question haunting him: When will it be my turn? His immersion in New York City is not that of a tourist. Times Square is a point of unstable equilibrium that attracts a generation of young people addicted to drugs and alcohol, engulfed in the solitude of the big city after returning from the war. Kerouac blends in with them, but continues to write.

On the Road depicts the immediate aftermath of the war, when "anything goes," after the title of the Cole Porter musical comedy composed in 1934, with the 1929 crash as its backdrop: let yourself go, pull out all the stops! The reaction to post-war McCarthyism would soon be followed by anti-Vietnam protests. Kerouac writes about everything. Everything is true, nothing is fabricated. In 1946, after the death of his father, who fought in the Great War, he starts to write *On the Road*.

On the Road

He calls his book an *epos*, and he knows what he is doing when he channels the passion that impels him to portray America into an epic form of writing. He takes on the role of Sancho Panza, "shambling after" Dean, Carlo Marx and the other characters. Just as Cervantes refused to be identified with the picaresque character of his era, the Sancho-like narrator, Sal Paradise, is not a picaro. But they are his companions on the road. First among them is Dean Moriarty, alias Neal Cassady, the car thief and former hustler on the streets of Denver. There is also Old Bull, alias William Burroughs, a real murderer, and others of the same ilk.

Kerouac "turns author" – as Laurence Sterne says – when Dean meets Carlo Marx, alias Allan Ginsberg. After several attempts at fictional narrative, he invents a poetic novel – or narrative poem – free from European influences. His rhapsody is a patchwork of things sown together, like a New England quilt – things that come into being on their own, to the rhythm of jazz, and create spontaneous prose, sustained by mastery of the breath. The reader can hear this mastery from the very first pages:

> They rushed down the street together, digging everything in the early way they had, which later became so much sadder and perceptive and blank. But then they danced down the streets like dingledoodles, and I shambled after as I've been doing all my life after people who interest me, because the only people for me are the mad ones, the ones who are mad to live, mad to talk, mad to be saved, desirous of everything at the same time, the ones who never yawn or say a commonplace thing, but burn, burn, burn like fabulous roman candles exploding like spiders across the stars and in the middle you see the blue centre light pop and everybody goes "yawww!"

The sexual seduction scene between Dean Moriarty and Carlo Max is replaced in the Viking edition by a reference to Werther:

> What did they call such young people in Goethe's Germany? The first thing you know, Dean, wanting dearly to learn how to write poetry like Carlo, was attacking him with a great amorous soul such as only a conman can have.

In the space of the marvel, where the fool dwelt in the Middle Ages, three hours could last three years. Having rejected the nonsense about structure and automatic writing, Kerouac took a long time to develop his own way of putting trauma into writing. The same is true of analytic work. The fact that in a lineage the name of the father has been destabilised does not necessarily mean that a psychotic structure develops. Inscribing truths that insist precisely because they have been cut out takes a long time.

All the more so when time has stopped in zones of death where words are frozen, like in Chapter 55 of Rabelais' *The Fourth Book*.[25] On board a ship sailing in search of the Oracle of the Holy Bottle, Pantagruel and his friends hear voices. The ship's captain tells them that the previous winter, in this region of the frozen sea where they are sailing, "a great and bloody battle"[26] had taken place. Suddenly, wild words of different colours, spoken in different tones, fall onto the decks of the ships. When Pantagruel warms them up in his hands, the words become distinct. Red words emerge from sliced throats and speak in heraldic tones. How many analysts are refrigerators for frozen words, confusing them with signifiers instead of taking them into their hands, as Pantagruel did, to warm up speech that was numbed in the chaos of battle?

Kerouac chose to warm up his wild words, through lengthy effort, with his own breath, without recourse to trendy discourse. In the third version of his typed manuscript, the editors inserted quotation marks and semicolons everywhere, but the scroll typed in three weeks had emerged after a long period of preparation during which Kerouac made numerous attempts at finding his own voice. In 1946, he wrote a postcard using his own blood. Everything that was not going to change American literature radically was to be mercilessly discarded.

The IT

The truth is that Kerouac was not interested in the narrativity of a story with a plot. When his publisher asked him to compress the narration of the three journeys into one, he refused. The only thing he wanted was to inscribe the trauma without periods or commas, like madness succeeds in doing. "I came to literature very early," he said, convinced that "the straight line will lead you only to death." Laurence Sterne defended the same viewpoint, with the help of a diagram in *Tristram Shandy*.[27] Kerouac's literature is rooted in the now, the present tense of sensations, not in the telling of stories that make sense. "Knowing time" is IT, as Dean Moriarty says several times; this is the immediacy of the IT to which jazz gives access.

Kerouac's writing style sheds the constraints of cause-and-effect relations. His ultimatum to himself is to reject the absurdity of modern art, adhere only to the truth of sensory experience, and ignore everything that doesn't have to do with his sensations. The creative force converts "everything you are" into art. The body is part of this, through its vibrations. The scroll was typed in a trance-like state, while Kerouac was bathed in sweat, breathless, like the horn player "tenorman" saying "Blow!" in San Francisco when he had IT and was able to hold it, in Chapter 10 (Part 3). When Wilfred Bion was giving his seminars in Brazil, once he had repossessed his war experiences during his exile in the United States, he advised analysts not to spend too much time in seminars, if they were to attain this IT. An analyst has to be born, in that particular moment, out of the unique character of his story and his personality.[28]

The subject of the IT comes up in the next chapter, in the car while they are driving east:

> We were telling these things and both sweating. [...] Dean and I both swayed to the rhythm of the IT of our final excited joy in talking and living to the blank tranced end of all innumerable riotous angelic particulars that had been lurking in our souls all our lives. "Oh, man! Man!" moaned Dean. [...] we know what IT is and we know TIME and we know that everything is really FINE.

> (pp. 208, 209)

The riotous angel who calls forth the particulars lurking in Kerouac's soul is his older brother. In *Visions of Gerard*,[29] he praises Gerard's kindness, "riotous" towards any form of cruelty. For Kerouac, finding the IT means getting hold of time that stands still and setting it in motion in his writing, thanks to the "pulse," not to the meaning. On the road, he meets Americans, "We the people," who are left by the wayside of the path forged by the pilgrims who landed in Plymouth, immigrating, like his own family, from France to Canada and then to the United States, with the Greeks, Blacks, Italians, Polish, Irish, Chinese, Jews and Quebeckers who lived in Lowell. In 1957, Kerouac wrote: "I am not a romantic poet or a surrealist. I am a linguistic poet." He was interested in the invigorating accents of other languages – Celtic, Latin, Greek and even Aztec – when the road took him to Mexico.

Kerouac questions the shadows

These accents constitute the erased traces of his history: "*Majoresque cadunt altis de montibus umbrae*: from the mountain summits longer shadows drop."[30] Kerouac has read the verse that closes Virgil's first Eclogue. When he summons the spirit of the mountain above Denver, he sees the shadow of the Rockies stretching towards the east (p. 55). The Eclogues are not simply a pastoral about shepherds blowing in their reed pipes, but also a story about the war that threatened to drive Virgil's father from his farm, after the decree granting land to veteran Roman legionaries.

In Lowell, Kerouac liked to read *The Shadow* magazine, whose hero, The Shadow, "knew the evil that lurks in the hearts of men." *On the Road* took shape after the death of Kerouac's father, to fill in the silence about his downfall and about his service in World War I. When Kerouac meets Neal, they set out in search of Neal's father, a vagrant who used to sing: "Hallelujah! I am a bum, bum again!" They did not find him, but on the road they met other vagrants, the schlemiels – to use Arendt's word – left out on the street like many veterans and immigrants are today. Their stories, which no one wants to hear, can take refuge in a syncopated rhythm in which silences mark the traces that have been erased.

When Jonathan Shay, psychotherapist at the Boston Veterans Hospital, was invited by his daughter to attend a course given by Gregory Nagy on the *Iliad* at Harvard, he recognised in the scansion of the hexameters of the epic tale the rhythm of his patients' profanities: "Fuck, fuckin' mother, motherfucker," the iambic rhythm of anger. The silence between the words needs to be heard outside the frame of psychiatric or even psychoanalytic discourse, which reduces these words to automatisms and "fuckin'" neologisms, leaving the patients in the depths of loneliness. After the success of *On the Road*, Kerouac had the same experience: his world went through what Kurt Vonnegut, another veteran of World War II, calls a timequake.

Like the Althing in Iceland – located in an ever-widening fault zone, chosen by the Vikings for their parliamentary sessions – Kerouac chose to settle on the Big Sur coastline to watch himself sink into alcoholic dementia, while trying to loosen its hold through poetic writing.[31] Lacan once said: "What has been foreclosed from the symbolic reappears in the real [...] it never ceases not to be inscribed." As if to prove him right, Kerouac never stopped writing on the rift between two tectonic plates. At night, he went down to the beach from Lawrence Ferlinghetti's cabin overlooking the ocean, and wrote in his notebook, under a feeble light, what the white mouth of the Pacific told him. The poem entitled "Sea," at the end of his book, reproduces the crashing of the waves: "Cherson! Cherson! Go on die salt light, Shaw ... Shoo ..."

In his solitude, he speaks to flowers, trees, the brook and the animals: a little mouse – the reincarnation of Gerard – a racoon, blue jays, a sacred mule named Alf, and they all answer him when humans cannot: "and my soul screams a thousand babbling words, oh – it's hard to explain and best thing to do is not be false" (p. 24).

A cathedral of words

"What is a book," he asks in *The Dharma Bums*, published in 1958, in his Buddhist period, "if not the creation of history among lunatics?"[32] He had happened upon Buddhism by chance, while reading sutras in a library. He wrote: "I can't wait to become disembodied in rhythm." For him, this discovery had nothing to do with the New Age fad that would sweep over California. Instead, it gave shape to the founding experience of his first four years of life, intensely lived through Gerard's imminent death. During this period, Kerouac translated Buddhist texts[33] and wrote haikus.[34]

Visions of Gerard, written in 1957 and published in 1963, followed *Some of the Dharma*, written between 1953 and 1956, but only published forty years later. He called these Dharma "illuminations" in both senses of the word: manuscript drawings and visions that enlighten the soul. Gerard seldom cried. When you cannot cry, things may feel in your place: like the little mouse whose life Gerard saved until the cat caught it, or the clouds he watched from his bed "fighting their wars."A year before his death, he saw the Virgin Mary taking him to Heaven in a white wagon pulled by two little lambs. The nuns at his school considered him a saint.

Kerouac describes the saga of his lineage, which he calls the *Duluoz Legend*, as his cathedral of words, which he describes in the prologue of *Big Sur* as "seen through the eyes of poor Ti Jean (me): the world of raging action and folly and also of gentle sweetness seen through the keyhole of his eye." The building of this cathedral is a victory over fate.

In *Oedipus at Colonus*, the choir proposes a solution to the impasse of those whose lineage is a heavy burden: "*Mè phunai ton apanta nika logon*" ("Not to be born at all is a victory over speech").[35] Lacan's double misinterpretation consists in having translated the infinitive as an optative spoken by Oedipus: "Would that I had not been born," when what the choir asserted was that not being born is a victory over *logos*: no more words. But Sophocles' tragedy[36] teaches us that the unborn children will have to wrestle with destiny – *atè,* from the verb *aô* – to drive somebody crazy, thanks to the power of words, emerging, Kerouac says, "in a rush of truth." *Phumai* means "to be born," in the sense of burgeoning or flourishing, like the land, like life.

When Lin Tsi, the Zen master, asks: "What was a child like before he was born?"[37] one may answer: he was like new potential, charged with the time long before his birth, breaking through the doctrine of causality which claims that life is not worth living. Hannah Arendt calls children *"oi neoi, the new ones."*[38] Gerard's brief life served to bequeath to his brother the energy to write. Similarly, Tristram Shandy's embryo – whose birth was imperilled by his parents' carelessness – asserts that not being born is no victory over the *logos,* and would, moreover, have deprived us of the narrative of his life and opinions.

In the style of Tex Avery

The scene reminds us of a Woody Woodpecker cartoon in which the woodpecker keeps running after having gone past the edge of the cliff. On the edge of a cliff, in 1956, Kerouac practises Zen, reads Suzuki and Zen koans, and has talks with Gary Snyder, a mountaineer from Oregon, an erudite lumberjack well versed in Chinese and Japanese culture and poetry, who takes him on hikes and challenges him to write. When they climb the 4,000-metre-high peak of the Matterhorn in the Rockies, Kerouac is exhausted at 30 metres from the top and thinks he will die, but continues to climb while asking himself what he is doing there. Still, he keeps going to find firm ground for his writing. Unfortunately, Gary leaves for Japan after taking him to a refuge on Desolation Peak, to be a forest fire lookout. There, Kerouac experiences extreme loneliness, which the success of *On the Road* would intensify two years later.

Writing is the road when there is nothing solid to stand on. When Sterne "turns author" at the worst moment of his life, he creates a new style punctuated by direct addresses to the reader. Kerouac chooses to replace traditional English prose that is of no use to him, by short sentences without conjunctions such as "and," "therefore," and so on, as we see in *Good Blonde and Others,*[39] a 1993 collection of texts from the same period as the publication of *On the Road.* The writing he creates becomes the ground on which he stands.

For him, madness is not structured by the foreclosure of the name of the father, but by his typewriter. The surface on which he makes his inscription is his own life, Dean's life and the lives of the other Dharma bums. The name Tristram comes from that of a tramp whose statue stood in front of the church, near the Yorkshire school where Sterne's father brought him from Ireland when he was 11 – a symbol of his abandonment. His father went to war and died; he never saw him again. Following in Cervantes' footsteps, he was to create the quixotic character of Uncle Toby, a veteran of the wars against the French, and the boy's only interlocutor.

According to Wilfred Bion, in this context "transference is transient" because it depends on an "interaction." In *On the Road*, the interaction is between two children who have seen too much. Sal Paradise and Dean Moriarty experience together the instantaneity of the present, the subversion of the adult world, the immediate fulfilment of desires, and they talk, talk, talk about their ghosts, about what they have in common, although they come from very different worlds, with a childlike indulgence for each other's whims, but not childishly. Their "premature knowledge," as Bion calls it, impels them to write. The same thing was true for Samuel Beckett; when a journalist asked him why he wrote, he answered: "All I'm good for."

When I am asked why, as an analyst, I am interested in madness and trauma, I can say the same thing: "All I'm good for," and not every day, because with each patient I am an analyst once a year, when it's a good year! Martin Cooperman, an analyst of psychosis at the Austen Riggs Center, and a veteran of Guadalcanal, made the same observation:

> The analysis of psychosis lasts a week, but it takes years to get to it. And all that time, the analyst hides behind his theories and the patient behind his symptoms, until the day they come out of hiding and can finally meet.

Then, trauma speaks to trauma, from their respective zones of catastrophe. Castaway truths, in "thoughts without a thinker," wandering in search of a co-researcher, meet to fight against the erasure of their traces by denial.

The frog pond

To illustrate this transient moment, both critical and decisive, I will use the example of a frog pond. Let us imagine the surface of a pond on a very calm day, a smooth surface without a ripple. But this immobility is only apparent since the water in the pond has a very low-frequency undulatory rhythm. A ripple will form every 100 years. Let us imagine two ponds fairly close to each other, with the same telluric properties. One looks smooth, as if nothing will change its structure, unless there is recourse to mechanical means; the frequency of the other pond is slightly different. At some point, flooding can occur, creating a channel between the two ponds. The equation of the appearance of their ripples will now be completely different, since what is involved are not distinct waves, but an interference.

This is what takes place in our work with patients. All of us have known some turmoil that impelled us to become analysts. When we speak of lands of exile imposed by plagues, famines and wars, of people who sail away with no hope of return, what can happen to a child who bears the name of these people? Harry Stack Sullivan, the psychoanalyst who worked with schizophrenics, was the grandson of Irish immigrants who left on a ship on which his grandmother lost her first husband and gave birth to a son.[40] These catastrophes are not causes, but are points of origin of ripples or tidal waves we know nothing about.

A patient arrives with a big blank, a vast void. He and the analyst are in their respective frog ponds, sometimes as distant from each other as France is from Amazonia. The patient can say to himself, like Shakespeare's King Richard II in his prison: "I am still king of my griefs." Sometimes, even analysts seek reassurance by electing a king, like La Fontaine's frogs did, and end up choosing a log.[41]

If the patient persists in coming to see the analyst, after many twists and turns while the analyst tries to keep control of his pond, a catastrophic flood could risk happening. Then the analyst can either hospitalise the patient, or can recognise the emergence of something, IT, in a pulse lasting a thousandth of a second that touches him in places of which he is most often unaware, causing a ripple they should investigate together.

Or this might not happen. And that would be a shame, because this co-research is the only way in which the traces of beings and events cut out of history may come into being, in a new time-space between them, enabling the birth of a transitional subject, as Benedetti calls it. To go back to Martin Cooperman, flight surgeon on the Wasp when it was shot down at Guadalcanal, analysts would be better advised to learn to swim with their patients instead of drowning in a glass of water.

Especially when a "timequake" takes place in the session, a subject on which Kurt Vonnegut will enlighten us in the next seminar.

Notes

1 Kerouac, J., *On the Road*, Viking Press, 1957.
2 Wittgenstein, L., *Philosophical Investigations*, Blackwell, 1956, paragraph 21.
3 Kerouac, J., *The Town and the City*, Harcourt Brace, 1950.
4 Gifford, B., *Jack's Book: An Oral Biography of Jack Kerouac*, Penguin Books, 2012.
5 Kerouac, J., *Visions of Gerard*, Penguin Books, 1991.
6 Benedetti, G., *Psychotherapy of Schizophrenia*, New York University Press, 1987. See *infra* Seminar 2 on Gaetano Benedetti.
7 Kerouac, J., *Satori in Paris and Pic*, Grove Press, 1985.
8 Malamoud, C., *Cooking the World: Ritual and Thought in Ancient India*, Oxford University Press, 1996.
9 Renou, L., *The Destiny of Veda in India*, Motilal Banarsidass, 1965.
10 Kerouac, J., *The Town and the City*, op. cit.
11 Mallarmé, S., *Collected Poems of Mallarmé*, University of California Press, 2011.
12 Rulfo, J., *Pedro Paramo*, Grove Press, 1994.
13 Kerouac, J., *Vanity of Duluoz*, Penguin Books, 1994.
14 Baillet, A., "Olympica," in *La vie de M. Descartes*, CreateSpace, 2015.
15 Descartes, R., *Discourse on the Method*, SMK Books, 2009.

16 Sullivan, H. S., "Schizophrenic Individuals as a Source of Data for Comparative Investigation of Personality," in *Schizophrenia as a Human Process*, W. W. Norton & Company, 1944.

17 Baudelaire, C., *The Flowers of Evil & Paris Spleen: Selected Poems*, Dover Publications, 2010.

18 Proust, M., *Remembrance of Things Past*, Modern Library, 1999.

19 Sterne, L., *The Life and Opinions of Tristram Shandy, Gentleman*, Wordsworth Editions, 1999.

20 Kerouac, J., *Atop an Underwood*, Penguin Books, 1999.

21 Allen, W. (Dir.), *The Purple Rose of Cairo*, 1985.

22 Kerouac, J., *The Town and the City*, op. cit.

23 Damasio, A., *Descartes' Error*, Penguin Books, 2005.

24 Barrois, C., *La psychanalyse du guerrier*, Hachette, 1993; Shay, J., *Achilles in Vietnam*, Scribner, 1995.

25 Rabelais, F., *Gargantua and Pantagruel: The Fourth Book*, Penguin Classics, 2006, Chapter 55. See *infra* Seminar 12 on François Rabelais and Yvette Guilbert.

26 Rabelais, F., *Gargantua: The Fourth Book*, CreateSpace, 2015.

27 Sterne, L., *The Life and Opinions of Tristram Shandy, Gentleman*, op. cit., Chapter XL.

28 Bion, W., *Clinical Seminars and Other Works*, Karnac Books, 1994, p. 15.

29 Kerouac, J., *Visions of Gerard*, op. cit.

30 Virgil, *The Eclogues of Virgil*, Ferry, D. (Trans.), Farrar, Straus & Giroux, 2000.

31 Kerouac, J., *Big Sur*, Penguin Books, 1992.

32 Kerouac, J., *The Dharma Bums*, Penguin Classics, 2006.

33 Kerouac, J., *Some of the Dharma*, Penguin Books, 1999.

34 Kerouac, J., *Book of Haikus*, Penguin Books, 2003.

35 Sophocles, *Oedipus at Colonus*, Dover Publications, 1999.

36 Saïd, S., *La Faute tragique*, Maspero, 1978.

37 Watson, B. (Ed.), *The Zen Teachings of Master Lin-Chi*, Shambhala, 1993.

38 See *infra* Seminar 7 on Hannah Arendt.

39 Kerouac, J., *Good Blonde and Others*, Grey Fox Press, 2001.

40 Swick Perry, H., *Psychiatrist of America: The Life of Harry Stack Sullivan*, Harvard University Press, 1982.

41 De La Fontaine, J.,"The Frogs Who Ask for a King," in *The Complete Fables of Jean de La Fontaine*, University of Illinois Press, 2007, p. 60.

Seminar 14: 2013–2014
Kurt Vonnegut (1922–2007)
Timequake:[1] the hard reality of fiction

Kurt Vonnegut published his last novel, *Timequake*, ten years before his death, thumbing his nose at his biographer Charles Shields,[2] who had met him a year earlier. Shields had already written the biography of Harper Lee (1928–2016), although she had refused to meet him.[3]

With the publication of *Slaughterhouse-Five* in 1969,[4] Kurt Vonnegut became a bestselling author. The title of his biography, *And So It Goes*, takes up the refrain of the novel, punctuating the narration, of the effects of the destruction of Dresden in February 1945 on a former prisoner of war. Kurt Vonnegut was drafted in June 1944 – one month after his mother's suicide on Mother's Day. He was assigned to a division sent to France as reinforcement to troops fighting in the Ardennes. Taken prisoner on December 15, 1944, just before the Battle of the Bulge, he was part of a convoy of about 100 American prisoners forced to march and take trains to Dresden, where they were locked up, in January 1945, in the second basement of a slaughterhouse of the city, *Schlachthof-Fünf*, so that their lives were saved.

On February 14, the city was completely destroyed by the firebombs of the British and American air forces. The prisoners were assigned to clear the rubble. In April, they were taken to the Czech border. Vonnegut was sent back to the United States in June. The fact that he wrote his novel 24 years later, when he was 47, testifies to the time necessary to inscribe trauma. For six months, between January and June, his father, who had been told that he was missing, did not know if he was dead or alive.

Timequake appears to be the rewriting of a previous manuscript, about which the reader is told nothing other than the recurring phrase: "This is from *Timequake One*." An initial text disappears – like the first manuscript of *Don Quixote*, lost in Chapter 8 and found in the following chapter in a pile of old newspapers written in Arabic;[5] like Chapters 18 and 19 of Volume 9 of *Tristram Shandy*,[6] which Laurence Sterne left blank because he had thrown them in the fire by mistake; and like the *War Memoirs*[7] that Bion wrote at the front, then lost, wrote again, lost once more, and found and reread, so that he could finally recount his war experience when he was in exile in Los Angeles in 1968, at the age of 71. There, he must have read

Kurt Vonnegut's *Slaughterhouse-Five*, since the expression "memories of the future" appears several times in the book, echoing the title of Bion's work of fiction *A Memoir of the Future*, written in the United States. All these books originating in war trauma are the product of a "memory that doesn't forget," as Bion says.

Genesis of *Timequake*

The epigraph of the novel – "All persons, living and dead, are purely coincidental" – brings to mind the question often asked by patients who have emerged from madness: "How did it happen that I met you?" How did it happen that Kurt Vonnegut rescued a text from the trash bin of History, as he recounts at the start of the novel? It was thanks to a chance encounter he describes to his biographer, "a spectral incident" that took place when he was speaking at the University of Rochester in 1996.[8]

The lecture series coordinator took him to Mount Hope Cemetery, where they saw the graves of famous people like Frederick Douglass (1818–1895), former slave and leader of the abolitionist movement, and Susan B. Anthony (1820–1906), a feminist militant for civil rights. Then she took him to the military plot and showed him the grave of Edward Crone, the model for Billy Pilgrim in *Slaughterhouse-Five*. Vonnegut was stunned, since he had seen Crone buried in Dresden in a paper suit, for no real clothes could be had. After the war, Crone's parents wrote hundreds of letters and finally went to East Germany to bring back his remains. Vonnegut himself had waited until they died before confirming that this young man with the childlike face was indeed the model for his quixotic hero. He described Crone to his biographer as "definitely unsoldierly" and so awkward that someone always had to "pick up the utensils falling out of his backpack." But he never complained. He was "a kind of holy fool" who "kept expecting a rationale" for the madness of war – confirmed by Billy's delusions in the book.

Standing before the grave, Vonnegut asked his host to let him have a few minutes to himself. From a distance, she saw him light a cigarette, glance around him, and talk to the gravestone, "having a conversation across a gap of fifty years." He wept, but when he joined the woman again he seemed content: "Well, that closes the book on World War II for me." After having been Crone's second in combat during the war, he could now carry out the second function attributed to the *therapon* in the *Iliad*: that of "ritual double," in charge of funeral rites. He sends a cheque to the cemetery for flowers to be placed on the grave each year on Memorial Day, celebrated on the last day of May in honour of soldiers fallen in battle.

Timequake is the outcome of texts that "never cease not to be inscribed" – Lacan's definition of the Real – but which, paradoxically, tend towards their inscription. The action begins with a "timequake" which suspends temporality for ten years, between 1991 and 2001, so that events are inexorably repeated.

This situation, called a "rerun," is familiar to analysts working with madness and trauma who, becoming discouraged by lack of progress, are tempted to diagnose irrevocable psychic structures. Indeed, the main character in *Timequake* is also taken for a madman, since he never stops writing and keeps throwing his manuscripts into the garbage can. His name is Kilgore Trout, a science fiction writer we already met in *Slaughterhouse-Five*, who has become a bum since then. But he escapes the predetermined fate "once a madman, always a madman" when the author ends the book with public recognition for Trout's writings.

This "closes the book on World War II for me," Vonnegut says, thanks to a coincidence, the only thing that can set time in motion again when causality is to no avail. In the novel, the rerun unfolds unchanged, and the characters are helpless to influence events. Only chance can interfere with the mechanism of repetition. The Rochester lady guessed how important it was for the writer to know that his buddy had a proper gravestone. The tormented soul of the Dresden prisoner has found peace, which had been refused to Billy Pilgrim at the end of *Slaughterhouse-Five*. Now Kurt Vonnegut can stop writing about the war.

After the timequake of World War I and a year spent at Monte Cassino as a POW,[9] Wittgenstein returned to Vienna and struggled for ten years with the rerun of traumatic revivals, until 1929 when, by happy coincidence, the young philosopher George Moore invited him to return to Cambridge, where he had studied before the war. He could now take up philosophy, abandoned during the rerun, "as a therapy," as suggested in paragraph 133 of the *Philosophical Investigations*: "there is not a single philosophical method, though there are indeed methods, different therapies." One effect of his new therapy was to change the last desperate sentence of the *Tractatus* written on the Eastern Front,[10] from: "Whereof one cannot speak, thereof one must be silent," to: "When one cannot speak, one cannot help showing what cannot be said." This is Vonnegut's purpose in *Timequake*: to show how relentless repetition can suddenly engender free will, but not without creating mayhem.

This sudden transition takes the form of repression in the case of traumatic memory that doesn't forget anything. Freud hypothesises primary repression, *Urverdrängung*,[11] in a mythical dimension, unrelated to "repression as such." Several times, in the *Gradiva* and *The Uncanny*, where madness is concerned, he speaks of an unconscious that is not repressed. We assume that this is the missing text, always lost, in the field of trauma where nothing can be inscribed in the symbolic chain due to timequakes that destroy the sphere of language with the symbols which make it possible to calculate time and reach a reliable other.

The subject of speech seems to have disappeared. Yet he exists in the effort made by delusion to show what cannot be said to another who will allow him to emerge from what Benedetti calls "a delirious masterpiece." In a series of lectures delivered in Cambridge in 1956, published under the title *Mind and Matter*, quantum physicist Erwin Schrödinger stressed this paradox:

> On the one hand, the mind is the artist who has produced the whole [be that a delirious masterpiece]; in the accomplished work, however, it is but an insignificant accessory that might be absent without detracting from the total effect.[12]

This apparent insignificance often causes psychiatrists and psychoanalysts to treat patients as accessories of their theories, neglecting the creative work of this cut-out unconscious.

In the Amiens Cathedral, on the armrest of a stall, a small figure represents the architect, hammer in hand. He goes unnoticed, yet without him the cathedral would not stand. The same is true when the analyst can glimpse the subject in the split-off fragments of a cut-out unconscious. But to reach him, and build an alterity that allows a transitional subject to emerge in the session, he must go, with his patient, through "time doors" or "time windows."

Slaughterhouse-Five

Chapter 2 of the novel begins: "Listen. Billy Pilgrim has come unstuck in time." The verb suggests the take-off of a spaceship – the flying saucer that takes him to the planet Tralfamadore – as well as becoming unstuck from the glue of denial. The formulation has sacramental overtones: "*Audite omnes et expavescite*" ("Listen all and be filled with dread"), says the first verse of a motet in François Couperin's *Lessons of Darkness*, composed for Holy Week – also called *Semaine de la Passion*, in French.

Billy Pilgrim has come unstuck in time to enter the delirious narration of his Passion. He:

> has gone to sleep a senile widower, and awakened on his wedding day. He had walked through a door in 1955 and come out another one in 1941. He has gone through that door to find himself in 1963. He has seen his birth and death many times, he says, and pays random visits to all the events between. He says. Billy Pilgrim is spastic in time. He has no control over where he is going next, and the trips aren't necessarily fun. He is in a constant state of stage fright, he says, because he never knows what part of his life he is going to have to act in next.
>
> (p. 34)

To inscribe his kidnapping by aliens, he has a communiqué published in the newspaper of his home town. His daughter is flabbergasted: "You are making a laughingstock of us," she says. Billy merely answers: "It's all true" (p. 37).

The initial cut-out event is the destruction of Dresden between February 13 and 15, 1945. The asphyxiated corpses, the collapsed houses, the architectural masterpieces abolished in one night, the unbearable stench, the deafening noise, all come back to him now. "I was there," he wants to shout. But no one cares, just as they didn't care about the Battle of Lepanto when Cervantes came back to Spain after five years of slavery in Algiers, ten years after going to war in Sicily.[13]

Billy Pilgrim was born in 1922, like Kurt Vonnegut. Drafted into the army in World War II like Vonnegut, he came back in April 1945. Ten years later, he married the overweight daughter of the owner of an optometry school, became rich and had two children. The year 1968, where he finds himself after going through another time door, is the year he was the sole survivor of a plane crash. Another collateral catastrophe stemming from the accident is the death of his wife by carbon monoxide poisoning, in her own car, while she was rushing to the hospital to see him. This was not his first hospitalisation.

At the time when he was engaged, in 1948, he had already travelled in time, and was hospitalised for shell shock in a ward for non-violent mental patients, where he received shock treatment. It was then, in Chapter 5, that he discovered the writings of Kilgore Trout, thanks to the man in the bed next to his, who loved science fiction. This man, Eliot Rosewater, is the hero of Vonnegut's previous book, *God Bless You, Mr. Rosewater*.[14] For Rosewater, a former infantry captain in the war, science fiction was the only literature possible, now that they "both found life meaningless," as he told Billy, after "the greatest massacre in European history, which was the firebombing of Dresden. So it goes."

Kilgore Trout has written many books, most of them unpublished. As fate would have it, he lives in a basement two miles from the pretty white house where Billy Pilgrim lives, and Billy visits him when he is released from the hospital (Chapter 8): "Trout's paranoid face was terribly familiar to Billy. [...] Trout certainly looked like a prisoner of war." Billy's intuition was right. Kilgore Trout's war in Europe would be the theme of *Timequake*. But when they met, Kilgore was stunned – it was the first time he was meeting a fan: "He did not think of himself as a writer for the simple reason that the world had never allowed him to think of himself in this way" (p. 215). Never had a book of his been "advertised, reviewed or on sale." Billy invited him to his eighteenth wedding anniversary, during which he would step out through a time window again.

At the party, a quartet sang "That Old Gang of Mine." Billy Pilgrim felt upset, since he had never had an old gang of his own. The song went on:

So long for ever, old fellows and gals,
so long for ever old sweethearts and pals,
God bless 'em.

(p. 220)

Suddenly, the chords of the quartet were sour, then sourer still, then very sweet, and then sour again. Billy had a violent response to the changing chords. His face became grotesque, as if he was being tortured. When he sat down heavily in a chair, people thought he was having a heart attack.

There was silence around him. He kept saying: "Really – I'm OK," but he could not find any explanation for what happened. "He had supposed for years that he had no secrets from himself. Here was proof that he had a great big secret somewhere inside, and he could not imagine what it was." Kilgore Trout comes closer, looking at him shrewdly, as if he knew. Billy's wife says: "You looked as though you'd seen a ghost. – 'No', said Billy. He hadn't seen anything ..." Kilgore asks: "Can I make a guess? You saw through a time window" (p. 221). The interpretation hits home since it comes from the man on whom Billy had recognised the traces of war at first sight: "He suddenly saw the past or the future" (p. 222). Although he feels his secret is out, Billy acts as if everything is normal. He gives his wife the sapphire ring he has prepared for the occasion. And Trout comments: "You looked as though [...] you were standing on thin air." After all, most of his science fiction novels "dealt with time warps and extrasensory perception."

The Dresden prisoner of war has found his second in combat to help him face a past that will not pass. The quartet continues to sing the song that tortures him. The lyrics speak of cotton and meat, of a bar burnt down by lightning. But beyond the words, what torments him has to do with the four musicians, with their expressionless faces, not with what they are singing.

Billy fled upstairs, telling Kilgore not to follow him. In his bedroom, he remembered. He heard giant footsteps – high-explosive bombs above the meat locker, he remembered the four guards with expressionless faces:

> Before the raid, the other guards had gone to the comfort of their own homes in Dresden, where they were now being killed with their families. So it goes. He also remembered the girls he had seen earlier, who were killed in their much shallower shelters. So it goes.
>
> A guard would go to the head of the stairs [...] to see what it was like outside, then he would come down and whisper [that] there was a fire-storm out there. Dresden was one big flame [that] ate everything organic. [...] When [they] did come out the next day, the sky was black with smoke. [...] Dresden was like the moon now, nothing but minerals. The stones were hot. Everybody else [...] was dead. So it goes.
>
> (pp. 226–227)

The four guards drew close together, standing with their mouths open, like the musicians in the quartet: "So long forever, old sweethearts and pals. So long forever."

For the little children

The delusional account sent to the local newspaper by Billy Pilgrim to testify to his kidnapping by extraterrestrial beings is unacceptable. His aim is to inscribe historical events, but that kind of truth has no place in the social link. Lacan has defined four discourses as being social links: that of the master, that of the hysteric, that of the university and that of the analyst, which supposes repression.[15] But what happens to analytic discourse when repression is not possible, when the unconscious, defined as the discourse of the Other, is silent because there is no other?

The objective of this seminar entitled "Madness and the Social Link" is to show that the aim of madness is to create otherness on the very site where it has been destroyed. A first mirror is set in place where everything exploded, constructed from analogous elements in the analyst's history, often cut out from his own analysis. This allows the emergence of a social link around a historical truth denied by perversion. The *Madres Locas* ("Mad Mothers") – the Mothers of the Plaza de Mayo in Buenos Aires – were demanding the return of their children alive, after they disappeared during the military dictatorship between 1977 and 1983. The grandmothers, *Avuelas*, are still carrying out organised action to reunite "adopted" grandchildren to their real families, after they were stolen from their murdered mothers. Marc Hillel revealed similar Nazi practices in his book *Of Pure Blood*.[16]

In December 1915, Debussy, who was suffering from cancer, composed his "Christmas of the Homeless Children," sung by the *Petits Chanteurs de Paris*:

> Our houses are gone!
> The enemy has taken everything,
> Even our little beds!
> They burned the school and the schoolmaster. [...]
> Of course, Papa has gone to war.
> Poor Mama died before she saw all of this.
> What are we going to do?

Sometimes a century is needed to inscribe history. Historian Annette Becker's book *Les cicatrices rouges* (*The Red Scars*)[17] reveals the torment inflicted on civilians during World War I in the occupied territories of Belgium and Northern France. Historian Marion Pignot's book *Allons enfants de la Patrie* (*Onward, Children of the Fatherland*)[18] is based on letters found in schools and family homes, written by children to fathers, uncles and godparents, like those written by the child analyst Françoise Dolto to her godfather, who died in 1915 on the front line when she was 7. At that age, she declares that she was a widow, like all the women around her, who went mad after losing their husbands and sons. Eighty years later, historian Timothy Snyder's book *Bloodlands*[19] draws the present-day maps of territories – extending from the Baltic states to the Ukraine, where 14 million civilians were killed between 1933 and 1945 by Stalin's regime, and then by the Nazis.

In the meantime, original manuscripts have been tossed into oblivion, like the black Moleskine notebooks discovered at the back of a drawer or in an attic, and brought to me – because I ask for them – written by a grandfather or a great-great aunt who became an old maid at 20. Their wait to be read by a witness extended over several generations.

This is what happens to Kurt Vonnegut. Despite the success of *Slaughterhouse-Five* and his other novels, he has writer's block. A portion of his "book about the war" has remained unfinished, although he tried to write it. After his visit to the grave of Edward Crone, alias Billy Pilgrim, he discusses his problem in a letter to poet Edward Muir, whom he met by chance on several occasions – first at the University of Chicago after World War II, then in New York State when he was a publicist at General Electric. Finally, he met Muir again when he was living in Cape Cod with his first wife and their children, as well as his sister's children, orphaned after the death of both their parents.

Edward Muir transforms Vonnegut's letter into a poem:

> I cover paper with words every day
> But the stories never go anywhere . . .
> And now believe that writer's block
> Is finding out
> How lives of loved ones really ended
> Instead of the way we hoped they would end
> With the help of our body English.
> Fiction is body English.
>
> *(Timequake*, p. 40)

The word "block" refers to both the writer's difficulty and to capital letters. The expression "body English" refers to the literary corpus, as well as to the body, given by fiction to the truth about the death of those we love, rather than to its falsification. Hannah Arendt played somewhat similarly with the opposite meanings of the word "fiction," by differentiating fictional characters in literature from the fictitious *Figuren* people become in a totalitarian system.

The rhythm the poet gives to Vonnegut's letter reminds me of how the Ramayana came to be written.[20] A wise man, angered to see a hunter kill the female of a pair of birds he had been stalking, cursed the man in rhythmic phrases. When he was back in his hermitage, Rama appeared to him and said: "those [angry] words emanated from you, at my will. Compose the epic of Rama." The wise man objects, saying he can't write. The god answers: "[the] deeds and thoughts will all be made known to you, by my grace." He gives him the epic rhythm of his anger.

Edward Muir rouses Vonnegut's anger against the destruction of children, mentioned in the subtitle of *Slaughterhouse-Five, The Children's Crusade.* This theme occurs in the story he tells about his friend, whose name is also that of a famous Scottish poet who died in 1959. One day, a woman asks the American Edward Muir: "Are you *the poet*?" Disappointed to learn that he is not, she tells him that one of her favourite poems is "The Poet Covers His Child." The end of the story provides the key to his future novel: "Get a load of this: It was the American Ed Muir who wrote that poem" (*Timequake*, p. 41).

When he takes up his writing again at the poet's prompting, Kurt Vonnegut finds inspiration in a play about children and death, which provided his first example of a timequake. Written by Thornton Wilder (1897–1975), it is called *Our Town*, and was staged for the first time on Broadway in 1938.

Our Town[21]

Chapter 12 of *Timequake* begins, like *Tristram Shandy*, with "I wish": "I wish I'd written *Our Town*, as sweet a play as can ever be" (p. 130). Kurt Vonnegut saw it five or six times (Chapter 6). Thornton Wilder said he wanted to show "the life of a village against the life of the stars." Located in New Hampshire, the town is made up of families that arrived in the late seventeenth century, as well as Polish immigrants and Canucks – French-Canadian families from Quebec, like that of Kerouac, who also wrote about his home town of Lowell in Massachusetts, comparing it to New York in his first novel, *The Town and the City.*[22] The play is composed of three acts, with minimal decor: two tables, chairs, and two stools in Act 2. The lighting indicates the time of the day, as the hours pass. The characters speak with a New Hampshire accent.

Act 1

The spectators are seeing an empty stage where the stage manager is placing a table and three chairs on each side. He announces the title of the play, the date (May 7, 1901, at dawn), and the name of the town (Grover's Corners), which he describes briefly: its railway station, its town hall, its churches, its factory, its main street, its stores and its schools. A rooster crows. Two families are living their lives on opposite sides of the street: on the right Dr Gibbs' family, and across the street the family of the editor of the local newspaper, Mr Webb. The stage manager concludes: "Nice town, y'know what I mean? Nobody very remarkable ever come out of it, s'far as we know" (p.7).

Doc Gibbs is coming back from delivering a baby during the night. He speaks with the newspaper boy and to the milkman, stroking his horse. In both houses, Mrs Webb and Mrs Gibbs are busy setting the table and preparing breakfast. They call the children like they do every morning, but, as always, they're in no hurry to come down; George and Rebecca Gibbs in one house, and Emily and Wally Webb in the other, gobble down their breakfast and dash off to school. The two mothers get together for a chat. Mrs Gibbs dreams of going to Paris, instead of the regular trips she takes with her husband to the battlefields of the Civil War.

The stage manager steps in to interview a local historian about the history of the town, and the newspaper editor about the political as well as cultural inclinations of the inhabitants. Once again, there is nothing remarkable to report. Aside from *Robinson Crusoe*, the Bible and Handel's *Largo*, their culture is the beauty of the majestic mountains around them.

Act 2

Three years later, on July 7, 1904, George Gibbs and Emily Webb are getting married. The stage manager acts as the clergyman who performs the church ceremony. The families and friends of the bride and groom are seated on either side of the aisle. The "minister" stops officiating to tell the story of how love was born between the two youngsters. The two high stools facing each other represent them in their respective rooms, shyly confessing their feelings through their open windows.

The stage manager then addresses the audience to speak of what really matters to him: to inscribe for centuries to come the daily life of the town, ignored by historical accounts – for instance, marriages celebrated right after high school graduation. Emily is a brilliant student, while George loves baseball and wants to become a farmer. The marriage ceremony resumes, to the sound of music played by an organist who is an alcoholic. As Emily walks to the altar in her wedding dress, she wonders what she is doing there; George, meanwhile, is afraid he might not be up to this. Once they've exchanged rings, they walk up the aisle, radiant.

The minister/stage manager now addresses the audience to speak about his experience of weddings. Despite appearances, he says, "there's a lot of confusion way down deep in people's minds" about a wedding. But the true hero of the event is not on stage: "And don't forget all the other witnesses at this wedding – the ancestors. Millions of them." And he adds: "Well, that's all my sermon. T'wasn't very long, anyway."

Act 3

Nine years later, summer 1913. The action is set in the town cemetery, on a hilltop offering a splendid view. The stage is once again divided into two parts. On the left, the dead sit quietly on chairs, without looking to the right or to the left. The stage manager explains:

> You know as well as I do that the dead don't stay interested in us living people for very long. Gradually, gradually, they [...] get weaned away

from earth – that's the way I put it – weaned away. [...] they slowly get indifferent to what's going on in Grover's Corners.

(pp. 80–81)

Among the dead, we see Mrs Gibbs who passed away recently, Emily's brother who died of appendicitis, the organist who hanged himself, and many others. On the right side of the living, the undertaker is talking to a young man who just arrived from Buffalo, a cousin who left town twelve years ago. Their conversation reveals that Emily died giving birth to her second son.

The funeral procession arrives at the cemetery. Emily leaves it, to go over to the dead. For a while, she remains in "the space between two deaths." Dead in the eyes of the living, she is not yet seated among the dead. Vonnegut's book *Timequake* takes place in this time-space where Kilgore Trout has withdrawn, away from the living. The dead greet Emily one by one: "Hello, Emily. – Hello, Mother Gibbs." Her mother-in-law reassures her: "They'll be gone soon, dear. Just rest yourself."

Emily wishes she was still one of them. She says she would like to go back there. Mrs Gibbs tells her: "Yes, of course you can. All I can say is, Emily, don't." The other dead join in to dissuade her, but she wants to try: "But [...] how can I *ever* forget that life? It's all I know. It's all I had." Mrs Gibbs suggests that, in that case, she should choose to relive "the least important day of her life. It will be important enough." Emily chooses her twelfth birthday, February 11, 1899.

This is the start of Emily's "rerun," which only lasts a morning, while Kurt Vonnegut's was extended over ten years, from February 17, 1991 to February 13, 2001. This February date insists, since between Thornton Wilder's play and Vonnegut's last novel, the major timequake of the destruction of Dresden, began on February 13, 1945. When Vonnegut admitted to the woman in Rochester that he had not yet closed his book on World War II, did he mean that Billy Pilgrim's rerun was not yet over?

Of course, Billy Pilgrim's delusions transform his "rerun" into science fiction. His kidnapping by aliens reproduces the hijacking of the prisoners taken to Dresden, and his captivity in a zoo of their planet – where Tralfamadorians take their children to observe human specimens called *Earthlings* – is a re-enactment of his captivity in the slaughterhouse where the prisoners lived among carcasses, like animals. But he finds no way out, no free will to interrupt the rerun. Indeed, the novel ends with him being thrown out of a New York television studio, where he was trying to tell the American public about his extraterrestrial adventure.

By contrast, Emily's "rerun" leads to a tribute to life, offered from the beyond. She comes back home as a girl of 12 – like the ghost Beloved[23] dwelling in the house of her mother and sister – and she realises that her family has no time to see her. Her mother goes on preparing breakfast while she hugs her, looking away to watch the stove, stirring the porridge without listening to her. Same thing with her father and brother. But instead of exhausting them, like Beloved, who haunts the living with her endless demand for love, she draws a different conclusion from her disappointment, and decides to return among the dead. She tells her mother-in-law: "They don't understand, do they? – No dear. They don't understand" (p. 103).

The living don't understand anything about daily life. "They are blind" to its value measured against the finality of death. This is what the stage manager wants to inscribe in History, by telling the story of a small town. This message is carried by Emily's farewell to her life on Earth, which had a powerful effect on Kurt Vonnegut (*Timequake,* p. 21):

> It goes so fast, says Emily. We don't have time to look at one another. [...] So all that was going on and we never noticed. Take me back – up the hill – to my grave. But first: Wait! One more look. Good-by, Good-by, world. Good-by, Grover's Corners ... Mama and Papa. Good-by to clocks ticking ... and Mama's sunflowers. And food and coffee. And new-ironed dresses and hot baths ... and sleeping and waking up. Oh, earth, you're too wonderful for anybody to realize you.
>
> (*Our Town*, p. 100)

Kurt Vonnegut repeats Emily's question: "Do any human beings ever realize life while they live it? – every, every minute?" Like Flaubert when he admitted "Madame Bovary is me," Vonnegut confesses:

> I myself become a sort of Emily every time I hear that speech. I haven't died yet, but there is a place, as seemingly safe and simple, as learnable, as acceptable as Grover's Corners at the turn of the century, with ticking clocks and Mama and Papa and hot baths and new-ironed clothes and all the rest of it, to which I've already said good-bye one hell of a long time ago now. Here's what that was: the first seven years of my life, before the shit hit the fan, first the Great Depression and then World War Two.

The solution found in *Timequake* is not simply *carpe diem*, "seize the day," but also gather up all the fragments of life and of writing that you've thrown in the dustbin. Do not scorn the child who comes back as a fool or a vagrant, outside of time. In an analysis of madness or trauma, a child in the analyst steps forward to stand beside the one who speaks with the dead about war, about their lineage and about daily life, so that their stories are told among the living.

Slaughterhouse-Five also resonated with Bion when he was exiled in America. It allowed him to hear the accents of the American and Canadian soldiers who fought alongside him. Afterwards, he was able to gather up the war memories that had been thrown away several times, and finish the story of his *Long Week-End*, thanks to a precise memory that does not forget.

The analyst speaks to the children whose houses are gone, and to the stars in a fourth dimension. This is how *Our Town* ends, and Kurt Vonnegut will remember this ending in the last chapter of *Timequake*: "Most everybody's asleep in Grover's Corners. [...] There are the stars — doing their old, old crisscross journeys in the sky."

A Memoir of the Future: "Talk about remembering the future!"[24]

At the end of the novel, the transference connecting Vonnegut to his fool, Kilgore Trout, leads to the recognition of the tramp as an author, after a rerun that lasted ten years. During the rerun, all the actors "know everything they are going to say and do, and how everything is going to come out in the end [...]. Yet they have no choice but to behave as though the future were a mystery" (p. 20). For the first time in his life, at 84, Trout is honoured on a beach in Rhode Island, at a writers' retreat, in the summer of 2001, during the famous clambake announced at the beginning of the book. There, Kurt Vonnegut meets not only friends, but also departed souls who were important in his life, represented by lookalike guests – like doppelgängers, he says. Trout has found a family. A year later, he would be ready to die.

At 10 o'clock, before retiring for the night, "the old, long-out-of-print science fiction writer" has one last thing to say and seeks a volunteer for an experiment. Kurt Vonnegut volunteers and is asked to pick two twinkling points in the sky, any two between which "for light to go from one to the other would take thousands or millions of years." Then he asks him to look precisely at one, then at the other. This only takes him a second. "Something [...] passed between where those two heavenly bodies used to be," at a speed greater than the speed of light. "What was it?" Vonnegut asks. "Your awareness. That is a new quality in the Universe, which exists only because there are human beings." And, after pushing in his upper dental plate with his left thumb, he adds: "I have thought of a better word [...]. Let's call it *soul*. Physicists must from now on factor [it] in when pondering the secrets of the Cosmos" (pp. 213–214).

Here, we have the humble character described by physicist Erwin Schrödinger in his book *Mind and Matter*:

> Sometimes a painter introduces into his large picture, or a poet into his long poem, an unpretending subordinate character who is himself. Thus the poet of the *Odyssey* has, I suppose, meant himself by the blindbard [...] in the hall of the Phaeacians. [...] In Dürer's *All-Saints* picture [among] a circle of humans on the earth [is] the portrait of the artist himself, as a humble side-figure that might as well be missing. To me this seems to be the best simile of the bewildering double role of mind [the artist and the insignificant accessory we mentioned earlier].

And Schrödinger goes on: "The physical world picture lacks all the sensual qualities that go to make up the Subjects of Cognizance. The model is colourless and soundless and unpalpable."[25] In *Timequake*, Vonnegut lets an analysis of madness and trauma unfold to its conclusion: regeneration – the title of Pat Barker's *Trilogy*[26] – of the child he is protecting.

The subject was absent from the psychiatric investigation when Billy Pilgrim committed himself to a hospital in 1948:

> The doctors agreed: He *was* going crazy. They didn't think it had any-thing to do with the war. [...] He was trying to prove to a willfully deaf and blind enemy that he was interesting to hear [when he said] "I was a prisoner of war."

The psychiatrist "sighed impatiently. – Do you believe me?" Billy asked. The psychiatrist returned his question: "Must we talk about it now? – We don't ever have to talk about it, said Billy. I just want you to know I was there."[27] The doctors "were sure Billy was going to pieces because his father had thrown him into the deep end of the [...] swimming pool" (*Slaughterhouse-Five*, p. 127).

The same misunderstanding is described by Arthur Blank, founder of Vet Centers in the United States.[28] When he returned from the Vietnam War, where he served as a military psychiatrist, he thought he would go crazy and consulted a dozen psychoanalysts who, without batting an eyelid, asked him to free-associate about his childhood. But the child who needs treatment is not the obvious one. Whatever his age, the child seeking help is the author of unborn speech, and is bereft of an other who can answer for it.

In *Timequake*, Vonnegut attributes Kilgore Trout's composure at the end of the "rerun" – when free will emerges after ten years and provokes catastrophes – to the fact that Trout fought in Europe as a forward observer for the field artillery: "His experiences [...] had taught him that panic only made things worse" (p. 9). Vonnegut knows what Trout is talking about, since he himself "was an intelligence and reconnaissance scout" in the Ardennes (p. 79). After the war, both of them saw "reputable" psychoanalysts, if we believe the caricatures in Kilgore Trout's short story *Dr. Schadenfreude* (Dr Badjoy).

Any resemblance between this "shrink" and actual persons living or dead is purely coincidental:

> This doctor had his patients lie on a couch and talk [...] ramble on about TV shows. [But] if a patient accidentally said "I" or "me" or "myself" or "mine," Dr. Schadenfreude [...] leapt out of his overstuffed leather chair [...] put his livid face directly over the patient [...] and barked things like this: "When will you ever learn that nobody cares anything about you, you, you, you boring, insignificant piece of poop?

Your whole problem is you think you matter! Get over that, or sashay your stuck-up butt the hell out of here!"

(p. 61)

Another version of this caricature is provided by therapists who listen to the stories of traumatised patients without a word, as if they were watching a television series. Kurt Vonnegut criticises those who are "humorless enough to regard psychiatry as a science" (p. 64). The same can be said of "shrinks" who think that psychosis is a personality structure. Because transference makes them fall out of their armchairs, they theorise that psychoanalysis is impossible, given the foreclosure of the name of the father. For Kurt Vonnegut, such a crisis, strangely similar to the initial breakdown, marks the moment when a new freedom emerges after years of relentless repetition.

Free will

This moment brings to an end the "rerun" in which the past is endlessly enacted in the present, until free will unexpectedly kicks in. On February 13, 2011, the universe expands again, after having shrunk and receded to February 17, 1991. When free will kicks in, pedestrians are knocked off their feet, people fall off escalators, cars and trucks smash into each other, gas pipes explode, the dead and the wounded are strewn across the city of New York (p. 122).

The only one who reacts appropriately, after spending "ten years on automatic pilot," is Kilgore Trout, the vagrant of the sacred "bums" – *The Dharma Bums,* as Jack Kerouac calls them.[29] Trout finishes the story he is writing; he is carried over the "yawning abyss" and senses what the universe is going to do after its hiccup.

The Greek word *khaos* means "the void before creation." Time before the origins of time is boredom that yawns, and from his gaping jaws the sky, the earth and the seas come into existence. In the same way, the end of the "rerun" during the transference stops the boredom of repetition, letting free will emerge, on condition, Trout says in *Slaughterhouse-Five,* that the psychiatrist gains access to the fourth dimension (Chapter 5). In his own book *Maniacs in the Fourth Dimension,* he analyses the problem of "three-dimensional Earthling doctors" who can't imagine the fourth dimension where the causes of mental diseases lie. Indeed, we were trained to focus on the sacred third dimension of the symbolic order, and to despise the dual imaginary dimension.

Kurt Vonnegut's self-diagnosis – "I am a monopolar depressive" (*Timequake,* p. 89) – mystifies analysts attached to a signifying chain that does not respond to their laborious word-games because it is broken, a hilarious situation he compares to two incidents described in *Timequake.* The first takes place during a performance of *Swan Lake* at the Royal

Ballet in London. When a ballerina leaves the stage dancing on her toes, "deedly-deedly-deedly, there is a sound backstage as if she had put her foot in a bucket and then gone down an iron stairway [...]. I instantly laughed like hell. I was the only person to do so." Likewise, the analyst who "deedly-deedly-deedly" dances on signifiers is generally thrown off his feet by his patient's boisterous delusion.

And Vonnegut goes on to say:

> A similar incident happened at a performance of the Indianapolis Symphony Orchestra when I was a kid. [...] There was this piece of music that was getting louder and louder, and was supposed to stop all of a sudden. There was this woman in the same row with me [...] talking to a friend [...] louder and louder. The music stopped. She shrieked, "I FRY MINE IN BUTTER!"
>
> (Chapter 30)

When the analysis suddenly stops at a critical moment, the patient hears clearly his analyst's cut-out unconscious, usually rendered inaudible by the hubbub of his theories. If the analyst can't laugh when this happens – "No Laughing Matter" is another of Kilgore Trout's stories – he misses the birth of a transitional subject, and potential inscriptions are once again thrown away.

PTA: post-traumatic apathy

Kilgore Trout is addicted to writing and speaks to the manuscripts he throws in the trash bin located in front of the homeless shelter where he lived in New York, situated in the former National Museum of the American Indian, next door to the American Academy of Arts and Letters. Intrigued by this character who looks like a bag lady with a blanket thrown over his head in babushka style, the guard of the Academy – an African American who had done jail time for a crime he didn't commit – retrieves the discarded manuscript and gives it to the lady at the head of the Academy. Soon afterwards, the rerun comes to an end. A fire truck smacks the entrance of the prestigious building, and in the ensuing chaos Kilgore Trout enters the space reserved for artists and writers, for the very first time.

His voluntary withdrawal from society followed the death of his son, a Vietnam War deserter accidentally decapitated in a shipyard accident in Sweden, where he had taken refuge (p. 46). Since he dressed like a hobo, people thought he was crazy, but he said: "It was the world that had suffered the nervous breakdown" (p. 54).

Kilgore Trout had registered at the shelter under the name Vincent Van Gogh. One day, he told Vonnegut:

The main thing about Van Gogh and me is that he painted pictures that astonished *him* with their importance, even though nobody else thought they were worth a damn, and I write stories that astonish *me*, even though nobody else thinks they're worth a damn.

(p. 96)

The momentous event of time being set in motion again did not affect him any more than "wars, economic collapses, plagues or TV stars." While people around him were devastated, he organised their rescue, like a true therapist familiar with disasters. But, once again, there was a gap between him and the others. While he foresaw "unlimited opportunities," they fell into a strange inertia.

Kurt Vonnegut invents PTA syndrome, post-traumatic apathy, on the model of PTSD, post-traumatic stress disorder, entered into the DSM-IV in 1986 to allow Vietnam veterans to obtain a pension. But be careful, Vonnegut says, not to confuse their psychic wounds with the process of healing – that would be like comparing a demolition site with a construction site. Kilgore Trout makes the difference very clear. Instead of singing despairing arias which, "as in Grand Opera, only make hopeless situations worse" (p. 111), he invents a watchword that should inspire us when we are paralysed by an end-of-the-world feeling. To those who are lying on the ground, he shouts: "Free will, free will! You've been very sick! Now you're well again, and there's work to do!" (p. 155). And he ends the discussion with his favourite expression: "Ting-a-ling."

The day of the clambake, Kurt Vonnegut asks him what this expression means. Trout tells him that it was what he shouted during the war when artillery fire hit its target after he had called for it from his position beyond the front line. To Vonnegut's surprise, "this innocent question triggered a horrible memory from Trout's childhood: 'My father murdered my mother [a housewife and poet] when I was twelve years old. Her body was in our basement.'" When his son came home from school, the father swore to him that she had disappeared (p. 50). He was an ornithologist and professor in Northampton, Massachusetts: "As wife-murderers often do – much too often nowadays – he swore he had no idea what had become of her."

At the psychiatric hospital, we met Mauricette, whose father had killed her mother, beating her to death with a broom, and had hidden her body in the cellar. Mauricette was diagnosed a "hysteric" and a "Dr Schadenfreude" had administered electricity to her uterus when she was young.

Kurt Vonnegut loves Kilgore Trout – since "men loving men can happen, in peacetime as well as war." He also loved his war buddy Bernard O'Hare, for the same reason: "indestructible self-respect" (p. 205). This "self" is the subject of the plural body of survival, which connects the soldier to his buddy, and the writer to his alter ego Kilgore Trout, like Don Quixote to Cervantes and Sancho Panza, and Captain Toby to Laurence Sterne and Corporal Trim.

In the *Symposium*,[30] through the voice of a woman, Diotima, Socrates calls Eros the bond of love in catastrophes, which he himself experienced on the battlefields of the Peloponnesian War. Eros' father is *Poros*, porosity, and his mother is *Penia*, poverty, the two attributes of Kilgore Trout, who keeps on writing everything that his porous psyche records. His indestructible self-respect is based on what Bion calls the "premature knowledge" of children traumatised in wartime or peacetime, speaking to voices or visions no one is interested in.

The Children's Crusade

This subtitle of Vonnegut's *Slaughterhouse-Five* was taken from a book published in 1841, *Extraordinary Popular Delusions and the Madness of Crowds*. In 1213, 30,000 children enrolled by two German monks in a crusade going to Palestine were sold as slaves in North Africa. Having set sail in Marseille, half of them died during the crossing and the others disappeared, except a small number that were given asylum in Genoa (*Slaughterhouse-Five*, Chapter 1). Billy Pilgrim is one of these children, as is Kilgore Trout, despite his advanced age. What they have in common is the self-respect that insists on saying: "I was there" when bearing witness is worthless.

"The poet covers his child," says Edward Muir. The analyst too covers his child, and the child in his patients, when they meet to bear witness to crusades without any witness, and can at last share the simple truth: "I was there," in the face of perversity or indifference.

Kurt Vonnegut imagines a war game played on the chessboard of Mendeleev's periodic table, on which the elements rebel, after World War II, against the tortures inflicted on children. They speak in turn: carbon first, since it is "an old veteran of the massacres of history," then nitrogen, weeping about its "involuntary servitude" in the gas chambers, then potassium telling dreadful stories about the Spanish Inquisition, calcium about the Roman Games, oxygen about African slaves, and many others used today to poison the planet. Sodium predicts that "All humans will die [and] all elements will be free of sin again." Its motion is passed by acclamation. Still, Vonnegut disagrees and protests against human extinction in the name of literature.

"The poet covers his child." When young Wilfred Bion went off to war in 1917, he took with him an anthology of poems compiled in 1916 by Robert Bridges, who had written in the preface: "The reader is asked to bathe in these waters, rather than fish in them." The anthology did not give titles or names of authors, to allow readers "to immerse themselves in different moods of mind." Kurt Vonnegut also objects to the apocalyptic prediction that books will disappear: "Many people are desperate to read the words: 'I feel and think like you. You are not alone.'" Freud conveyed the same message in the preface to *Moses and Monotheism*, after the burning of his books by the Nazis.

To counter the erasure of history, Vonnegut invokes the speech made by Abraham Lincoln on February 11, 1861, before leaving for Washington after his election (p. 228). It is recited on the beach of the clambake by a metis actor, a descendant of the man who killed Lincoln on April 14, 1865. When the speech is over, Kilgore Trout is heard sobbing. He mourns the death of American eloquence and then asks the others to look at the stars.

Fallen from the sky

In 1935, Antoine de Saint-Exupéry (1900–1944) crashes his plane in the Libyan Desert in an attempt to fly from Paris to Saigon. Before being shot down in July 1944 by a German plane during a reconnaissance mission for the Allied landing in Provence, he wrote *The Little Prince*, illustrated with his own watercolours, in New York, where an English version was published at once, in 1943.[31] Gallimard published the book in French in 1946. The same year, Charles Trenet referred to it in his song "Tombé du ciel" ("Fallen from the Sky"), which could be paraphrased:

> Listen to the song of the angel falling from the sky in his parachute,
> Listen to his strange song, listen, hush, hush. . .
> Falling from the sky.

During the Occupation, Trenet sung "Douce France," whose refrain, loosely translated, would be: "Sweet France, beloved land of my childhood," taken up by the audience like a hymn of resistance.

The Little Prince is dedicated to Leon Werth, novelist, journalist and art critic, whom Saint-Exupéry met in 1931:

> I ask children to forgive me for dedicating this book to a grown-up. I have a serious excuse: this grown-up is the best friend I have in the world. I have another excuse: this grown-up can understand everything, even books for children. I have a third excuse: he lives in France where he is hungry and cold. He needs to be comforted. If all these excuses are not enough then I want to dedicate this book to the child whom this grown-up once was. All grown-ups were children first. (But few of them remember it.) So I correct my dedication:
>
> to Leon Werth,
> When he was a little boy.

We would be well advised to remember this dedication when our patients bring us texts fallen from the sky, to be inscribed, along with the children we once were, on territories crossed off the map and in space-time that has been erased.

Leon Werth (1878–1955) enlisted in 1914. In 1919, he published *Clavel soldat* and *Clavel chez les majors*, whose anti-war tone created a scandal. He was Octave Mirbeau's secretary and counted many painters and writers among his friends. Between the two wars, he spoke out against colonialism, Stalinism and Nazism in his writings, and became a Gaullist in 1940. After Marshal Pétain came to power in June of that year and introduced the anti-Jewish Laws, Werth left Paris to take refuge in his little house in the Jura Mountains. Caught in the exodus of the French population, it took him and his wife thirty-three days to arrive at their destination. When Saint-Exupéry visited him in his hideout, Werth gave him the manuscript of *33 jours* (*33 Days*) – the account of this "debacle" as it is called in French – so that his friend could try to have it published in New York. But it became another lost text, found again and only recently published.[32]

The Little Prince goes back to his planet after he arranges to be bitten by a snake. Among the stars, he would be reunited with François, Saint-Exupéry's brother who died when Antoine was 17. Children who have been exposed to such timequakes are often attentive to voices and visions coming from the stars. The surviving image of the Little Prince and of his voice, telling the pilot in the desert: "Draw me a sheep," became known all over the world. In *Play and Reality*, Winnicot writes: "These phenomena which mean life and death for our schizoid or borderline patients who fluctuate between living and not living, are the same as the ones which emerge in our cultural experiences."[33]

When the child in the patient asks his psychoanalyst: "Do you believe me?" the answer is often: "What do you think?" Vonnegut answers that question by quoting the poet Samuel Coleridge (1772–1834), who recommends "that willing suspension, for the moment, of disbelief, which constitutes poetic faith" (Chapter 26). Coleridge does not say "for a moment," but rather for the specific moment when it is urgent to step in, *hic et nunc*, when time has stopped in a timequake, where poetic faith starts.

The Juggler of Notre-Dame[34]

The Feast of Fools, the Feast of Innocents and of Children, which opens *The Hunchback of Notre-Dame*,[35] was also the celebration of jugglers. Victor Hugo, who wrote his novel in 1831, at the age of 29, gave Pierre Gringoire (1475–1539), author of Sotties, a prominent place in the story. Although in the novel this celebration takes place on January 6, 1482, it was traditionally held on the December 26, 27 and 28, the week of the Roman Saturnalia when the slaves were given power. *Et exaltavit humiles!* The Magnificat, which exalts the humble and the humiliated – the madmen like Billy Pilgrim, the heavenly bums like Kilgore Trout, and the children abused by soul murderers – is enacted in the legend of the Tumbler of

Notre-Dame, handed down in written form since the twelfth century. It was rediscovered by Gaston Paris, the medievalist consulted by Yvette Guilbert for her new repertoire.[36] Let us suspend our disbelief and consent to be moved.

The Tumbler is a juggler famous for his acrobatics. Sick and tired of the life he leads, he knocks at the door of the Cistercian Abbey of Clairvaux, founded in 1115 by Bernard de Fontaine, the future St Bernard. Since he can neither read nor write, he is accepted among the lay brothers who are in charge of manual tasks. But it turns out that he is no good with his hands either. He faces the prospect of having to return to his previous occupation of juggler – *joculator*, from *jocus*, meaning "game" – whose gestures – those of the jester – are considered diabolical by the Church, for they evoke pagan rituals.[37] Seen as shiftless, vagrants and good-for-nothings, jugglers were considered no better than the prostitutes in brothels on the outskirts of cities. Although this was not always the case, King Louis XII protected them, just as Francis I of France granted royal favour to Rabelais, who carried on their legacy. At the monastery, the Tumbler tells himself: "Never shall I render any service here, for naught can I do or say. [...] If I am found out, I shall be utterly undone." He wept, wanting to die, and asked the Mother of God for guidance. His wish was granted when, his mind in turmoil, he wandered about the monastery until he happened on an abandoned crypt he entered. Crouching down by the altar, he saw the statue of Virgin Mary above it. Suddenly, the bell rang for Mass, and "he rushed forth from the crypt all trembling."

This timequake triggers the "rerun" of his former occupation: "I will do that which I have learned. [...] The others do service with song, and I will do service with tumbling." He took off his habit, laid his garments beside the altar, and "so that his body should not be uncovered, he kept on a tunic." Now the fourth dimension is present, so he is no longer alone and he hopes – expectancy – to be able to offer his Lady his "best tricks in great number." Right away, he turns somersaults, high and low, forwards and backwards, without any indecency, "like a kid which frisks and gambols before its mother." Growing bolder, he spins on his head in ecstasy and then performs dances of different countries: those of France, Lorraine, and Brittany, Champagne, Spain and Rome. Turning a cartwheel as perfect as the heavenly vault, he weeps, saying: "Lady, I do homage to you with my heart, and my body, and my feet, and my hands, for naught beside this do I understand. Now would I be your gleeman."

His dancing, punctuated by the rhythm of the monks' singing in the distance, exalts him to the point of exhaustion. He invents a new somersault and says: "Lady, so help me God, never before have I done this!" As long as the Mass lasted, "[he] ceased not to dance, and to jump, and to leap, until that he was on the point to faint [...] and thus he fell to the ground." And "the sweat issued from him all over, from head to foot." Prayer has become a sacrificial ritual; the Tumbler offers his whole being:

> I do this not for mine own sake [...] but for yours [...] and truly do I here declare unto you, that but little pleasure have I in it. [...] Lady, receive me in your [...] mansion! [...] I do this for your sake.

Setting all self-love aside, he gives himself to the Virgin, acting like the athletes of antiquity who offered their performances to Zeus or Apollo during the Olympic and Pythian games.

The years passed. Each day, "he repaired to the image, to render service and homage [...] with right and good will." But one of the monks started to "pursue him, and follow him, and keep watch on him." Telling himself that "he has a good time of it," he went to inform the abbot of what he had seen. The abbot, a shepherd of souls, not interested in the clinical presentation, wants to know what is in the Tumbler's heart, to prompt his strange behaviour. He says: "I command that you keep silence [...] and we will both go thither, and we shall see ..." Hidden in a covert nook, they observed all the somersaults and turns of the Tumbler until, almost fainting with fatigue, "he fell heavily to the ground, and so exhausted was he, that he sweated all over from his efforts so that the sweat ran all down the middle of the crypt."

This is when the marvel takes place: "And anon the abbot [...] saw descend from the vaulting so glorious a lady, that never had he seen one so fair." The angels who accompanied her surrounded the minstrel. The Lady took a white cloth and with it she "fanned his neck and body and face to cool him." But he knew nothing of this, for the marvel only showed itself to the abbot and the monk. The scene was repeated at least four times, when they came back to be sure they were not hallucinating. "And thus passed the time" – the abbot was not in a hurry – until he sends for the novice, who thinks he will be ousted from the monastery. "Alas, I am found out." The abbot orders him to "wholly reveal [his] thoughts and tell [him] in what manner [he] serve[s] in [the] monastery." Expecting to be banished, the Tumbler tells the truth. That is when the unexpected occurs. The transference has reached the fourth dimension.

Without revealing what he saw, "the holy abbot turned to him, and, all weeping, raised him up. And he kissed both his eyes." He promises that he will be safe in the community, and speaks to him like a brother: "I beseech and command you, my sweet friend, that you forthwith render this service openly, just as you have done it, and still better even, if that you know how." The Tumbler can't believe his ears: "Sire, are you in good earnest? – Yes, truly, said the abbot." After this, he performed his service "without ceasing, morning and evening." The last thing that remains to be done is to inscribe publicly his sacred ritual in the history of the monastery.

"At last it came to pass that he died." And the marvel took place once again. Everyone was there, and all those present:

> quite clearly [saw] a right wondrous miracle. [...] the angels, and the Mother of God, and the archangels, were ranged around him. And there were also the very evil and cruel and violent devils, for to possess them of his soul. [...] And forthwith his soul quitted his body [and] the Mother of God received it.

After burying him with great honour, the abbot told the monks all about his life, and what he had seen the worthy tumbler do.[38] This novice was "given" to the community – as children used to be "given" to convents, like the future St Hildegard of Bingen (1093–1179), author, painter, composer and healer, loved by St Bernard.

Disbelief has been replaced by poetic faith. "It cannot be misdoubted, for the truth bears witness to it," the medieval poet says. Some psychoanalysts we might call *losangiers*, as smooth talkers were called in Old French, will perhaps interpret the Tumbler's actions as Oedipal orgasms. But Vonnegut would answer: "Give me a break!" – one of the short phrases that punctuate his book. He would argue that it would be more useful to ask what the analyst saw and what he dreamed in such circumstances.

"Learned explanations," Socrates says in the *Phaedrus*:

> are amusing enough, but they are a job for a man I cannot envy at all. He'd have to be far too ingenious [...]. I am still unable, as the Delphic inscription orders, to know myself. [...] I accept what is generally believed.[39]

Let us stick to the legend that resonates with future echoes of Verlaine's "My Recurring Dream": "I often have this strange and striking dream: Some woman, whom I love, and who loves me; Loves me and understands; not utterly Different each time, not utterly the same."[40] She is the faraway Lady of Thoughts exalted by warrior poets in courtly love in the era of the Juggler. She was to become Don Quixote's Dulcinea and other feminine agencies who smile at the threshold of the fourth dimension, enabling survival when the third dimension of the law of the father has collapsed.

This story also provides a lesson through the transference between the abbot and his fool. The former's perspective is that of the analyst at crucial moments when a patient is in danger of being banished from the analysis. Despite the prohibition of gestures advocated by bigots of neutrality, the analyst must take a step to enter the dance, with his own dreams, which Benedetti calls "therapeutic," and with the simplicity of this legend.

Ragtime, the rags of time

Faced with perversion, which condemns jugglers to the gallows, the mad to electroshock and children to psychotropic drugs, administered under the pretence of psychoanalysis, one must do what the abbot did: trust one's impressions, the voices and visions coming from the fourth dimension of a cut-out unconscious. This is the start of a new freedom that is not without risk – which is why Bion compares it with going into action.

He speaks of sessions when the patient rebels: "I've been going over the same old memories for ten years, like a broken record. I have nothing else to say. Good-bye!" This rage makes me think of Neptune's wrath when he discovered, in the *Aeneid* Book I that the wineskin where he had imprisoned the winds had been emptied by Juno to stir up the waves under Aeneas' ships: "*Quos ego* ...! I shall ... you!" (verse 135). This fury is addressed to me, the analyst who has let the breath of the patient's psyche run off in the routine of the sessions. The temptation is great to send the rebel to a psychiatrist who will calm him down, before taking up the analysis again.

In the 1920s, Harry Stack Sullivan thought the opposite way: the more violent the crisis, the better the prognosis,[41] since it explodes like a clap of thunder in a clear sky, to force the analyst to see what is not in the landscape, and to discover the rest of the gods' wrath.

"So it goes," Kurt Vonnegut would say. And everything would be for the best in the best of all possible worlds, if the emergence of the subject of speech would not trigger his rage against the faithless, lawless, ruthless agency in whose place I am standing. And I want to throw in the towel. But wait, wait! Coleridge says: "Let's suspend disbelief in favour of poetic faith." If I admit my errors, then bits of torn time, rags thrown into the trash by this agency, emerge out of this rage and create a syncopated rhythm – ragtime – to match the rhythm of the crisis. In this brief interference of the transference – "transference is transient," Bion says – I can say, like Billy, the Pilgrim-in-arrested-time: "I was there," and the time immobilised in the timequake can take up its flow once again.

Notes

1 Vonnegut, K., *Timequake*, Berkley Books, 1997.
2 Shields, C., *And So It Goes: Kurt Vonnegut – A Life,* Henry Holt & Company, 2011.
3 Shields, C., *Mockingbird: A Portrait of Harper Lee*, St. Martin's Press, 2006.
4 Vonnegut, K., *Slaughterhouse-Five*, Random House, 1969.
5 De Cervantes, M., *Don Quixote*, Ormsby, J. (Trans.), Canterbury Classics/Baker & Taylor, 2013.
6 Sterne, L., *The Life and Opinions of Tristram Shandy, Gentleman*, Wordsworth Editions, 1999.

7 Bion, W., *War Memoirs, 1917–1919*, Karnac Books, 1997. See *infra* Seminar 8 on Wilfred Bion and Seminar 9 on Leo Tolstoy, Vasily Grossman, W. G. Sebald and Eric Kandel.

8 Shields, C., *And So It Goes*, op. cit., pp. 393–394.

9 Monk, R., *Ludwig Wittgenstein: The Duty of Genius*, Penguin Books, 1990.

10 Wittgenstein, L., *Philosophical Investigations*, Anscombe, G. (Trans.), Basil Blackwell, 1958; *Tractatus Logico-Philosophicus*, Dover Publications, 1998.

11 Freud, S., *Repression*, S.E. 14, Hogarth Press, 1915, pp. 143–158.

12 Schrödinger, E., *Mind and Matter*, Cambridge University Press, 1989, p. 148.

13 Garces, M. A., *Cervantes in Algiers: A Captive's Tale*, Vanderbilt University Press, 2006.

14 Vonnegut, K., *God Bless You, Mr. Rosewater*, Library of America, 2011.

15 Lacan, J., *The Seminar of Jacques Lacan: The Other Side of Psychoanalysis*, W. W. Norton & Company, 2007.

16 Hillel, M. & Henry, C., *Of Pure Blood*, Pocket Books, 1978.

17 Becker, A., *Les cicatrices rouges*, Fayard, 2010.

18 Pignot, M., *Allons enfants de la Patrie*, Seuil, 2012.

19 Snyder, T., *Bloodlands: Europe between Hitler and Stalin*, Basic Books, 2012.

20 Menon, R., *The Ramayana: A Modern Retelling of the Great Indian Epic*, North Point Press, 2004.

21 Wilder, T., *Our Town*, Harper & Row, 1957.

22 Kerouac, J., *The Town and the City*, Harcourt Brace, 1950. See *infra* Seminar 13 on Jack Kerouac.

23 Morrison, T., *Beloved*, Alma Classics, 2017. See *infra* Seminar 4 on Toni Morrison.

24 *Timequake*, p. 24.

25 Schrödinger, E., "The Oneness of the Mind," in *What Is Life? with Mind and Matter*, Cambridge University Press, 2013, p. 148.

26 See *infra* Seminar 6 on Pat Barker.

27 Vonnegut, K., *Slaughterhouse-Five*, op. cit., p. 247.

28 Sonnenberg, S. and Blank, A. (Eds.), *The Trauma of War: Stress and Recovery in Vietnam Veterans*, American Psychiatric Press, 1985.

29 Kerouac, J., *The Dharma Bums*, Viking Press, 1958.

30 Plato, *Symposium*, CreateSpace, 2013.

31 De Saint-Exupéry, A., *The Little Prince*, Harcourt Brace, 1971.

32 Werth, L., *33 Days: A Memoir*, Melville House, 2015.

33 Winnicott, D., *Playing and Reality*, Routledge Classics, 1971.

34 Ziolkowski, J. M., *The Juggler of Notre-Dame and the Medievalizing of Modernity*, Open Book Publishers, 2018; France, A., *The Juggler of Notre-Dame*, Dumbarton Oaks Research Library, 2018; *Le jongleur de Notre-Dame*, Massenet (opera), 1902.

35 Hugo, V., *The Hunchback of Notre-Dame*, Wordsworth Editions, 1998.

36 See *infra* Seminar 12 on François Rabelais and Yvette Guilbert.

37 Schmitt, J.-C. (Ed.), *Gestures*, Routledge, 1984.

38 Anonymous, *The Tumbler of Our Lady and Other Miracles*, Kemp-Welch, A. (Trans.), In Parentheses Publications, 1999.

39 Plato, *Phaedrus*, Focus Philosophical Library, 2003, pp. 229–230.

40 Verlaine, P., "My Recurring Dream," in *Selected Poems*, Sorrell, M. (Trans.), Oxford World's Classics, 2009.

41 Sullivan, H. S., *Schizophrenia as a Human Process*, W. W. Norton & Company, 1974.

Index

For Product Safety Concerns and Information please contact our EU
representative GPSR@taylorandfrancis.com
Taylor & Francis Verlag GmbH, Kaufingerstraße 24, 80331 München, Germany

www.ingramcontent.com/pod-product-compliance
Lightning Source LLC
Chambersburg PA
CBHW050708280326
41926CB00088B/2867

* 9 7 8 0 3 6 7 5 2 3 3 4 3 *